Canada's Age of Industry, 1849-1896

Readings in
Canadian Social History
Volume 3

Edited by
Michael S. Cross
and Gregory S. Kealey

Reprinted 1989

McClelland & Stewart Inc.
The Canadian Publishers
481 University Avenue
Toronto, Ontario
M5G 2E9

Canadian Cataloguing in Publication Data

Main entry under title:
Canada's age of industry, 1849-1896

(Readings in Canadian social history; 3)
ISBN 0-7710-2458-4

1. Canada – Economic conditions – 19th century – Addresses, essays, lectures. 2. Canada – Social conditions – 19th century – Addresses, essays, lectures. 3. Canada – Industries – History – 19th century – Addresses, essays, lectures
I. Cross, Michael S., 1938- II. Kealey, Gregory S., 1948-
III. Series.

HC114.C36 330.971'05 C82-094076-3

Printed and bound in Canada by Webcom Ltd.

Contents

Abbreviations

APQ	Archives de la Province de Québec
CHAR	Canadian Historical Association *Report*
CHR	*Canadian Historical Review*
OH	*Ontario History*
PAC	Public Archives of Canada
TPL	Toronto Public Library

General Introduction — The Series

The emergence of social history has been perhaps the most significant development of the last fifteen years in Canadian historical writing. Historians young and old have brought new approaches and new perspectives to Canada's past, revealing areas previously overlooked and offering new interpretations of old areas. The result has been what historian Ramsay Cook has called the discipline's "golden age." This five-volume series of readers in social history is intended to make the fruits of that "golden age" readily available to teachers, students, and general readers.

Modern social history is an approach rather than a specific subject matter. Where once social history was seen as what was left over after political and economic history was written, social history now is a "global" discipline, which can embrace politics and economics as well as the history of social groups or charitable institutions. The ideal of social history is to write the history of society, to study all of the ways in which people, groups of people, and classes of people interact to produce a society and to create social change. Such a global picture may never be drawn but its goal of an integrated history underlies recent study in Canada. The social historian, then, may write about a small subject over a limited period of time. However, that historian must be conscious of the links to the larger reality; of how local politics, say, indicate the relations of social classes, how they react with ideological assumptions of provincial politicians, how they affect local social customs.

It is a new field and that means its effort has been scattered. Canadian social history has embraced everything from the study of women's groups to computer analysis of population changes to the history of disease. It also has been marked by some sharp differences of opinion. The editors of this series, as practitioners and partisans, make no claim to objectivity in assessing these differences. Broadly, some historians treat social history as an extension of previous historical writing and share its assumptions about the general sweep of Canadian development: its liberal-democratic character; its fluid class structure; its peaceful and orderly growth. Others, however, break from that interpretation and argue for a different picture: a more rigid and influential class structure; a greater degree of conflict and violence; an emphasis on the working class. Which interpretation will prevail remains to be seen. The essays chosen for the series attempt to present as many viewpoints as possible, but the overall structure clearly reflects the judgment of the editors, which favours the second approach, the "working class" approach.

Rather than being structured along the traditional political divisions, the volumes in the series have been organized around dates which seemed most appropriate to social history:

- I New France to the Conquest, 1760
- II Pre-Industrial Canada, from the Conquest to the end of the imperial economic system, 1760 to 1849
- III Canada's Age of Industry, from the coming of the railway to the full flowering of industrialism, 1849 to 1896
- IV The Consolidation of Capitalism, from the beginnings of economic monopoly to the Great Crash, 1896 to 1929
- V The Emergence of the Welfare State, from the origins of large-scale state intervention to the present, 1930 to 1981.

Again, the internal divisions of the volumes have been chosen to illustrate basic themes that represent building blocks in social history. Not all themes could be included and some historians might argue with the particular choices made here. We would suggest several rationales for the selection: these themes seem important to us; the volume of writing and research on them, completed and underway, suggests that many others find them important; and they have proven useful in teaching social history.

Different periods and the availability of good literature require some variance from volume to volume. The general structure, however, is consistent. Each volume begins with an essay on the major economic developments of the period, for we work from the assumption that changing economic forms underlie most social changes. The second theme is that of social structure and social institutions, of the classes and groups of Canadian society and the way in which they interact. This theme will embrace subject matter as diverse as politics, religion, and landholding patterns.

Certain groups have emerged to centre stage historically in recent years. One is workers, the third theme in each volume. Workers and their work have been perhaps the area of richest development in historical writing in the last decade; social history has made its most profound impact in reshaping historical knowledge in this area. The fourth theme is one in which social history has had a similarly important influence, if only because interest in it is so recent. That is violence and protest, now receiving close attention from historians, sociologists, and criminologists. Violence and protest involved many Canadians and touched the lives of many more, and therefore are significant in their own right. However, they also provide a sharply defined picture of the structures and values of the society in which they occurred. The things people consider important enough to fight and protest about give us some indication of the values of particular groups. The attitudes of the leadership of society emerge in the fifth theme, social control. This theme studies the checks placed on violence and protest and inappropriate behaviour, as well as the institutions created to mould appropriate behaviour.

Along with workers, the other group to receive due attention from social history is women. No area, perhaps, was so neglected for so long as the study of women, outside of occasional writing on the suffrage movement. Recently, however, there has been a flood of literature, not just on feminism and women's organizations, but on women's productive and reproductive work. In a field devoted to creation of an integrated picture of society, this is a welcome and exciting development. Some of the trends in women's history, and some of the major achievements, are illustrated in these volumes.

The structure adopted here is offered as a useful one which will open to teachers and to students an exciting area of Canadian studies. It makes no claim to comprehensiveness; it is very much a starting point for that study. The additional readings suggested will help to move beyond that starting point and to introduce the controversies which cannot be reflected adequately in the small number of essays reprinted here. These volumes, however, do serve as a report on some approaches we have found helpful to students of social history and on some of the best literature available in this new field. More, they are collected on the premise that the investigation of social change in Canadian history, the ideas exposed and the questions raised, may allow students to understand more fully the nature of the Canadian society in which they live.

M. S. Cross

G. S. Kealey

Halifax and
St. John's,
July, 1981

Introduction to Volume 3

In the years between 1849 and 1896 the British American colonies experienced their Industrial Revolution. In the process of this vast transformation came the creation of a new nation-state–Canada–and territorial expansion from sea to sea. By the end of the period Canada looked forward to the twentieth century with considerable enthusiasm under a new set of political leaders, but underneath the optimistic facade lay deep concerns about the nature of the new industrial capitalist society and all the social problems it had engendered. Moreover, the deep depression of the early 1890's had shaken business confidence. One response to this crisis was the concentration and centralization of capital. Thus the initial signs of a new stage of capitalist development–monopoly capital–were becoming manifest. The story of that period in Canadian history will be the subject of volume 4 in this series, *The Consolidation of Capitalism, 1896-1929.*

None of these developments were evident to participants in the exciting events of 1849 in the Canadas. Extensive rioting greeted Britain's dismantling of the old colonial system and general gloom and doom prevailed among colonial merchants. Yet the élite's dire predictions of disaster and its frenzied flirtation with annexation to the United States came to nought. Instead, under the capable direction of Inspector-General and later Prime Minister of the United Canadas, Francis Hincks, an economic boom was set off by an orgy of railroad building financed largely by British capital. The government of the Canadas did its best to insure these investments and the concomitant prosperity through such statutes as the Railway Guarantee Act (1849), which made railroad building a lucrative proposition for capitalists, and the Municipal Loan Fund (1852), which encouraged local boosters to enlist their towns, villages, and counties in the near-hysteria which surrounded the coming of the steel horse. The railway mania had many tangible economic side effects: it recruited vast amounts of foreign capital, which then became available for other uses; it enabled the further concentration of capital and labour in urban centres; it encouraged new industries, such as rolling mills for rails, and led to the expansion of foundries and machine shops; it allowed farmers to diversify their production by opening up new urban markets. The new railway corporations also had many less tangible results. They further cemented the close ties between business and the state. Samuel Zimmerman, perhaps the most corrupt of the railway contractors, had declared: "Had it not been for the financial ability of the Hon. Francis Hincks, I would not be what I am at present." In addition, the new railways pioneered new labour relations policies and other managerial devices, which were later to spread to all forms of entrepreneurial activity. Finally, they captured the public's imagination and symbolically linked progress, science, and capitalism together in a Victorian trinity of seemingly God-given articles of faith.

The 1850's also saw the apparently contradictory Reciprocity Treaty of 1854 with the United States and then the Galt-Cayley and Galt tariffs of 1858 and 1859, which established for the first time a significant level of protection for Canadian manufacturers. These arrangements – free trade on the one hand, protection on the other – actually were not contradictory. Reciprocity in natural products (1854) was not contradicted by protection against foreign manufacturers (1858-59). The advocates of an "infant industry" strategy understood all of this well and promoted it as Canada's major aim and as a solution to the depression which set in during the late 1850's. These men argued that a young nation had to provide considerable protection for its new industries to allow them to reach maturity before facing competition from the advanced industrial nations of the time, especially England and the United States. British and American manufacturing interests were unhappy about the tariffs of the late 1850's, but their displeasure did not deter the Canadian government of the day. Indeed, proponents of protection pointed to the United States as a successful example of the benefits of protection.

The following decade saw a shift in the preoccupations of central Canadian statesmen. With a completed railway network, an increasingly menacing neighbour to the south, and a sharp hunger for the lands in the West, central Canadian businessmen and politicians (the line was never sharply drawn, if drawn at all) began to turn their attention to nation-building. A new nation from sea to sea would not only resolve the political crisis of the Canadas but it would also open up vast opportunities to central Canadian businessmen. The few residents of the West were, of course, ignored totally in the process and only an armed uprising, the Red River Rebellion of 1869-70, won them any notice. Meanwhile, the residents of the Atlantic British American colonies were split in their attitudes. Many opposed Confederation, but significant pockets of support existed, especially in the industrial areas of Nova Scotia. Popular attitudes mattered little in this particular event anyway, and the Canadian nation was created in 1867 at the height of the great age of nationalism without benefit of any significant popular enthusiasm - a peculiar nation from its birth.

The new nation had a difficult time reaching its majority. On its twenty-first birthday in 1888 it looked back on a decade of economic disaster (the 1870's) and one of moderate prosperity (the 1880's). Already significant regional protest had arisen to challenge Ottawa. Yet, despite this and the depression of the 1870's, the late nineteenth century witnessed steady industrial growth in Canada. The National Policy tariff of 1879 encouraged a minor industrial boom especially in textiles, but it also allowed the continued healthy expansion of extant industries - boot and shoe, furniture, agricultural implements, foundry products, tobacco, wood products, meat-packing, etc. Initially this industrial growth was not limited to central Canada as the Maritimes, too, enjoyed considerable industrial development. Nevertheless, even as Maritime industry expanded, the seeds of potential difficulty were being sowed as the region became increasingly integrated through the Intercolonial Railway into the new Canadian nation centred on the St. Lawrence system.

The 1870's and 1880's did not see the great growth in the Canadian population which statesmen and politicians had expected. Despite an extremely high rate of natural increase and a steady, if unspectacular, inflow of immigrants from the British Isles, Canada grew only slowly. The major reason for this was the significant emigration of Canadians to the United States - Maritimers to New England or "the Boston States," as they called them; Québécois to the New Hampshire, Vermont, and Massachusetts mill towns; and Ontario farmers to the midwestern farming frontier and urban artisans to the burgeoning American industrial cities. Only in the late 1890's and early 1900's, with the arrival of large numbers of new European immigrants, would the dreams of extensive western settlement and vibrant industrial cities come to fruition.

The third plank of Sir John A. Macdonald's famous National Policy, after tariffs and western settlement through immigration, was the completion of a transcontinental railway. Macdonald's first attempt at this project was partially led by our old friend Sir Francis Hincks, who was brought back from English retirement to consolidate the Canadian banking system and to help recruit capital and capitalists for the great railway project. Not surprisingly, given the events of the previous railway boom of the 1850's, the first CPR scheme ended in the Pacific Scandal which helped bring down the Conservative government. Nevertheless, in his second attempt, in the 1880's, Macdonald did oversee the completion of the CPR. Combined with the Intercolonial, these two railways created a new national market to correspond to the new nation-state. Both, however, proved to be controversial in operation as well as in construction. The CPR with its special monopoly rights made its captive clients pay high rates, while the ICR quickly developed into a one-way line–central Canadian goods in and, later, Maritimers out.

The Industrial Revolution also wrought significant changes in the Canadian class structure as an increasingly distinct and sometimes conscious class of wage earners emerged in the rapidly growing Canadian cities and towns. Although some craft union activity had been present in the major urban centres in the 1820's and 1830's, it was the 1850's which saw trade unions begin to play a more significant role in Canadian life. This growth, halted abruptly by the depression of the late 1850's, gained new momentum in the 1860's and reached its first peak of organized activity in the early 1870's with the Nine Hour Movement of 1872 and the creation of the Canadian Labor Union the following year. The CLU, the first Canadian labour central and a grandparent of the present Canadian Labour Congress, played a prominent role in the politics of the mid-1870's but was soon swamped both by the hard times of the depression and by the subsequent rush of workers to support Macdonald's National Policy, which they believed would bring employment and prosperity.

With the prosperity in the early 1880's came renewed working-class activity and the creation of the Trades and Labour Congress of Canada, which met for the first time in 1883, again in 1886, and annually thereafter until the 1956 merger which created the new Canadian Labour Congress. The TLC was initially central Canadian exclusively but by the end of the century both westerners and Maritimers were taking part.

The other great labour movement of the 1880's which swept across Canada (with the exception of the Maritimes) organizing all workers – not just the craft workers of the trade unions – was the Knights of Labor. Born in Philadelphia in 1869, the Knights of Labor led a covert existence until the 1880's when they burst upon the Canadian scene. In Canada they organized locals from Cape Breton to Vancouver Island and were particularly strong in Quebec (especially Montreal), Ontario (especially Toronto and Hamilton, but also London, Ottawa, St. Catharines, and St. Thomas), Winnipeg, and British Columbia. The Knights believed in the all-inclusive organization of the working class and attempted to organize workers without regard to race, sex, or skill. They pioneered in organizing women and black workers, although it should be noted that they had a far less enviable record in their attitudes to Chinese labour. At their peak in 1886, the year of the "Great Upheaval," it was the Knights who made "The Labour Problem," as it was so quaintly termed, the major social question of the day. The "Great Upheaval" saw unprecedented heights of class conflict in both Canada and the United States culminating in the infamous Haymarket explosion in Chicago where a bomb killed a number of policemen. Anarchist labour leaders were blamed and a panic-stricken American bourgeoisie began to take the "labour problem" seriously. The Knights, like the shorter-hours movement of the previous decade, occupied centre stage for a brief but significant moment before beginning a precipitous decline. The Order, however, retained a significant following in eastern Ontario and in Quebec and even enjoyed a brief flourish in the coal mines of Cape Breton in the late 1890's. In Ontario many of the Knights' ideologues, such as Phillips Thompson, A. W. Wright, and George Wrigley, also played prominent roles in helping the radical agrarian movement, the Patrons of Industry, in the

1890's. The Knights' legacy, however, remained long after its demise and provided an inspirational memory to socialists and industrial unionists on into the twentieth century.

Besides the labour problem, the woman question was one of the major social issues of the late nineteenth century. The rise of the feminist movement, albeit largely middle-class, in pursuit of suffrage forced the public to consider uncomfortable questions about women and their social role. A panoply of social organizations originating in the churches but soon embracing a wide range of secular concerns was the political vehicle of the movement. Radical in the 1880's, the later institutionalization of social reform into Progressivism and the Social Gospel would defuse much of this movement's potential.

Middle-class women were not the only ones whose lives were affected. Industrial capitalism absorbed many women into factory jobs, especially in textiles, boot and shoe, tobacco, and garments. Generally young, single women, they worked until marriage and were often subjected to atrocious conditions and low wages. Domestic service provided the other major women's work but it, too, involved low wages and constant supervision which many working-class women resented. Thus, factory jobs appear to have been the choice of working women when and if they could choose.

These were not the only developments in Canada in the years 1849 to 1896. Many themes remain unexplored in these comments and in this collection of essays. For example, the period saw the first flourishing of a new Canadian nationalism which found diverse intellectual supporters in the Canada First movement. It also saw the growth of the Canadian education system and the rapid expansion of schooling to cover larger numbers of children and for longer periods of time. At the more exalted level of the university, Canadian scholarship began to develop a few blooms of achievement, although these grew mainly in theology and philosophy. This latter fact, of course, suggests the importance of Christianity in nineteenth-century Canada.

What we know as the Victorian age was one of emphasis on formal religion. In its love of the construction of huge churches, religion shared the characteristics of the secular world with its railways and great edifices of commerce. Religion shared a belief in the efficiency of bigness as the Methodists, for example, reunited their scattered sects in 1884 so as to be better able to pursue missionary work in the West then being opened by the railway. French Canada, at the same time, was becoming more like the stereotype that Anglo-Saxons held of it. Moved by the aggressive international Catholic revival which began in the 1860's, the so-called ultramontane movement, Quebecers became more influenced by the social and political views of their church than perhaps ever before.

Canada's Industrial Revolution, however, was the most significant historical development in the years from 1849 to the mid-1890's. The transformative process by which Canada became a mature, industrial capitalist society by the turn of the twentieth century affected all realms of Canadian life. Economic growth and the ambitions it engendered led to Confederation and to western expansion, events which in turn engendered the origins of the distinct Canadian regions we know today–a West born in native people's revolt against central Canadian imperialism, an East bitterly split on the merits of the scheme, and a Quebec wooed to the marriage by business interests. As the industrial transformation took root it created the two classes which would become the major actors in the subsequent course of Canadian history–a bourgeoisie with its eyes clearly focused on a prosperous (and profitable) capitalist Canada and a working class born in the emergence of factory production and slowly creating its own institutions to defend itself against the onslaught of capital. This onslaught and the social issues that arose in its wake brought forth a reform movement, the cutting edge of which was led by women. These women began as well to develop a critique of their own position in society, but this latter process stumbled in its inability to question the individualism of late-Victorian Canada.

The following essays develop these themes further and look specifically at a number of these questions in detail. The two readings on the Canadian economy explore the process of industrialization in Toronto and in the Maritimes. The latter piece also considers the question of the failure of Maritime industry and the subsequent underdevelopment of that region. We then turn to social structure to see in a study of one Ontario county how the process of agricultural development had reached a stage which made local farmers very receptive to the politicians' promise to open the West as a new settlement area. This western expansion would later create a whole series of difficulties which twice demanded the armed intervention of the Canadian state. Desmond Morton's article explores the creation of an ongoing police force to preempt the necessity of sending in the army. Meanwhile in the cities Canadian workers faced different adversaries as their employers mechanized and expanded production. In response, workers created trade unions and began to take an active part in the country's affairs. Some of the subsequent conflict is explored by Bryan Palmer. Women also found jobs in the new factories and their lives are explored by Susan Trofimenkoff. As well, middle-class women became increasingly aware of the social problems which accompanied industrial capitalism and began to try to ameliorate these evils. One group of this kind viewed drink as the major enemy, and their organization, the Woman's Christian Temperance Union, is explored by Wendy Mitchinson. The essays here explore the themes chosen for all volumes in this series. The two subsequent volumes in the series will show how the problems which first emerged in this period remained the major pre-occupations of Canadians in the twentieth century.

I
Economic Overview

The debate about the nature of Canadian economic development has been increasing of late. For many years the prevalent view was "the staples thesis" formulated in the 1920's and 1930's by W. A. Mackintosh and Harold Innis, which described the Canadian economy primarily in terms of the evolution of staples - cod, fur, timber, wheat, and, later, minerals. This view tended to obscure early Canadian industrialization. Gregory Kealey takes a close look at one of Canada's major urban centres in the second half of the nineteenth century and discovers an advanced state of industrial development in 1871. Moreover, he shows how this economic development was created by the active co-operation of industrial propagandists and the Canadian state. The argument here would suggest that the contemporary problems of the Canadian economy cannot be traced to the nineteenth century as has been argued by many Canadian left-nationalist scholars of late. Instead we might redirect attention to the early twentieth century when the Americanization of the Canadian economy really commenced in the industries of the "Second Industrial Revolution" such as autos, rubber, chemicals, and electrical goods.

Bill Acheson's essay alerts us to a number of important themes in Canadian political economy. It demonstrates well the crucial stimulus to Canadian industrial growth provided by the National Policy tariff of 1879, only one in a string of protective tariffs going back to the late 1850's and lobbied for by Canadian businessmen. This concerted activity in turn raises significant questions about the relationship between the state and private business interests in the promotion of industrial capitalist development. But perhaps of even more importance, this essay raises questions about the regional impact of industrial capitalist development in Canada. In the process it rebuts the old romantic view of the Maritime nationalists – that all was downhill after 1867 – by showing the significant industrial growth in the region in the 1880's. At the same time, however, Acheson shows that in the early twentieth century the forces of capitalist concentration and centralization were beginning to impede economic growth in the region.

This essay, then, is an important piece of regional analysis for two reasons. First, of course, it tells us much about the economy of the Maritime region which we previously did not know because of the centralist focus of Canadian national history. But perhaps of equal importance, it also puts to rest some hoary regional chestnuts about the decline of the Maritimes. In the process it demonstrates why regional history is so important. It not only fills in the spaces left out of the old national history but also reinterprets the whole picture to force a new conception of Canada which incorporates all its parts, not simply Ontario and Quebec.

FURTHER READING:

For new material on industrialization, see G. J. J. Tulchinsky, *The River Barons: Montreal Businessmen and the Growth of Industry and Transportation, 1837-1853* (Toronto, 1977), especially ch. 12; Bryan D. Palmer, *A Culture in Conflict: Skilled Workers and Industrial Capitalism in Hamilton, Ontario, 1860-1914* (Montreal, 1979), especially ch. 1. See also the pioneering arguments of H. C. Pentland, "The Development of a Capitalistic Labour Market in Canada," *Canadian Journal of Economics and Political Science*, 25 (1959), 450-61; and Stanley Ryerson, *Unequal Union* (Toronto, 1968). Pentland's important thesis appeared posthumously as *Labour and the Development of Industrial Capitalism in Canada* (Toronto, 1981). Also, a considerable econometrics literature now supports an industrial revolution view. See, for example, Gordon W. Bertram, "Historical Statistics on Growth and Structure of Manufacturing in Canada, 1870-1957," in J. Henripin, ed., *C.P.S.A. Conference on Statistics, 1962 and 1963* (Toronto, 1964), 93-146; Edward J. Chambers and Gordon Bertram, "Urbanization and Manufacturing in Central Canada, 1870-1890," in Sylvia Ostry, ed.,

C.P.S.A. Conference on Statistics, 1966 (Toronto, 1966), 225-55; G. W. Bertram, "Economic Growth in Canadian Industry, 1870-1915," *Canadian Journal of Economics and Political Science*, 29 (1963), 159-84; and Duncan M. McDougall, "Canadian Manufactured Commodity Output, 1870-1915," *Canadian Journal of Economics*, 4 (1971), 21-36. For a critical view, see Tom Naylor, *The History of Canadian Business*, 2 vols. (Toronto, 1976); and Larry MacDonald, "Merchants against Industry: An Idea and its Origins," *Canadian Historical Review*, 56 (1975), 263-81.

For specific studies of early industrial activity in the Maritime region, see T. W. Acheson, "The Great Merchant and Economic Development in St. John 1820-1850," *Acadiensis*, 8 (1979), 3-27; L. D. McCann, "Staples and the New Industrialism in the Growth of Post-Confederation Halifax," *Acadiensis*, 8 (1979), 47-79; and Robert Babcock, "Economic Development in Portland, Maine and Saint John, N.B. During the Age of Iron and Steam, 1850-1914," *American Review of Canadian Studies*, 9 (1979), 3-37. For a stimulating critique of prevalent views of regional problems, see David Frank, "The Nine Myths of Regional Disparity," *Canadian Dimension*, 13, 2 (1979), 18-21. On regionalism as a concept, see the special issue of the *Journal of Canadian Studies*, 15, 2 (1980), especially William Westfall, "On the Concept of Region in Canadian History and Literature," 3-15.

Gregory S. Kealey teaches history at Memorial University of Newfoundland and edits *Labour/Le Travailleur* and is the editor of McClelland and Stewart's Canadian Social History Series. **T. W. Acheson** is a member of the History Department of the University of New Brunswick and one of the leading Maritime regional historians.

Toronto's Industrial Revolution, 1850-1892

by Gregory S. Kealey

Between the late 1840's and the early 1890's Canada experienced its own Industrial Revolution. Toronto, Canada's second largest city, played a major role in this transformation. Its capitalists led the strategic drive for protective tariffs, enabling native industries to thrive and prosper; its working class provided the leadership for organized labour in central Canada.

Most Canadian economic history to date has dealt mainly with the role of staple exports in Canadian development.[1] They have been viewed as dominating the economy until the early twentieth century, when finally some attention is paid to industrial development.[2] Although suggestive when first pursued in the 1930's, this approach has obscured key components of the nineteenth-century Canadian economy, especially the emergence of industry. Attention to cod, beaver, pine, wheat, and to the rivers, the canals, and the railroads that carried them to market has unfortunately all but excluded the study of the mills and factories which grew on their banks and built their rails and locomotives.[3]

The few scholars who have studied early Canadian manufacturing have all too often restricted their attention to the published census returns. The aggregate data on industrial development disguises much that the available manuscript returns reveal. For example, Toronto in 1871 had 9,400 workers spread throughout

From Gregory S. Kealey, *Toronto Workers Respond to Industrial Capitalism 1867-1892* (Toronto: University of Toronto Press, 1980), 3-34.

approximately 560 shops and factories. This suggests that the average Toronto worker was employed in a relatively small shop situation with about sixteen other employees. But such an "average" totally obscures the reality of the Toronto economy in 1870. Actually, 38 per cent of Toronto's industrial work force was employed in factories of over a hundred workers. Another 21 per cent worked with between fifty and ninety-nine other employees and 11 per cent worked in shops with between thirty and forty-nine others. Thus, fully 70 per cent of Toronto workers in 1871 worked in shops or factories employing over thirty men and women (see Table 1). The old pre-industrial labour market revolving around personal contact between employer and employee in small shops no longer prevailed in Toronto. How had this new industrial capitalist labour market been created?

TABLE 1

Toronto Factories Employing Over 30 Workers, 1871

Number of workers	*Number of establishments*	*%of ests.*	*Number of workers*	*% of workers*
100+	19	3	3,594	36
50–99	30	5	2,074	20.7
30–49	28	5	1,046	10.5
Total 30+	77	13	6,714	67.1
0–29	495	88	3,285	32.9

SOURCE: Canada Census, 1871, Industrial Mss., Toronto. Calculations throughout are my own.

Answering that question first requires a discussion of the broader development of industrial capitalism in Canada. First I shall sketch the emergence of an industrial capitalist development strategy increasingly reliant on the use of the Canadian state. Then I shall focus on Toronto to trace its specific development from the 1850's to the early 1890's.

I

Recent Canadian economic historians,[4] especially Tom Naylor, have argued that Canadian industrial capitalism developed as a peculiar hybrid shaped by the colonial context and the Canadian bourgeoisie's inability to pursue industrial development as its primary aim. Here I shall argue that industrial capitalist development in central Canada in the period under study displays no such weaknesses. The Toronto case will provide the specific evidence, but it is important first to demonstrate the creation of a concerted and comprehensive industrial capitalist strategy of development in central Canada.

The late 1840's and 1850's mark the crucial transition years in the evolution of the Canadian economy. In the mid-1840's the British Industrial Revolution had proceeded sufficiently far that England began to dismantle its old colonial system. The system of preferential tariffs on timber and grain that had shaped the Canadian economy was systematically removed. Its removal caused a panic in Canadian merchant circles, which burgeoned with the arrival in the same year of hordes of Irish-Catholic famine migrants. The disembarking of huge numbers of impoverished, starving, and often diseased Irish threw Canadian cities into turmoil. The final blow came in 1849 when Lord Elgin signed the hated Rebellion Losses Bill, which recompensed all Canadians for their losses in 1837–possibly, opponents alleged, including even some of the rebels. This was too much for the Toronto and Montreal merchant élites who rioted a number of times in the summer of 1849 and began discussing annexation to the United States.

Yet, cooler heads prevailed and out of these crises emerged the major strategies that would transform the Canadian economy: protection, railways, and Confederation. The first had been present as a potential development strategy since the early 1830's. In both 1830 and 1831 Toronto cabinetmakers, led by Thomas Wallis, had petitioned the Assembly to prevent the importation of furniture which competed with the domestic product.[5] These petitions failed, and the subject disappeared until the early 1840's when shoemakers from Montreal, Kingston, and Belleville petitioned for protection against American imports.[6] The economic crisis precipitated by British free trade greatly increased interest in protection and in home manufactures. Robert Baldwin Sullivan, a former Canadian Legislative Councillor and Provincial Secretary in the Baldwin-LaFontaine ministry of 1848, became protection's most prominent promoter. In an inaugural address to the Hamilton Mechanics' Institute in November 1847, Sullivan strongly advocated a strategy of industrial development as the only solution to the current crisis.[7] In reviewing the economic history of the young country, he revised conventional wisdom, arguing that the fur trade had been of "no use to

Canada" since the "profits of their enterprise were realized at a distance, or were remitted thither."[8] Moreover, the timber trade was only slightly more beneficial to Canada, but "in proportion to its magnitude, it has been of little advantage." Finally, the operation of the current wheat and flour trade was dismissed in similar terms. The Canadian economy's historical problem was clear: "For many, very many, years, the people of this country manufactured nothing for themselves; and up to this day articles of the coarsest and most simple fabric, and in the most common use, are brought in ready-made in vast quantities." As a result Canada was not developing:

> And these towns would have furnished a home market for a large portion of the produce of the land, and have become as they did in the early times of English History, places in which the capital of the country would have accumulated. However slow and difficult the accumulation might have been, we still should have the fruits of industry ready to be expended in new enterprise. Capital would be reproducing capital, and town and country acting and re-acting on each other, to the advantage of both.

Instead, all "the profits of the manufacturers in this Province have accumulated in England." The remainder of the lecture polemicized in favour of home manufactures as the obvious and only solution to Canada's economic woes. Searching the province for favourable examples, Sullivan described the Marmora Iron Works, a few woollen mills, and some foundries, but the very paucity of examples helped demonstrate his thesis.[9] The solution lay in the recruitment of "more of the artizans, and more of the manufacturing capital of England" and then, when the country finally had something to protect, high tariffs. Although put extremely tentatively, the policy implication was clear:

> Instead of theorizing generally upon true or false abstract propositions, my mental constitution, a narrow education, leads me to particularize before acting–I do not know what is good or bad for England, in the way of Protection, or of free trade. But I do know that if the shoes and boots made by fifty tradesmen in Toronto, were supplanted in the market, by a like quantity of shoes and boots made in the state prison at

> Auburn, Toronto would lose two hundred of her citizens, who build houses, pay taxes, make money, and keep it . . . and the accumulation of profit from the industry of these fifty citizens, would be lost to the long future.

In 1849 protection became a key policy of the British-American League, a mainly Tory lobbying group which, while opposing Elgin, attempted to prevent the excesses of the Annexationists by proposing alternative economic and political strategies for Canada. Perhaps the most important plank in its platform demanded: "That it is essential to the prosperity of the country that the tariff should be so proportioned and levied as to afford just and adequate protection to the manufacturing and industrial classes of the country, and to secure to the agricultural population a home market with fair and remunerating prices for all descriptions of farm produce."[10] Later, at the league's convention at Kingston, this strategy was combined with a proposed union of all the British North American colonies. This suggestion flowed from "the necessity which exists for extending commercial intercourse with our sister colonies, thereby creating large home markets for the consumption of agricultural products and domestic manufactures." The league's *Address to the Inhabitants of Canada* was even more explicit:

> In her promulgation of Free Trade principles, she [Great Britain] has lost sight of the interests of her colonies, with the view of obtaining from all the nations reciprocal free trade, and thereby inundating the world with her manufactures. This new policy has produced in Canada its inevitable results. Unprotected by an adequate tariff, we have continued to consume a vast amount of British manufactures, whilst our produce, the principle source upon which we rely for their payment, rarely entered the English market except at a sacrifice. The result has been a monetary pressure, extensive bankruptcy, and general distress.[11]

The solution for these problems lay in protection:

> The true elements of your country's wealth – the certain indices of her prosperity – can only be developed by the adoption of measures which will fill her cities with the busy hum of industry, make her streams the outlet of that wealth which will be poured forth from the loom and the foundry, the teeming

> harvests of her soil, and the produce of her primeval forest. For the attainment of these results it is essential that a tariff . . . should be so proportioned and levied as to afford just and adequate protection to every industrial class . . . so as to create a Home Market for Home Industry, and enrich together consumer and producer.[12]

One of the major propagandists of this new protectionist sentiment and an important figure in the British-American League was John William Gamble. A Toronto Tory lawyer, he put into practice the theories of Robert Baldwin Sullivan. In the small community of Pine Grove on the Humber River, upstream from Toronto, Gamble erected a primitive industrial complex which combined a grist and flour mill with a sawmill, a distillery, and a small cotton textile manufactory.[13] At the British-American League meeting in 1849, Gamble gave the major theoretical speeches, justifying the move to protection. In an argument reminiscent of Sullivan, he showed that British colonial policy had favoured Britain at the expense of Canada and he pointed to the United States as proof of what could be accomplished with protection. Adam Smith had been his intellectual companion since his youth, "but practical experience had of late forced upon him the conviction, that the beautiful theory was not borne out by corresponding benefits." Thus he had come to adopt "the views of the American Protectionists as those most consonant with sound reason and common sense." The solution followed: "The proper remedy was to protect our native industry, to protect it from the surplus products of the industry of other countries . . . Where the raw material produced in any country is worked up in that country, the difference between the value of the material and the finished article is retained in the country."[14]

In a late fall meeting in Toronto, British-American League delegates degenerated into wrangling over the question of constitutional change. Compact Tory elements opposed a proposal for an elected legislative council. Unanimity remained, however, on the questions of union of the British-American provinces and the need for a protective tariff. Orange leaders Ogle Gowan and George Benjamin gave their support to Gamble who again led the fight for protection.[15]

The tariff was increased from 7½ to 12½ per cent in 1849, but this was not enough to satisfy the advocates of protection. Gamble continued his agitation in the legislature and introduced unsuccessful motions in 1852 and 1853 in favour of increased tariff protection.[16] He did manage, however, to have tariffs lowered on some raw materials, which were needed for home manufactures and could never be produced in Canada.

The campaign for higher tariffs gained strength in the 1850's with the rapid growth of Canadian industry which accompanied that decade's railroad boom. During this period the Canadian state pursued a systematic and vigorous policy of encouraging railroad-building, for which two major pieces of legislation provided the necessary guarantees of government financial support. Francis Hincks' Guarantee Act of 1849 allowed the government to guarantee the interest on half the bonds of any railway over 75 miles in length, provided that half the railway had already been built. Three years later, Hincks' Municipal Loan Fund Act created a government fund to back the municipal debentures, since the Canadian government was more highly regarded in international capital markets than local towns.[17] The railway boom that followed these government policies was an orgy of corruption and excess, but at the end of the decade the Canadas had over 2,000 miles of railway compared with only 66 in 1850. The railroad boom was of crucial importance to Canadian industrial development. It also demonstrates the important role the Canadian state played in augmenting domestic capital formation. There are various estimates of capital importation into the Canadas in the 1850's, but none are lower than a minimum of $100 million. This represented an inflow of foreign capital of at least four times the magnitude of any previous capital importation. Pentland has pointed out the importance of the "unintended effects":

> They represented, first, a commitment of fixed capital, overhead costs, and permanent staffs, that are the essence of metropolitan economies. By integrating the Canadian market, they opened the way for Canadian manufacturers to conquer it. Most important, the overflow of foreign capital into Canada made it possible at the second and third remove for Canadians to amass funds which could be invested in new enterprises. The water-power sites created by the canals, the metal industries necessarily introduced by the railroads, and the mass of labour with urban preferences drawn by the construction work, all had the same result.[18]

Capital was certainly accumulated in Canada, especially by contractors hired to build North American railroads in the nineteenth century and by Canadian politicians and their close friends and colleagues involved in countless shady deals in Canadian business. It is worth pointing out at this point that the Canadian state and business were, and remain, intertwined in ways that appear to extend beyond the interlocking in other capitalist societies.[19] The capital accumulated in railroads quickly was transformed into industrial development as a producer goods industry sprang up to feed the new railways. Locomotive manufacturing, rolling mills for rails, rolling stock construction, and other secondary metal manufacturing rose to meet the voracious appetite of the new transportation system. This new rail network also integrated the Canadian market and brought new areas into the exchange economy. Consumer goods industries, such as boots and shoes and clothing, centred in the rapidly growing cities and grew to service their immediate populace and an increasingly extensive hinterland. The railroads had an extensive impact on the Canadian economy, encouraging a rapid expansion in the 1850's which developed both a logic and a dynamic of its own.

Toronto entrepreneurs played major roles in this boom and the city benefited greatly. By 1853 the Northern Railway connected Toronto to Barrie and by 1855 was completed to Collingwood on Georgian Bay. One year later the Grand Trunk opened from Montreal to Toronto and the Great Western joined Toronto to Hamilton and points west.[20] The railway boom of the 1850's committed the Canadian state to a policy of industrial development. By the late 1850's Canadian capitalists, facing the depression conditions that spread rapidly after 1857, again began to agitate strenuously for protection. Montreal merchant William Weir arrived in Toronto in 1856 and began publishing the *Canadian Merchants' Magazine and Commercial Review* the following year,[21] which from its inception took the lead in advocating the development of "Home Industry."[22]

For three years Weir toured the Canadas, writing vivid descriptions of industrial successes.[23] To these he added initially didactic editorials explaining the benefits of home manufactures.[24] As the economic crisis of the late 1850's deepened, however, his pen became increasingly polemical. Among the protectionists, he was perhaps most persuasive in articulating what were to become the major themes:

> Canada is not in the same position as England, nor even as the United States. It has but few manufactures, and they are yet in their infancy. If, therefore, they do not receive here the benefit of that encouragement which was afforded to them . . . in those countries, and which the laws of the United States still accord to them, they will perish in their infancy, our resources will become of no avail, capital will be banished from our country, and the energies of our countrymen will be paralyzed by the want of that occupation which they need. Thus we drive them to a foreign land in search of what our foresight might have found for them at home; that labour which is a condition of their subsistence.[25]

This reasoning led him to call for "reciprocity in duties as well as free trade" with the United States, since the Canadian tariff should "ensure to the manufacturers such Protection as other Governments have accorded, and still accord."[26]

By April 1858 the sentiments for tariff reform had increased to the point that Weir described it as a "movement" and the august Montreal Board of Trade, which he had earlier identified as the major bastion of opposition to protection, agreed to co-operate with a committee founded to propose "legislative measures as may foster Native Industry."[27] In that same month Weir joined forces with Hamilton merchant Isaac Buchanan to create the Association for the Protection of Canadian Industry (APCI), which held a public meeting in Toronto's St. Lawrence Hall to commence its campaign.[28] This body lobbied systematically for a new tariff. The APCI rationale restated the earlier arguments of Gamble, Sullivan, and Weir, blaming the new economic distress of the late 1850's on

> the present tariff being based on erroneous principles, admitting as it does, at low rates of duty, the manufactures of other countries, that can be made by a class of labour now in Canada, unfitted for agricultural pursuits, and charging high rates on articles that cannot be produced in the country, thereby preventing the development of the natural resources of the colony, as well as injuring Canada as a field of immigration.[29]

The APCI proposed an alternative plan for: raw materials to enter at very low rates or even free; articles of consumption such as sugar, tea, coffee, molasses also to enter at very low rates; an intermediate list of goods not produced in Canada and only semi-processed to be charged at a medium rate of about 15 per cent; and finally that "all manufactures in Wood, Iron, Tin, Brass, Copper, Leather, India Rubber, etc., competing with our industrial products . . . [to] be charged a duty of about 25%."[30]

Prominent among the members of APCI were leading Toronto industrialists such as Robert Hay and William Lyman. Future Toronto manufacturer Hart Massey, then still manufacturing agricultural implements in Newcastle, was also active.[31] Buchanan's agitation for a concerted and consistent policy of protection increased over the next few years. An active propagandist, he published a series of books, pamphlets, broadsheets, and letters throughout the early 1860's.[32] In all of these writings, he lay the basis for the alliance of Tory and producer that figured so prominently in the politics of the 1870's and 1880's. On many occasions he cited, as evidence for the need to produce an alliance of industrial capitalists and workers to save the economy of the nation, the statement of a British labour radical in Hyde Park: "if political economy is against us then we are against political economy."[33] The pervasive influence of protectionist sentiments and, of course, the growth of industry can also be seen in the Toronto Board of Trade's gradual shift from a policy of free trade to one of protection. By the 1860's its enthusiastic reports on industrial development in Toronto marked its final conversion.[34]

William Weir continued his activities as well, as secretary of APCI and editor of the *Merchants' Magazine*. In the fall of 1858 he published a comprehensive essay on "The Manufactures of Upper Canada," which, after surveying the state of local industry, argued for a three-pronged government policy to aid manufacturers. In addition to a "sound commercial policy" which would admit needed raw materials free, raise the necessary government revenues by taxing luxury imports heavily, and strongly protect home manufactures, he also called for direct assistance to manufacturers through bounties and for active government promotion of Upper-Canadian prospects abroad to help recruit British and American capital.[35]

These campaigns – the propaganda work of Weir and Buchanan and the lobbying activities of APCI – were eminently successful. The Galt-Cayley tariff of 1858 and the Galt tariff of 1859 met the demands of Canadian manufacturers. There has been considerable debate recently as to whether these tariffs were actually protectionist. A recent rigorous econometric analysis has proved conclusively that they did represent an advanced example of tariff-building, employing a three-tier system of tariff levels to promote industrial development.[36]

Debate about these tariffs has centred on Galt's description of them as only "incidental protection." Historians who argue they were not protective on this basis ignore the fact that Galt made this argument while in Great Britain to offset the complaints of British manufacturers about the new Canadian policy of protection. His special pleading on that occasion was clear to the British manufacturers who were not satisfied by his explanations. He admitted that there was in Canada a large and influential party that advocated a protective policy, but claimed that the policy had not been adopted. He admitted, however, that "the necessity of increased taxation for the purposes of revenue has, to a certain extent, compelled action in partial unison with their views, and has caused more attention to be given to the proper adjustment of the duties, so as neither unduly to stimulate nor depress the few branches of manufacture which exist in Canada." Although denying that the tariff increase would lead to any considerable development of manufacturing industry, he did note that the government would be gratified if "the duties . . . should incidentally benefit and encourage the production of many of those articles which we now import."[37]

Despite recent arguments, then, the 1859 tariff was protective. Nineteenth-century commentators certainly had no doubts. In his autobiography, William Weir concluded that "for the first time was the principle of protection applied to Canadian manufactures."[38] Throughout the 1870's speakers in Dominion Board of Trade debates on protection identified the Galt tariff as protective.[39] And in 1880, John MacLean, a leading protectionist, described the 1859 tariff "as the first ever framed in this country for the avowed purpose of developing home manufactures, and in obedience to a popular demand."[40]

Moreover, the Upper-Canadian protection advocates were delighted. Weir, for example, observed that "our tariff is constructed upon principles, which, if not ultra-protective, yet afford a fair advantage to the home manufacturer against the foreigner . . . the consequence is that the manufacturers of Canada . . . may be safely regarded as the most successful and promising class that the country possesses at the present moment."[41] The next step, Weir felt, was to recruit immigrants who possessed capital and manufacturing experience.

Alexander Somerville, "The Whistler at the Plough" of Chartist fame, advanced this theme in the pages of the *Canadian Illustrated News* in the early 1860's. Frequently he argued that Canada needed a selective immigration policy, that British immigrants without capital or agricultural experience were of little use to the Canadian economy, and that what Canada needed was men of moderate capital. "We want more manufacturers in textile fabrics, iron work, pottery, glassware, leather, etc. We have abundance of raw material for all of these, and an extensive market as well, as only require the capital in order to commence their manufacture on a large scale. Let us secure that and labourers will follow it in abundance without any spasmodic efforts on our part to increase them."[42] He combined this interest with a fascination for the development of Canadian industry; the pages of the *Illustrated News* were crowded with engravings and descriptions of Canada's fledgling factories.

Both Somerville and Weir continually called for an active state role in industrial development. One response to these demands was the Board of Arts and Manufactures of Upper Canada. The board established and supervised mechanics' institutes and industrial exhibits, organized Canada's participation in overseas trade exhibitions, published the *Journal*, and in general promoted Canadian industrial development. Under the editorship of Henry Youle Hind, Toronto engineer, explorer, and scientist, and later of William Edwards, the major force behind the Toronto Mechanics' Institute, the *Journal* from 1861 to 1867 published educational, scientific, and descriptive materials for Canadian manufacturers. Predictably, Edwards advocated protection, since without it "no new country could succeed in establishing extensive manufactures."[43] Because of its status as a government publication, the *Journal* did not engage in an extensive commentary on the economic significance of confederation, but the old Hamilton politico, Isaac Buchanan, did.

On retiring from active politics, Buchanan issued a strong call for confederation in 1865, which he and many other central Canadian proponents of industrial capitalism saw as the natural option after the abrogation of the Reciprocity Treaty in natural products with the United States. He argued that it was vital to both the Maritimes and central Canada to have each other as markets to substitute for the loss of the United States. It was self-evident, he added, "that now we must either be drifted by industrial necessity into Annexation . . . or must find markets for our industry and an outlet for our trade through an intimate and indissoluble union of all the provinces of British North America."[44]

Unlike other promoters of confederation, Buchanan opposed the 1866 reduction in the Canadian tariff. This reduction was intended as a conciliatory gesture to the eastern provinces where there was little interest in protection, and where anti-confederate forces focused considerable attention on the dangers of protection for the Maritime economy. Buchanan reorganized the Association for the Promotion of Canadian Industry in September 1866, noting that "the immediate objects of this society [the old APCI] having been triumphantly arrived at, it was allowed to die out, after leaving to the country that tariff which we now seek to have restored."[45] Most of the province's important industrial capitalists gathered together in Toronto to protest the new tariff. Toronto representatives included Robert Hay, W. Gooderham, William Hamilton, J. J. Taylor; representatives from shoe firms such as W. Hamilton and Sessions, Carpenter and Co.; tobacco manufacturers such as A. Dredge and A. Schack; and woollens producer Joseph Simpson. At least twenty-two Toronto firms were represented at this meeting and joined the new association.

The declaration of the new APCI evidenced the increasing self-consciousness of the new industrial capitalist class. They complained bitterly that "we hear much of the shipping interest, also of the railroad interest; it is now full time that the manufacturers' interest should assume that place in public affairs, to which its importance fully entitles it." Their aims were simply "to obtain protection to a moderate extent, to endeavour to secure a permanency in our tariffs, to use every possible means to effect a return to the tariff list discarded at the last session of Parliament, and to avail ourselves . . . of all opportunities for enlightening the public mind [of] . . . the truth regarding the importance of manufacturers to this country." Unfortunately for them, the exigencies of creating the new nation were more immediate than their arguments and the tariffs were not readjusted in 1866.

The APCI re-emerged in the early 1870's as the Manufacturers Association of Ontario, which in turn transformed itself in the 1880's into the Canadian Manufacturers' Association, still the chief lobbyist for industrial interests in Canada.[46] In the 1870's the manufacturers also carried their fight for higher tariffs to the

Dominion Board of Trade where Toronto delegates led an annual battle against free-trade advocates. In 1871 William Elliott recommended a tariff increase on manufactured goods to 20 per cent in order to promote Canadian industry. In supporting the motion, Toronto Board of Trade colleague and textile manufacturer John Gordon pointed out that "there had been, in 1859, an intention to inaugurate a policy that would encourage manufacturers." This policy had met with considerable success, "but on the abrogation of that tariff, that capital languished and languishes still."[47] Elliott's motion failed, but Toronto provided three of the six favourable votes.

The onslaught of a depression in 1873 gave protectionist efforts more credibility, and in 1874 Toronto clothing manufacturer John Gillespie again moved for a tariff increase to 20 per cent.[48] This motion gained strong support in two position papers. The first, by Dr. L. S. Olle of St. Catharines, promoted "a generous policy of protection" and "liberal subventions in the shape of bonuses, bounties, grants of public land, etc." in order to develop a Canadian iron and steel industry. The second paper, titled "Buchanan's Postulates and Remedies," denounced "the imposition on Canada of the *Free Trade and Hard Money Heresies of England*, which simply amount to an ignoring, or abnegation, of practical patriotism." Instead, Isaac Buchanan called for "a *Patriotic Industrial Policy*" – either free trade with the U.S. or reciprocal duties (emphasis in original). Other Toronto delegates spoke in favour of Elliott's resolution, reminding those present that his nearly identical 1871 motion had been "in a considerable minority then." After a lengthy debate the board, by a vote of 42 to 12, accepted Thomas White's more moderate proposal, which requested that "the principle of protection to the manufacturing industries of the country be embodied in such revision of the tariff, so far as the same can be carried out consistently with the commerce and revenue requirements of the country."[49]

The failure of the Mackenzie government to respond favourably to this proposal and the deepening depression led to a more vigorous expression of protectionist positions at the 1876 meeting. There, Hamilton's Adam Brown, seconded by Toronto paper manufacturer Hugh Staunton, called for legislation to protect "the capital already invested in manufactures" against the effects of the depression, which was "mainly owing to the competition of American manufacturers, who make of Canada a slaughter market for their surplus products." Since "this system of unfair and unequal competition will . . . increase in intensity in the future," he resolved, "that in the opinion of this Board the true and patriotic policy for the Canadian Government would be to adopt a thoroughly national commercial policy, and with that view that in any readjustment of the tariff, reciprocal duties with the United States be adopted."[50] Citing Horace Greeley favourably, Brown argued "squarely for a national policy . . . the only true policy for a new country to build itself up." Toronto's W. H. Howland supported the motion, stressing the severe difficulties of Ontario manufacturers; moreover, confederation was failing, he argued, since old north-south trade patterns persisted and the provinces were little "more than a bundle of sticks loosely tied together." For these reasons, Howland also demanded a national policy. This strongly protectionist motion carried 22 to 14, with all Toronto delegates supporting it.

The 1877 meeting passed a similar motion after hearing lengthy descriptions of industrial distress throughout the nation, which included W. H. Howland's version of the near collapse of the Toronto furniture factory of Robert Hay.[51] Similar motions were endorsed in 1878 with the addition of a more specific call for aid to the nascent iron and steel industry. Finally, in 1879 Montreal's Thomas White, Jr., smugly summed up the experience of the 1870's: "It must be a matter for very great congratulation that this subject which has occupied our attention at this Board during the last five years, is now being discussed not as a controversial question at all, but as to the manner in which our views are to be carried into effect."[52] The lonely position held by Toronto Board of Trade delegates in 1871 not only had become the accepted orthodoxy of the Dominion Board of Trade but also was about to be enacted as part of the National Policy by the triumphant Macdonald government.

The difficulty of winning control of the Dominion Board of Trade had also led to the formation of the Manufacturers' Association of Ontario in 1875. Leading roles in that association were played by Toronto manufacturers Lyman (drugs), Staunton (paper), Gurney (stoves), Hay (furniture), W. Hamilton (machinery), and W. B. Hamilton (boot and shoe). At their meeting in November 1875 they complained bitterly of the impact of U.S. goods being dumped on the Canadian market and called for increased protection. Significantly, this call for higher tariffs, at least back to the level of the Galt 1859 tariff, came from both

Liberal and Tory manufacturers.[53] This economic stance led to the creation of purportedly non-partisan associations, such as the Dominion National League, which threw its support behind the Tories in the crucial national policy election of 1878. William Fraser, the secretary and major force in the league, held the same position in the Manufacturers' Association of Ontario, and was a vociferous delegate at Dominion Board of Trade meetings.[54]

The 1878 Tory election triumph led to the closer ties between manufacturers and the Canadian state that were to anger western farmers and Maritime nationalists for the following century. Manufacturers met in Toronto and Montreal in 1879 and decided upon tariff levels.[55] Delegations made their wishes known to the new Tory government, and a complicated process of trade-offs then commenced. Critics were certain that the famous "Red Parlour" meetings in Toronto's Queen's Hotel between Macdonald and the industrialists revolved more around campaign funds for the Tories than the good of the country.[56] Be that as it may, by 1879 Canadian industrial capitalists had come to dominate the state and were able to dictate their self-interested policies in the name of the common good. John A. Macdonald had pledged himself to this policy in a speech in 1878 when he announced, "I cannot tell what protection you require. But let each manufacturer tell us what he wants, and we will try to give him what he needs."[57]

Toronto industrial capitalists played prominent roles in all these developments. Besides creating the strong and important lobbying bodies such as APCI, the Manufacturers' Association of Ontario, and later the Canadian Manufacturers' Association, they were also active in the Dominion Board of Trade. In addition, in 1878, because of the importance of the National Policy election, one of their leaders, furniture manufacturer Robert Hay, formerly a Liberal, ran for office in support of protection and sat as one of Toronto's members of parliament for two terms.

The National Policy was modified only slightly in the 1880's. All tariff adjustments were in aid of home industry and the only major change came in 1887 when iron and steel interests received substantially increased protection. Thus from 1850 to the early 1890's, the period in which industrial capitalism transformed Canadian society, the Canadian bourgeoisie played an active role in using the state to further capitalist accumulation. This period of considerable economic growth, but most importantly of qualitative transformations, has been too long ignored by the staples interpretation of Canadian economic history and by the nationalist focus on Confederation. The four decades which followed the crisis of 1849 lay the foundations for the twentieth-century Canadian economy, and without an understanding of the development of industrial capitalism in Canada it would be impossible to understand the present situation.[58]

Let us now turn to a specific analysis of the transformation and growth of the Toronto economy.

II

The triumphant march of industrial capitalism is apparent in any analysis of the Toronto economy in the years 1850 to 1890. By the 1840's capitalist handicraft production had firmly established itself in the city. The 1850's witnessed a consolidation of handicrafts into manufactories either through uniting various different craftsmen as in carriage-making (wheelwrights, blacksmiths, carpenters, painters, and others), or through an ever-increasing division of labour, as in shoemaking (cutters, fitters, makers, and so on). Although much larger than the artisan's shop and displaying an increased division of labour, the manufactory was still largely dependent on hand production. From the 1860's to the 1880's the modern factory emerged with the introduction of machinery.

This process of economic transformation underlay the strategies of Toronto capitalists analysed above. If Toronto capitalists with a strategy of industrial development had not spoken for the nation in 1849, by 1879 there could be little question that their views reigned triumphant under the guise of the National Policy.

Data on the Toronto economy in the 1840's are slight but it is clear that production was centred in small shops and perhaps a few manufactories.[59] The 1846 *Canadian Gazeteer* listed numerous artisans, such as thirty-seven blacksmiths, forty-nine shoemakers, and twenty-five cabinetmakers, but the *Gazeteer* listed no businesses of a substantial size.[60] The sketchy 1848 census listed seventy-five "factories" in Toronto but the more detailed census of 1851 found only fifty-five.[61] Most of these were probably artisan shops employing a few journeymen and apprentices. A closer look at four Toronto industries – cabinetmaking, metallurgy, shoe manufacturing, and tobacco manufacturing – will illustrate the shift to manufactories and finally to modern industry.

Cabinetmakers were present in Toronto quite early. Perhaps the key development in the industry was the unheralded arrival in 1831 of two British journeymen cabinetmakers, Robert Hay and John Jacques.[62] Hay, born in Scotland in 1808, apprenticed as a cabinetmaker at the age of fourteen; Jacques, born in England in 1804, began learning the trade at six. On their arrival in York, both went to work as journeymen, and in 1835 they joined forces to buy the shop of William Maxwell, Jacques' boss. Besides themselves they employed only two apprentices, and they were so successful that by the 1840's they had accumulated sufficient capital to build their first manufactory. There were two other relatively large cabinetmaking shops in Toronto in the 1840's: the City Chair Factory, which employed between eight and ten men, and the cabinet works of the O'Neill Brothers, which employed fifteen to twenty men. Jacques' and Hay's factory outdid their rivals', however; by the early 1850's it employed between ninety and one hundred men and had its first steam engine to power substantial new machinery. In 1853 they expanded once again into a new factory employing two hundred men and bought a bigger engine. A disastrous fire destroyed the plant in 1854, but with a generous loan from the city of Toronto, they rebuilt it. After a second fire and rebuilding, in 1857 the company diversified by buying forests north of Toronto and erecting a saw mill and rough factory in New Lowell to process wood for the Toronto plant. In 1861 they reported a total capitalization of $200,000, and employed two hundred men and fifty women in Toronto and thirty men in New Lowell.

By 1865 the Jacques and Hay factory complex in Toronto included a building housing the boiler and 35 hp steam engine, the factory proper, a warehouse, and a retail store and office. In the factory the operation was divided by floors: on the first was the heavy machinery and the turning department where for much "the hand still guided the tool"; the second was the location of chair production from which came most of the chairs and desks for the expanding Upper-Canadian school system; the third was another "place of comparative quiet" where the finer cabinetmaking was done, some of the best of which reached export markets in Scotland and England; the top floor was reserved for design and repair. Thus, although there were still pools of handicraft labour left in the factory, the basic organization was industrial with a highly developed division of labour, separate management and design functions, and extensive mechanization. Employee lists demonstrate both the advanced division of labour and the maintenance of skill in the factory. Along with the many labourers and managers (including a timekeeper) typical of the factory were found cabinetmakers, chairmakers, carvers, turners, carpenters, finishers, sawyers, and upholsterers.[63]

Although a few small shops remained in the 1850's and 1860's, by the early 1870's Jacques and Hay dominated the furniture market in Toronto. The Industrial Revolution had transformed the Toronto furniture industry.

The foundry and iron business in Toronto developed steadily if less spectacularly. There were a number of small foundries in the 1830's and 1840's, some substantial enough to build large steam engines.[64] The new railway age gave the industry its major impetus. The foundry of James Good, for example, which had previously specialized in stoves, manufactured the second locomotive for the Northern Railway.[65] Money made in railway contracting by entrepreneurs such as Casimir Gzowski and D. L. Macpherson was wisely reinvested in producer goods industries that could supply the growing railway network of Ontario. These two men set up the Toronto Locomotive Works in the 1850's and in 1860 the Toronto Rolling Mills, which by 1866 employed over 300 men. Although primarily involved in rerolling old rails, the Rolling Mill also puddled new iron for the head of the new rails. Powered by a 500 hp engine, the mill was the most spectacular of Toronto's mid-century industries.[66] The unusual painting of the mill by William Armstrong suggests how far industrialization had proceeded by 1864 and how far it had to go, especially in terms of labour management.[67]

The Toronto economy in this period developed the producer goods that are essential for a strong industrial base. Most of the machinery which powered the new Toronto factories was built at home. Important producer goods manufacturers were the Toronto Car Wheel Co., Currie Boilers, the Soho Foundry, and Dickey, Neill and Co.-the makers of engines for Jacques and Hay and twenty-five other Toronto factories. Currie employed around forty workers and Dickey over 100 by the mid-1860's.[68] Millwright and machinist Francis Metcalf opened his Don Foundry in the late 1840's and specialized in steam engines and heavy castings for grist and saw mills.[69] Perhaps the most important of these early manufacturers was William Hamilton, a Scottish-born, English-trained machinist. He arrived in Toronto in 1850 and found work at James Good's foundry because of his knowledge of steam-driven machine tools. In 1852 he established the

St. Lawrence Foundry, Engine Works and Machine Shop. Although work there in the 1850's was primarily restricted to castings of various kinds, he still employed over 400 men by 1861.[70]

The American Civil War provided a major impetus to the Canadian machine industry as manufacturers there turned to war production. The St. Lawrence Foundry especially benefited and expanded swiftly in the early 1860's. It constructed a complete machine system for the new Toronto Rolling Mill, machinery for Joseph Simpson's Toronto Knitting Co., and, most importantly, nearly all the power presses for the rapidly expanding Toronto tobacco industry.[71] The foundry also pioneered new processes:

> Hamilton's production techniques differed markedly from those then most current in Toronto. Good, for example, had been producing what were virtually handmade machines since the 1830's. Hamilton used a larger number of machine tools while retaining numerous well-trained artisans; his techniques attracted machinists, inventors, and moulders of high calibre.[72]

A more specialized secondary-metal manufacturer was the J. J. Taylor Safe Works. An American immigrant, Taylor arrived in Toronto in 1855, and exported safes to the United States until the outbreak of the Civil War. Even after that trade failed, his company continued to grow and by the mid-1860's employed fifty workers. One enthusiastic observer noted that they had "reduced their business to a system" and used "machinery made on the most approved principles." These included turning lathes, drilling machines, pinching and shearing machines, and a "powerful" steam engine. In addition, they had their own cabinet shop (for the interior woodwork) and separate paint and blacksmith shops, as well as a filing and engine room.[73]

Other metal consumer goods production included a large number of foundries specializing in stoves. The largest of these, the Phoenix Foundry, employed over 100 men. Other large foundries were the Beard Brothers, James Armstrong, and after 1868 E. C. Gurney and Co.

With the exception of the Toronto Rolling Mill, all the producers we have described so far grew from small shops into increasingly larger enterprises. Jacques and Hay, for example, had begun production as artisans, as had most of the Toronto founders and machine builders. This was of course Marx's "revolutionary path" to the factory, but other industries developed differently.

The industrial development of Toronto's shoe industry, for example, although displaying the transformation from shop to manufactory to factory, also shows that that transformation was not always linear for the artisans involved. In 1846 one investigator discovered forty-nine shoemaker shops in Toronto.[74] The 1851 census reported two shoe "factories" in the city.[75] In the early 1850's the introduction of sewing machines revolutionized the structure of the industry. A Montreal firm, Brown and Childs, which had pioneered machine production in Montreal, introduced sewing machines to Toronto as well.[76] Their Toronto branch, Childs and Brown, originally established as a retail shop for Montreal goods, began to manufacture for the growing western market and by 1858 employed 100 workers. By 1856 two other companies had also commenced manufacturing shoes in Toronto: Gilyat, Robinson, and Hall; and E. K. Paul and Co.[77] They were quickly followed by Sessions, Carpenter and Co.[78] All of these firms had previously "imported most of their goods, but the high tariff had induced them to turn their attention to manufacturing at home."[79]

The introduction of the sewing machine was the first step in bringing the factory to shoe production. Steps leading to the emergence of the central shop, a "manufactory" in our terms, included an ever-increasing division of labour, the development of pegged shoes, and standardization of the product. These three developments, however, had gone on within the general framework of craft production. The sewing machine of the early 1850's, the pegging machines of the later 1850's, and finally the McKay machine of the early 1860's ended craft production as the major method of manufacturing shoes.[80]

A rapid increase in Toronto shoe production occurred in the late 1850's and early 1860's. The major impetus came from the growth of the Canadian market. Agricultural specialization and the improved transportation network allowed the new urban interests to triumph over former rural production.[81] The tariff also played an important role in the development of the shoe industry. In the 1850's, when the tariff stood at 12½ per cent, New England goods apparently competed successfully, but the 25 per cent tariff of 1859 combined with the dislocations of the Civil War to close off American shoes to the Canadian market.[82] The tariff was lowered in 1866 but was subsequently raised to 17½ per cent in 1874 and to 25 per cent in 1879 to meet manufacturers' self-interested demands.[83]

By 1860 Childs and Brown, which had become Hamilton and Childs in Toronto, employed forty men and fifteen women in its four-storey establishment on Wellington Street East. These workers "were kept constantly employed in cutting, fitting and stitching, besides a number – generally over a hundred – who work in their own homes at what is termed bottoming – so that upwards of 150 hands are engaged." The company owned ten sewing machines and utilized all the other "latest appliances in labour-saving machinery." The factory occupied only the top flats; the other two were given over to sales and storage.[84] The coming of the McKay machine in the early 1860's ended the "putting-out" of bottoming for the large factories like Hamilton and Childs. As we shall see, however, not all Toronto shoe companies transformed their production so totally.

The 1861 census reported a total of seven shoe factories, but directories identified only four competitors of Childs and Hamilton in the wholesale trade. Nevertheless, the rapid growth of shoe manufacturing was proudly described in the Toronto Board of Trade reports, and in 1860 Erastus Wiman wrote of the "decrease of the manufactures of small towns over the country," speculating that these shops would slowly become little more than cobblers' shops for the repair of city manufactures. The following year he stated that "the large shoe shops in each village where from five to ten men were wont to be employed" were a thing of the past.[85] Two years later he reached a new eloquence in describing the industry's transformation:

> Eight years ago there was only one regular traveller from Montreal and one from Toronto who solicited orders from the country trade, and these seldom left the line of the railroad. Now it is no uncommon thing to meet from fifteen to eighteen in a single season – all keenly alive to business, and pushing into all sections of the country, remote or otherwise . . . business formerly distributed over a thousand workshops in the country districts . . . [had become] the eighteen or twenty establishments of the five cities of the provinces.[86]

Major Toronto manufacturers quickly implemented the latest changes in production. J. M. Trout enthusiastically described the wonders of these new devices that reduced all to a system: "Childs and Hamilton's establishment is a perfect beehive of activity, and the admirable order and arrangement of the whole is as perfect as long experience and the best business tact can make it."[87]

Other manufacturers grew rapidly in the mid-1860's. Sessions, Carpenter and Company doubled its production in 1865 and hoped to redouble it again in 1866. Employing 250 hands in 1867, it expanded to 400 in 1868 and then to 510 in 1870, when the firm, now Sessions, Turner and Cooper, opened its new Front Street factory. This 1870 factory demonstrated the complete transition to machine production. Built at a cost of $30,000, the new three-storey building "utilized machinery to an extraordinary extent." The basement was used for storage, the ground floor for offices and shipping, and the first floor for cutting and finishing. This floor also housed the channelling machine, which shaved and cut the sole, removed strips, and left the leather ready for the sewing machine. The seventy-eight sewing machines were located on the second floor; they were operated by 119 women who had their own separate entrance and were completely segregated from the male employees on the other floors. The men's work was done on the third floor and involved the heavier sewing, peg work, and the larger McKay machines used in bottoming.[88]

The development of the tobacco industry reveals a somewhat different experience. Insignificant before 1862, it enjoyed a rapid growth due to the dislocation caused by the American Civil War. By 1863, Wiman reported four separate companies in Toronto, each employing more than 100 workers and using "the latest and best machinery." This industry, with its more than 500 workers, rose in response to the U.S. war tax; two of the companies in Toronto were American firms trying to retain their control of the Canadian market.[89] The extent of mechanization was impressive:

> A steam engine of ten horse power, complete steam warming and drying apparatus keep the temperature to the requisite height throughout the building. . . . Two immense hydraulic presses and nine smaller ones from the St. Lawrence Foundry, together with a hydraulic pump, compresses, packing apparatus, etc. are all of the best and most complete kind, quite as good, if not superior to anything that could be got in St. Louis or Louisville, where the manufactory of this class of machinery is a long established trade.[90]

The above description of S. S. Preston and Co., which employed 125 men, applied also to competitors, J. D. King and Co. (150 to 160 men), Withers and Wright (125), Rossin and Brothers (95), and Lewis and Thompson.[91]

The rapid expansion of the tobacco industry, however, quickly created a situation that reoccurred frequently in Canada's early industrial history: over-production. With the end of the Civil War and the re-entry of U.S. products, the industry faltered. In 1865 the Board of Trade noted that both Rossin Brothers and S. S. Preston and Co. were under new management, and that J. E. Withers and Co. had suspended production in May because of the glutted market. By 1871 the industry had levelled off, but it was never to be as large as it had been in the Civil War boom years. One of the major tobacco manufacturers, J. D. King, who had employed 160 workers in 1862, transferred his accumulated capital into the manufacture of boots and shoes. King's decision demonstrated both the demise of tobacco as an important Toronto industry as well as the emergence of the type of industrialist who invests only capital and general management skills and does not possess a detailed knowledge of production.

Thus by the 1870's modern industry had come to Toronto, albeit unevenly. In furniture, shoes, machinery, and tobacco, factory production had to some degree displaced the craftsman. The factory was not limited to these industries, but these are the sectors of the Toronto economy most fully described in the extant sources. An analysis of Schedule Six of the 1871 census provides us with a summary of the total Toronto industrial picture and allows us to analyse the sectors for which other sources are

TABLE 2

Annual Production, Toronto Factories, 1871

No. of employees	*No. of factories*	*Value of product in $000's*	*% of Toronto product*	*Value added in $000's*	*% of Toronto value added*
100 +	19	5,320	39	2,083	54
50–99	30	2,507	18	562	15
30–49	28	1,499	11	443	12
0–29	495	4,360	32	738	19
Total	**572**	**13,686**	**100**	**3,826**	**100**

SOURCE: Unless otherwise specified the source for tables is Canada, Census, 1871, Industrial Mss.

TABLE 3

Steam Power by Industry, 1871

	0–19 employees		20+ employees			
Industry	*No. of factories*	*Horsepower*	*No. of factories*	*Horsepower*	*Total horsepower*	*% of total*
Metal	8	79	16	608	687	31
Woodworking	12	119	7	267	386	17.3
Brewing and distilling	9	134	1	116	250	11.3
Flour	2	130	1	50	180	8.1
Pork packing	2	17	2	95	112	5.1
Publishing	0	0	6	84	84	3.8
Chemicals	5	52	1	20	72	3.2
Furniture	4	23	1	40	63	2.8
Clothing	0	0	3	43	43	1.9
Baking and confectionary	3	17	1	25	42	1.9
Musical instr.	0	0	2	40	40	1.8
Tobacco	0	0	3	36	36	1.6
Boot and shoe	0	0	2	30	30	1.4
Brass, tin, etc.	4	22	1	8	30	1.4
Carriage	0	0	1	12	12	.5
Other	12	66	4	87	153	6.9
Total	**61**	**659**	**52**	**1,561**	**2,220**	**100**

slight. This reconstruction is not possible for either the previous period or the following decades because of the inadequacies of earlier censuses and the destruction of the later returns.

We have already summarized the growing concentration in employment in Table 1. Table 2 shows how dominant the largest factories were in terms of total Toronto production and especially in terms of value added. Factories with over fifty workers accounted for 57 per cent of Toronto's value produced and 69 per cent of her value added. Size and production levels of a work force employed in a given factory are of course only two of many measures of the arrival of industrial capitalism. Sources of power and the extent of mechanization are other important indicators.

If we analyse the use of steam power in Toronto, many interesting patterns emerge. Table 3 shows how very uneven the spread of steam power was in Toronto. As one would expect, the machinery, foundries, and metal-working industries were the

TABLE 4

Toronto Industries Using Steam Power, 1871

No. of workers	*No. of factories using steam*	*No. of factories not using steam*	*Total no. of factories*	*% using steam*
Over 100	13	6	19	68.4
50–99	15*	12	27	55.6
30–49	13	15	28	46.4
20–29	11	26	37	29.7
0–19	61	388	449	13.6
Total	**113**	**447**	**560****	**20.2**

* One unit (Globe Printing Co.) has been added. The census was clearly in error here.
** Two factories which utilized water power not counted.

TABLE 5

Toronto Industries Without Steam Power, Employing More Than 20 Workers, 1871

No. of employees	*Clothing*	*Boot and shoe*	*Other*	*Total*
100+	3	2	1	6
50–90	5	4	3	12
30–49	11	2	2	15
20–29	13	0	13	26
Total	**32**	**8**	**19**	**59**

largest users. But perhaps surprising is how little it was used in the clothing and shoe industries–Toronto's largest employers in 1871. Also surprising is the evidence of Table 4, which suggests that the size of the work force was not totally able to predict whether a firm would utilize steam power. Table 5, however, which sets the clothing and shoe industries off, demonstrates that when they are excluded, the predictive value of number of employees rises dramatically. Indeed, only six other factories employing more than thirty workers did not avail themselves of steam power.

Our initial surprise at these findings should be allayed considerably by consideration of the mid-Victorian industrial context in both the United States and England. In a recent article Raphael Samuels warns: "Steam power and hand technology may represent different principles of industrial organization, and to the historian they may well appear as belonging to different epochs, the one innovatory, the other 'traditional' and unchanging in its ways. But from the point of view of 19th century capitalist development they were two sides of the same coin."[92] Samuels contrasts England's maintenance of hand technology with the relatively more rapid acceptance of mechanized production in the United States; recent studies of the maintenance of craft traditions and workers' successful resistance to machinery in the United States, at least for a time, should enlighten our analysis of the Toronto industrial structure. A more specific sector-by-sector survey of the 1871 Toronto industrial setting will allow us to consider the nature of "combined and uneven development."

The clothing industry led the city in number of workers employed, in value of product, and in the number of women employed. Factory production was less dominant here because of the industry's continued dependence on outwork and subcontracting. The two straw works and Joseph Simpson's knitting factory were definitely modern factories with steam-powered engines. The clothing, tailoring, and millinery firms are more difficult to classify; little descriptive information is available for these firms in the 1860's and 1870's but their dependence on child and female labour is quite apparent. In the firms employing more than fifty workers, 81.6 per cent of the work force consisted of women and children. For the clothing industry as a whole, this figure fell only slightly to 74.6 per cent. It employed 17 per cent of all child workers and 63 per cent of all women workers in Toronto.

Boot and shoe exemplifies "combined and uneven development" within one industry. On the one hand, there were modern factories such as Sessions and Turner, and Damer, King that used the most advanced machinery and fully centralized operations; Childs and Hamilton certainly, and probably many of the other large producers, had McKay machines and channelling machines as well as the ever-present sewing machines. On the other hand, some of them (including Childs and Hamilton) continued to put out some of their bottoming work. In addition to this putting-out, there still existed a market for custom-made shoes, and some of the manufacturers (Dack, for example) specialized in this line. This uneven development accounts for the large differences in the shoe industry in which ten producers employed 90 per cent of the workers and produced 86 per cent of the value added, whereas the other thirty-nine shops (80 per cent) employed only 11 per cent and produced only 14 per cent of the value added. The failure of all the largest producers to mechanize fully, as indicated by their lack of steam power, might also suggest the competitive problems the Toronto industry would have to face in the following decade.

Metal works in Toronto, primarily focused on the engineering industry and stove foundries, dominated the industrial scene. Although it trailed the clothing and shoe industries in size of work force, metallurgy led in value of product and value added. It was also the most consistently mechanized with nearly all producers, large and small, employing steam power and machine tools. Yet, as we shall see, its workers, especially machinists and moulders, maintained both their skills and their customary work habits throughout the period covered by this study. Thus, even here, at the very heart of the Industrial Revolution with huge boilers, fiery furnaces, and powerful trip-hammers, metallurgy also displayed the characteristic mix of old and new which typified Victorian industry everywhere.

Other large Toronto industries in 1871 included publishing and furniture. The city's many newspapers were complemented by an emerging publishing industry that employed extensive numbers of women in bookbinding. The furniture industry showed the dominance of Robert Hay and Co., the development of which we have described earlier.

Brewing and distilling showed an extremely high value added for the number of workers involved. The industry was dominated by Gooderham and Worts, which employed 63.6 per cent of the industry's workers and accounted for 82.6 per cent of the value added. Emigrating from England in the early 1830's, Gooderham and Worts gradually transformed their tiny mill and distillery into one of Toronto's major industries and one of the city's most important fortunes. Their activities diversified to include a linen mill in Streetsville as well as other mills at Meadowvale and Pine Grove.[93] Their only competition in Toronto, by 1871, was a small distillery employing only seven workers.

Data on the brewing industry are obscured by its classification with distilling. All nine Toronto breweries had under twenty workers in 1871. Together they accounted for a value added of nearly $160,000. In the next decades this industry grew in importance, with the advent of refrigeration.

The major sectors of the Toronto economy in 1871 then were highly industrialized with large concentrations of workers, extensive mechanization, and an elaborate division of labour. Industrialization did not extend to all production in Toronto, however. Numerous artisanal pursuits remained, in which production was still centred in small shops with very few employees and a minimal level of mechanization. As we have seen, even within the most industrialized trades, such as boot and shoe, there were still many small shops producing custom-made goods for the luxury consumer market. Examples of crafts in which mechanization had made little impact included baking, carriage-making, harness-making, and brass, tin, and sheet-iron work. Small production was also the rule of Toronto coopers. The unevenness of industrial development had major repercussions for the emerging working-class movement. A city that just twenty years before had possessed only artisan shops and few manufactories now saw 71 per cent of its industrial work force employed in units larger then thirty workers, and its major factories – boot and shoe, engineering, furniture – making extensive use of the most advanced machines. By 1871, Toronto had experienced its industrial revolution and the following two decades would see the continued growth of the city's manufacturing.

The years immediately following 1871 were quite prosperous for Toronto industrial capitalists and the future looked bright. Then disaster struck. The world-wide depression of the mid-1870's began to affect Toronto seriously in 1874, and business failures throughout Canada soared to almost double their pervious rate.[94] Especially hard hit by the depression was the Canadian boot and shoe industry in which over-production and American dumping led to numerous failures.[95] The depression also caused failures in Toronto's basic metal production. Gzowski's Rolling Mill, the St. Lawrence Foundry's expansion into railroad car manufacturing, Hugh Allan's Canada Bolt and Nut Co., and the Toronto Car Wheel Co. all failed.

The decline in the boot and shoe industry never reversed itself. The depression caused a further decline in the already troubled tobacco industry. In both of these industries, Toronto producers succumbed before the flood of cheaper Quebec goods into the Ontario market. Montreal and Quebec producers, perhaps because of the availability of cheaper labour, won the bulk of the Ontario tobacco and shoe markets. In the 1880's significant Toronto factories in boots and shoes, such as Hamiltons' and Charlesworth, shut their doors for good.[96] A slight decline in production in the 1870's in other industries such as furniture and distilling, however, was quickly offset by rapid growth in the 1880's.

Tactics for dealing with the depression did not reflect a retreat from a strategy of industrial development. Indeed, as has already been seen, Canadian manufacturers, in general, and Toronto industrialists, in particular, sought a solution to the troubled 1870's in a policy of high protective tariffs. This, they argued, was the key to restoring prosperity.[97] Similar tactics were reflected in the increased number of schemes to recruit more industrial capital to Toronto. Substantial civic bonuses were offered in 1876 (between $100,000 and $200,000) for any entrepreneur willing to undertake the smelting of iron in Toronto.[98] This scheme found no takers, but the city was successful in wooing the Massey Agricultural Implements Works away from Newcastle in 1879.[99] Additional recruitment brought the Abell Agricultural Implements Works from Woodbridge in 1880 but failed to find an industrialist willing to start a locomotive works in the east end of the city in return for a ten-year tax waiver.[100] The whole strategy of bonuses to foster industrial growth became very controversial in the 1880's. In 1888, for example, a controversy broke out in city council over the Masseys' offer to build a malleable iron works in return for ten taxless years.[101] The Toronto labour movement in the late 1880's opposed all bonus schemes, arguing that they were simply a method of taxing the general public to increase the profits of industrial capitalists.[102]

The impact of the National Policy tariff on the development of Toronto manufacturing was substantial. A comparison of the industrial sector of the Toronto economy before and after the

TABLE 6

Major Toronto Factories, 1878 and 1884

	No. of factories	*No. of hands*	*Wages in $000's*	*Value of annual product in $000's*	*Capital invested in $000's*
1878	55	3,195	1,045.5	4,109.0	2,430.5
1884	91	6,852	2,378.2	9,715.3	4,761.5
Increase 1878-84	36	3,657	1,332.7	5,606.3	2,331.0

SOURCE: Canada, Parliament, *Sessional Papers*, 1885, no. 37, 9-10, 17

National Policy, conducted in 1885, showed significant growth between 1878 and 1884 (see Table 6). Toronto benefited, for example, from the significant growth in the musical instrument industry, a growth which Alfred Blackeby attributed solely to the impact of the National Policy tariff. Blackeby, the commissioner entrusted with the investigation of Canadian manufacturing in 1884, argued:

> Prior to the change in tariff, [the musical instrument industry] was very insignificant . . . but as soon as efficient protection was afforded against outside competitors the trade increased surprisingly. . . . Prior to the change in fiscal policy, the Canadian trade was almost entirely in the hands of the United States manufacturers, now at least 70% of the trade of Ontario and 50% of the trade of Quebec is done by Canadian makers.[103]

TABLE 7

Toronto Industrial Growth, 1871-91

Year	*No. of estabs.*	*No. of employees*	*Capital in $000's*	*Raw materials in $000's*	*Wages in $000's*	*Annual product in $000's*	*Value added in $000's*
1871	561	9,400	4,036	7,169	2,691	13,686	3,826
1881	870	12,708	11,502	9,761	3,721	19,100	5,617
1891	2,109	24,470	29,261	21,228	9,042	42,489	12,219

SOURCE: Canada, Census, 1871, 1881, 1891

Another clear case of the utility of the new protection was the foundry and engineering industry, which recovered rapidly in the

1880's.[104] Yet the National Policy tariff only reinforced the industry already in existence in Toronto; it did not create an industrial revolution in any sense but only augmented the one which had already taken place. Moreover, the National Policy was further evidence of industrial capitalists' power; their interests now were identified as those of the Canadian state.

Aggregate data, all that are available, from the 1881 and 1891 published censuses allow further analysis of the growth of Toronto industry in these years. By 1881, prosperity had returned and the census showed an increase in manufacturing in the 1870's despite the dislocations of the depression. The following decade saw even greater growth (see Table 7). A closer look at the data shows that the various segments of the garment industry together continued to make clothing the largest industry in number of workers employed, in value produced, and perhaps most importantly in value added. The two other major growing sectors were engineering and publishing. Engineering growth slowed greatly in the depression of the 1870's but recovered rapidly in the 1880's. Publishing grew steadily throughout the two decades. Agricultural implements rocketed to prominence; by 1891 the Massey plant alone accounted for 3 per cent of Toronto's annual product and 5.3 per cent of her value added. No other single company played so large a role, although, as we have seen, in 1871 Gooderham and Worts had. Furniture and musical instruments showed steady growth with major increases in the 1880's. Meat packing in 1891, although growing in employment and value produced, actually fell beneath its 1871 value-added total.[105] Distilling decreased somewhat but brewing grew rapidly in the 1880's with the new possibilities for concentration that refrigeration brought; Toronto brewers were quick to innovate.[106] Tobacco, after a slight recovery in 1881, continued its precipitous decline. Meanwhile the boot and shoe industry, increasingly monopolized by J. D. King and Co., declined in employment and value produced but managed to increase its value added.

Although we cannot reproduce, from the aggregate returns, as detailed a breakdown of the Toronto economy for the 1880's, the pattern of continued overall growth is still apparent. Increasing specialization into relatively skilled and well-paid industries is also evident with the significant growth of publishing machinery, musical instruments, and agricultural implements. (The garment industry represented an important exception to this pattern.) Toronto's major industries did not dominate the economy in

1891 to the same extent as they had in 1871. This can best be seen in their decreased contribution to Toronto's annual product and value added.

Piano manufacturing was often cited, along with agricultural implements, as an example of Toronto's pre-eminent position in Ontario. Heintzman and R. S. Williams were joined by the new firm of Mason and Risch where, the *Globe* noted, "every department is organized under a perfect system [according to] thoroughly scientific principles and methods." Such firms transformed the Canadian market: whereas in 1876 90 per cent of pianos were imported, by 1891 95 per cent were produced at home.[107]

Other sources make clear that increased concentration of capital of two kinds was taking place in Toronto between 1871 and 1891. Toronto workers continued to be gathered into larger production units; and, in addition, Toronto became the centre for the production of many commodities that had been previously manufactured throughout Ontario. Economic geographers working with historical data have provided us with considerable evidence of this process, and it was well illustrated by moves such as those undertaken by the Massey and Abell firms in the early 1880's.[108]

In the 1880's the enlargement of production units began to take place in segments of the economy that were run on a small scale in 1871. For example, the confectionery industry was transformed by the introduction of factory production (although baking remained a small-shop operation in 1891). Small shops still remained, but the number of workers employed in them as a proportion of the total Toronto work force became less and less significant as the century passed.

The increased concentration of capital led to considerable concern about the evils of monopoly. Although cartelization had not emerged as a significant force in the Canadian economy in the 1880's, both industrialists and anti-monopoly forces began to anticipate its arrival. Cotton manufacturers attempted to create a price-fixing arrangement in the mid-1880's which anticipated their mergers of the 1890's. In 1881 the Masseys bought out their major Toronto competitor, the Toronto Reaper and Mower Co. Ten years later they merged with the Harris Company of Brantford to create the Massey-Harris Co. Ltd., which was to dominate the agricultural implements field in Canada. Six months after that merger, their two major remaining competitors, Patterson and Brothers of Woodstock and J. O. Wisner Son and Co., realizing they could not compete, sold out.[109] Anti-monopoly sentiment in the 1880's and early 1890's was sufficiently strong that a Tory MP from the Toronto area, Clarke Wallace, instituted a select committee in 1887 to investigate combines. The following year he introduced legislation which, in its original intent at least, attempted to prevent the growth of combinations in Canada.

By the late 1880's and early 1890's, Toronto had experienced her industrial revolution, and a new set of economic forces and political responses were emerging. As the centralization and concentration of capital increased, Toronto stood poised on the brink of the next stage of economic development – monopoly capitalism. That phase of development lies beyond the scope of this study.

NOTES

1. For an early description of this school, see J. M. S. Careless, "Frontierism, Metropolitanism, and Canadian History," *CHR*, XXXV (1954), 1-21. See also W. T. Easterbrook and M. H. Watkins, *Approaches to Canadian Economic History* (Toronto, 1967), ix-xviii.
2. The following discussion owes much to the brilliant pioneering economic histories of H. C. Pentland and Stanley Ryerson. Pentland's "The Role of Capital in Canadian Economic Development before 1875," *Canadian Journal of Economics and Political Science* (1950), 457-74, and his "Development of a Capitalistic Labour Market in Canada," *Canadian Journal of Economics and Political Science* (1959), 450-61, are examples of fine, innovative, scholarly work. This is even more true of his "Labour and the Development of Industrial Capitalism in Canada" (Ph.D. thesis, University of Toronto, 1960). Stanley Ryerson, Canada's leading Marxist historian, attempted a brave synthesis (*Unequal Union* [Toronto, 1968]) which, despite its dismissal by bourgeois historians and the recent attacks on it by left-wing nationalists, remains the best overview of Canadian economic development in the nineteenth century. My debts to both these scholars are evident throughout this work.
3. The new econometrics literature in Canada, while problematic in many respects, has made recent strides in debunking some of the older notions of Canadian economic development. Three areas of work have importance for the arguments made here. First is the recent discussion of the impact of the Reciprocity Treaty of 1854,

which de-emphasizes it as a factor in colonial economic growth. See L. H. Officer and L. B. Smith, "The Canadian-American Reciprocity Treaty of 1855 to 1866," *Journal of Economic History*, 28 (1968), 598-623; and Robert Ankli, "The Reciprocity Treaty of 1854," *Canadian Journal of Economics*, 4 (1971), 1-20. Second is the important literature which re-evaluated the period 1878 to 1896 and reasserted that economic growth took place especially in manufacturing. See O. J. Firestone, "Development of Canada's Economy, 1850-1900," in *Trends in the American Economy in the Nineteenth Century* (Princeton, 1960), 217-52; Gordon Bertram, "Economic Growth in Canadian Industry, 1870-1915," *Canadian Journal of Economics and Political Science*, 19 (1967), 159-84; and Duncan M. McDougall, "Canadian Manufactured Commodity Output," *Canadian Journal of Economics*, 4 (1971), 21-36. Third is the work which indicates that the "wheat boom" of the years after 1896 has been given a disproportionate place in Canadian economic history and that continued manufacturing growth was of great import in the prosperity of the Laurier years. See Edward J. Chambers and Donald F. Gordon, "Primary Products and Economic Growth," *Journal of Political Economy*, 74 (1966), 315-32. For a useful survey of all this literature, see Peter J. George and Ernest H. Obsanen, "Recent Developments in the Quantification of Canadian Economic History," *Histoire Sociale*, 4 (1969), 76-95. See also Trevor J. O. Dick, "Frontiers in Canadian Economic History," *Journal of Economic History*, 36 (1976), 34-9.

4. This new group of left-wing nationalist scholars is avowedly attempting "to stand Creighton on his feet." One can only assume Harold Innis has always stood on solid ground in this view. The major member of this school is Tom Naylor, whose "The Rise and Fall of the Third Commercial Empire of the St. Lawrence," in Gary Teeple, ed., *Capitalism and the National Question in Canada* (Toronto, 1972), 1-41, was the first major work. More important is his *The History of Canadian Business,* 2 vols. (Toronto, 1976). Another scholar working along these lines is Daniel Drache, who has argued the critical strength of the staples approach in his "Rediscovering Canadian Political Economy," *Journal of Canadian Studies,* 11 (1976), 3-18. Glenn Williams in "Canadian Industrialization: We Ain't Growin' Nowhere," *This Magazine,* 9, 1 (1975), 7-9, and "Canada-the Case of the Wealthiest Colony," *This Magazine,* 10, 1 (1976), 28-32, has corrected some of Naylor's excesses and has reinserted labour into this discussion of political economy quite beneficially. Most important is his recent "The National Policy and Import Substitution Industrialization," unpublished Canadian Political Science Association paper, 1978, which includes a devastating critique of Naylor. Other substantive critiques of Naylor are L. R. MacDonald, "Merchants against In-

dustry: An Idea and Its Origins," *CHR*, LVI (1975), 263-81; and Stanley Ryerson, "Who's Looking After Business: A Review," *This Magazine,* 10, 5 and 6 (1976), 41-6. Robert Storey, "Industrialization in Canada: The Emergence of the Hamilton Working Class, 1850-1870s" (M.A. thesis, Dalhousie University, 1975) and Bryan Palmer, "Most Uncommon Common Man: Craft, Culture and Conflict in a Canadian Community, 1860-1914" (Ph.D. thesis, State University of New York at Binghamton, 1977), provide excellent accounts of Hamilton's industrial revolution. See also Stephen Langdon, "The Political Economy of Capitalist Transformation, Central Canada from the 1840s to the 1870s" (M.A. thesis, Carleton University, 1972); Leo Johnson, *History of the County of Ontario,* 1815-1875 (Whitby, 1973).

5. Joan MacKinnon, *A Checklist of Toronto Cabinet and Chair Makers, 1800-1865* (Ottawa, 1975), 3, 165.
6. Pentland, "Labour and the Development of Industrial Capitalism," 341-3.
7. Robert Baldwin Sullivan, *Lecture Before the Mechanics' Institute, on the 17th November, 1847* (Hamilton, 1848[?]). Quotations are from pages 6-7, 7-8, 9-10, 40, 41.
8. See also his "Memo, re: Corps of Military Labourers," in Sir Arthur G. Doughty, ed., *Elgin-Grey Papers,* IV (Ottawa, 1937), 1436ff.
9. Sullivan, *Lecture,* 20-36. One of the only discussions of commodity production in the 1840's is Ryerson, *Unequal Union,* ch. 9.
10. British-American League, *Minutes of the Proceedings of a Convention of Delegates,* (Kingston, 1849), 8. For the only detailed discussion of the League, see Gerald A. Hallowell, "The Reaction of the Upper Canadian Tories to the Adversity of 1849: Annexation and the British-American League," *OH,* 62 (1970), 41-56.
11. British-American League, *Proceedings,* 20.
12. *Ibid.,* 21.
13. For a detailed biography, see Barrie Dyster, "John William Gamble," *Dictionary of Canadian Biography* (Toronto, 1972), X, 299-300.
14. Text of speech is from Samuel Thompson, *Reminiscences of a Canadian Pioneer for the Last Fifty Years* (Toronto, 1884), 251-60.
15. British-American League, *Minutes of the Proceedings of . . .,* Toronto, 1849, 5, ii, xiv-xvi, and *passim*. In addition to the British-American League, there was also a Montreal association for home manufactures which advocated protection. For a description of their 1849 meeting, see William Weir, *Sixty Years in Canada* (Montreal, 1903), 98-104. This organization also presented a 4,000-name petition to the Legislative Assembly in 1849 in favour of protection. See Elizabeth Gibbs, ed., *Debates of the Legislative Assembly of United Canada* (Montreal, 1976), viii, part I, 1849, 699.

16. For a discussion of Gamble in the legislature, see Edward Porritt, *Sixty Years of Protection in Canada, 1846-1912* (Winnipeg, 1918), 174-80.
17. On capital imports, see Leland H. Jenks, *The Migration of British Capital to 1875* (New York, 1927), 198-206. The best discussion of the railroad era is probably still G. P. de T. Glazebrook, *A History of Transportation in Canada* (Toronto, 1938). For details on the connection of business and government, see Gustavus Myers, *History of Canadian Wealth* (Toronto), and H. V. Nelles, ed., *The Philosophy of Railroads* (Toronto, 1972). The most insightful discussions of the broad impact of railroads on the Canadian economy are predictably Ryerson, *Unequal Union,* chs. 12 and 13, and Pentland, "The Role of Capital," 463-70.
18. Pentland, "Role of Capital," 463.
19. Leo Panitch, "The Role and Nature of the Canadian State," in Leo Panitch, ed., *The Canadian State* (Toronto, 1977), 3-27. See also Peter Baskerville, "Professional vs. Proprietor: Power Distribution in the Railway World of Upper Canada/Ontario, 1850-1881," paper delivered at the Canadian Historical Association, 1978.
20. *Report of the Toronto Board of Trade* (Toronto, 1856), 9-10; John E. MacNab, "Toronto's Industrial Growth in 1891," *OH,* 47 (1955), 61. For a useful discussion of the importance of railroads to industrial development, see Albert Faucher, *Quebec en Amérique au XIXe siècle: Essai sur les caractères économiques de la Laurentie* (Montreal, 1973), chs. 3, 7.
21. On Weir, see his *Sixty Years in Canada.*
22. *Canadian Merchants' Magazine,* I (1857), 1. Weir later (in *Sixty Years,* 248) described it as "a monthly magazine advocating the development of Canadian Industry."
23. *Ibid.,* I (1857), 29-30, 163-5, 215-1; II (1858), 205-9; III (1858), 97-106, 407-40.
24. *Ibid.,* I (1857), 193-6; II (1858), 198-205.
25. *Ibid.,* II (1858), 198ff.
26. *Ibid.*
27. *Ibid.,* III (1858), 35, 26.
28. Weir, *Sixty Years,* 105-18. Buchanan's importance has not yet been sufficiently understood, but his influence over an entire generation of Canadian economic thinkers was profound. The major work on him to date, Douglas McCalla, "The Buchanan Businesses, 1834-1872: A Study in the Organization and Development of Canadian Trade" (Ph.D. thesis, Oxford University, 1972), unfortunately ignores Buchanan's role as an economic thinker. Craufurd D. W. Goodwin, *Canadian Economic Thought* (Durham, North Carolina, 1961), 49-51, treats Buchanan in passing but is not very useful. A more useful brief treatment is Peter Warrian, " 'Sons of Toil': The Impact of Industrialization on Craft Workers in Late

19th Century Ontario," in David F. Walker and James H. Bater, eds., *Industrial Development in Southern Ontario* (Waterloo, 1974), 69-99, which discusses two of Buchanan's publishing ventures: *The Workingman's Journal* (1864) and *The Peoples' Journal* (1869-72). See also Storey, "Industrialization in Canada: The Emergence of the Hamilton Working Class."

29. *Report of the Public Meeting of Delegates . . . and Proceedings of the Association for the Promotion of Canadian Industry.* Toronto, 1858, 5.
30. *Ibid.,* 6.
31. *Ibid.,* 4, 7, 14. There was an overt attempt to keep the profile of manufacturers low for fear that they would appear too self-interested. See Weir, *Sixty Years,* 130; PAC, Buchanan Papers, Isaac Buchanan to W. H. Howland, 2 October 1878.
32. See among others his: *Letters Illustrative of the Present Position of Politics in Canada* (Hamilton, 1859); *A Permanent Patriotic Policy* (n.p., 1860); *Britain the Country versus Britain the Empire. Our Financial Distresses – Their Legislative Cause and Cure* (Hamilton, 1860); *Relations of the Industry of Canada with the Mother Country and the United States* (Montreal, 1864); and *The British American Federation, A Necessity. Its Industrial Policy also a Necessity* (Hamilton, 1865).
33. Buchanan, *Britain the Country,* I, xxiv.
34. Douglas McCalla, "The Commercial Politics of the Toronto Board of Trade, 1850-1860," *CHR,* L (1969), 51-67; and Toronto Board of Trade, *Reports,* in the 1860's.
35. *Canadian Merchants' Magazine,* III (1858), 407-40. This essay won the Board of Arts and Manufacturers of Upper Canada's essay contest in 1858. For more about the board, see below.
36. D. F. Barnett, "The Galt Tariff: Incidental or Effective Protection?" *Canadian Journal of Economics,* 9 (1976), 389-407. Compare this convincing view, based on a detailed analysis, which concludes that "evidence strongly supports the protective character of Galt's tariff changes," with Tom Naylor's argument that "the objectives of the tariff were in fact clearly revenue-oriented." This is a good example of the empirical weakness of Naylor's polemical *The History of Canadian Business, 1867-1914,* 2 vols. (Toronto, 1975). The quotation is from I, 28.
37. Hon. A. T. Galt, *Canada 1849 to 1859* (Quebec, 1860), 33-4.
38. Weir, *Sixty Years,* 115.
39. Dominion Board of Trade, *Proceedings,* 1871, 26; 1877, 116-17, and *passim.*
40. John MacLean, *The Complete Tariff Hand-Book* (Toronto, 1880), 3.
41. *Canadian Merchants Magazine,* IV (1859), 321-2.
42. *Canadian Illustrated News* (Hamilton), 20 December 1862.

43. *Journal of the Board of Arts and Manufacturers of Upper Canada,* III (1863), 12-15.
44. Buchanan, *British American Federation,* 4.
45. *Association for the Promotion of Canadian Industry, Its Formation, By-Laws* (Toronto, 1866). Quotations are from pages 7, 6.
46. For a very sketchy account, see S. D. Clark, *The Canadian Manufacturers' Association* (Toronto, 1939), 1-7.
47. Dominion Board of Trade, *Proceedings,* 1871, 24-8.
48. *Ibid.,* 1874. Quotations are from pages 65-6, 73-84, 113-15.
49. The convention rejected a free-trade resolution by a vote of 34 to 20.
50. *Ibid.,* 1876. Quotations are from pages 109-11, 135-8, 175.
51. *Ibid.,* 1877, 116-18, 126, 133.
52. *Ibid.,* 1878, 72-9, 88, 200.
53. Manufacturers' Association of Ontario, *Proceedings of Special Meeting . . . 1875* (Toronto, 1876), 2-4.
54. *Ibid., passim.*
55. Dominion National League, *Country Before Party* (Hamilton, 1878). See also the earlier *Home Industries. Canada's National Policy. Protection to Native Products. Development of Field and Factory. Speeches by Leading Members of Parliament* (Ottawa, 1876). Although this pamphlet fails to identify its source, considerable advertising by Ontario manufacturers suggests that the MAO was involved.
56. Clark, *Canadian Manufacturers' Association,* 7.
57. For perhaps the most comprehensive western indictment, see Porritt, *Sixty Years of Protection in Canada,* especially ch. XI.
58. For a totally unapologetic defence of the staples theory see Mel Watkins, "The Staple Theory Revisited," *Journal of Canadian Studies,* 12 (Winter, 1977), 83-95.
59. For general works on the economic history of Toronto, see: Edith Firth, ed., *The Town of York,* 2 vols. (Toronto, 1962, 1966); F. H. Armstrong, "Toronto in Transition: The Emergence of a City, 1828-1838" (Ph.D. thesis, University of Toronto, 1965); Armstrong, "Metropolitanism and Toronto Reconsidered, 1825-1850," *Canadian Historical Association Annual Report* (1966), 29-40; Barry Dyster, "Toronto 1840-1860: Making It in a British Protestant Town" (Ph.D. thesis, University of Toronto, 1970); E. C. Guillett, *Toronto from Trading Post to Great City* (Toronto, 1934); D. C. Masters, *The Rise of Toronto, 1850-1890* (Toronto, 1947); Masters, "Toronto vs. Montreal," *CHR,* XXII (1941), 133-46; and G. P. de T. Glazebrook, *The Story of Toronto* (Toronto, 1971).
60. W. H. Smith, *Canadian Gazeteer* (Toronto, 1846), 193-7.
61. Canada, *Census,* 1848, 1851.
62. MacKinnon, *Toronto Cabinet Makers,* 69-77, 184-91.

63. *Journal of the Board of Arts and Manufacturers of Upper Canada,* IV (1864), 193-6. See also testimony of R. Hay to the Select Committee on the Extent and Condition of the Manufacturing Interests of the Dominion, *Journal of the House of Commons,* 1874, Appendix III, 46-8.
64. Bruce Sinclair *et al., Let Us Be Honest and Modest: Technology and Society in Canadian History* (Toronto, 1974), 158-9.
65. *Ibid.,* 138; Glazebrook, *Story of Toronto,* 113.
66. *Journal of the Board of Arts and Manufacturers of Upper Canada,* IV (1864), 1-3.
67. For a discussion of Armstrong's painting, see Gregory S. Kealey, "Toronto Rolling Mills," *Canadian Labour History,* 7 (1975), 1-2.
68. Toronto Board of Trade, *Report,* 1865.
69. Barrie Dyster, "Francis Henry Medcalf," in *Dictionary of Canadian Biography,* (Toronto, 1972), X, 503-4.
70. George Mainer, "William Hamilton," *ibid.,* 330-1.
71. Toronto Board of Trade, *Report,* 1863.
72. Mainer, "Hamilton," 331. For a general description of developments in iron and secondary metal which is generally in agreement with my line of argument, see William Kilbourn, *The Elements Combined* (Toronto, 1960), chs. 1-3.
73. *Canadian Illustrated News* (Hamilton), 3 January 1863.
74. Smith, *Canadian Gazateer,* 196.
75. Canada, *Census,* 1851.
76. For developments in the Montreal shoe industry, see Jean Hamelin and Yves Roby, *Histoire économique du Québec* (Montreal, 1971); and Joanne Burgess, "L'industrie de la chaussure à Montréal: 1840-1879," *Revue de l'histoire de l'amérique française,* 31 (1977), 187-210.
77. Toronto Board of Trade, *Annual Report,* 1856.
78. *Canadian Merchants' Magazine,* III (1858), 418-19.
79. *Ibid.*
80. For a brilliant discussion of the shoe industry, see Ross Thomson, "The Origin of Modern Industry in the United States: The Mechanization of Shoe and Sewing Machine Production" (Ph.D. thesis, Yale University, 1976). For an equally useful local study, see Alan Dawley, *Class and Community: The Industrial Revolution in Lynn* (Cambridge, Mass., 1976).
81. Hamelin and Roby, *Histoire économique du Québec, passim.*
82. Canada, Parliament, *Sessional Papers,* 1885, no. 37, 28.
83. Canada, Parliament, House of Commons, *Journals,* 1874, Appendix 3, 63ff, and 1876, Appendix 3, 90-115.
84. Toronto Board of Trade, *Report,* 1860, 41.
85. *Ibid.,* 28; and *Report for 1861,* 1862.
86. Toronto Board of Trade, *Report for 1863,* 1864, 24.
87. Toronto Board of Trade, *Annual Report for 1865,* 1866, 39-40.

88. *Globe,* 18 November 1870.
89. Toronto Board of Trade, *Annual Report for 1862,* 1863.
90. *Ibid.*
91. *Journal of the Board of Arts and Manufacturers of Upper Canada,* III (1863), 84-5, 321-5.
92. Raphael Samuels, "Workshop of the World: Steam Power and Hand Technology in Mid-Victorian Britain," *History Workshop,* 3 (1977), 57.
93. *Canadian Illustrated News* (Hamilton), 25 April 1863.
94. J. Clarence Ingram, "The Financial Depression of 1873 and Its Effects on Canadian Industry" (M.A. thesis, Queen's University, Kingston, 1929); and Edward J. Chambers, "Late Nineteenth Century Business Cycles in Canada," *Canadian Journal of Economics and Political Science,* 30 (1964), 391-412.
95. William Wycliffe Johnson, *Sketches of the Late Depression* (Montreal, 1882); and Sarah Common, "A History of Business Conditions in Canada, 1870-1891" (M.A. thesis, Queen's University, Kingston, 1930).
96. *Globe,* 13 January, 1883; *Canadian Labor Reformer,* 13 November, 25 December 1886. See also Hector Charlesworth, *Candid Chronicles* (Toronto, 1925), 68-70, for a description of his father's failure.
97. Canada, House of Commons, *Journals,* 1874, Appendix 3, and 1876, Appendix 3.
98. *Globe,* 9, 23 February 1876.
99. *Ibid.,* 24 May 1879; 17 April 1880. On the agricultural implement industry in Canada, see Merrill Denison, *Harvest Triumphant: The Story of Massey-Harris* (Toronto, 1949); and W. G. Phillips, *The Agricultural Implement Industry in Canada* (Toronto, 1956).
100. *Globe,* 17 May, 26 June, 17 July 1880.
101. Clipping Files, Volume One, Massey Archives. From *Mail,* 9 March, 1888; *News,* 10 March 1888; *Empire,* 27 December 1888; *World,* 25 October 1888.
102. Toronto Trades and Labor Council, *Minutes,* 1888-9, *passim.*
103. Canada, Parliament, *Sessional Papers,* 1885, no. 37, 5.
104. *Ibid.,* 20-2.
105. For a discussion of the early Toronto meat-packing industry, see Michael Bliss, *A Canadian Millionaire: The Life and Business Times of Sir Joseph Flavelle* (Toronto, 1978), esp. 27-52.
106. James M. Gilmour, *Spatial Evolution of Manufacturing: Southern Ontario, 1851-1891* (Toronto, 1972), 153-68.
107. *Globe,* 5 September 1891.
108. Gilmour, *Spatial Evolution of Manufacturing,* especially ch. 7; David F. Walker and James H. Bater, eds., *Industrial Development in Southern Ontario* (Waterloo, 1974); Peter Goheen, *Victorian Toronto, 1850 to 1900* (Chicago, 1970); Warren R. Bland,

"The Location of Manufacturing in Southern Ontario in 1881," *Ontario Geography,* 8 (1974), 8-30; Warren R. Bland, "The Changing Location of Metal Fabricating and Clothing Industries in Southern Ontario, 1881-1932," *Ontario Geography,* 9 (1975), 35-57; J. David Wood, ed., *Perspectives on Landscape and Settlement in Nineteenth Century Ontario* (Toronto, 1975), chs. 9-10. See also J. Spelt, *Urban Development in South-Central Ontario* (Toronto, 1972).

109. Denison, *Harvest Triumphant,* chs. 5 and 6.

The National Policy and the Industrialization of the Maritimes

by T. W. Acheson

The Maritime provinces of Canada in 1870 probably came the closest of any region to representing the classic ideal of the staple economy. Traditionally shaped by the Atlantic community, the region's industrial sector had been structured to the production and export of timber, lumber products, fish, and ships. The last was of crucial significance. In terms of the balance of trade, it accounted for more than one-third of New Brunswick's exports at Confederation. In human terms, the manufacture of ships provided a number of towns with large groups of highly skilled, highly paid craftsmen who were able to contribute significantly to the quality of community life. Against this background, the constricting British market for lumber and ships after 1871 created a serious economic crisis for the area. This was not in itself unusual. Throughout the nineteenth century the region's resource-based economy had suffered a series of periodic recessions as the result of changing imperial policies and world markets. Yet, in one respect, this crisis differed from all earlier; while the lumber markets gradually returned in the late 1870's, the ship market did not. Nova Scotians continued to build their small vessels for the coasting trade, but the large shipbuilding industry failed to revive.

In the face of this uncertain future the National Policy was embraced by much of the Maritime business community as a new mercantilism which would re-establish that stability which the region had enjoyed under the old British order. In the first years

From *Acadiensis*, 1 (Spring, 1972), 3-28.

of its operation the Maritimes experienced a dramatic growth in manufacturing potential, a growth often obscured by the stagnation of both the staple industries and population growth. In fact, the decade following 1879 was characterized by a significant transfer of capital and human resources from the traditional staples into a new manufacturing base which was emerging in response to federal tariff policies. This development was so significant that between 1881 and 1891 the industrial growth rate of Nova Scotia outstripped all other provinces in eastern Canada.[1] The comparative growth of the period is perhaps best illustrated in Saint John. The relative increase in industrial capital, average wages, and output in this community significantly surpassed that of Hamilton, the Canadian city whose growth was perhaps most directly attributable to the protective tariff.[2]

Within the Atlantic region the growth of the 1880's was most unequally distributed. It centred not so much on areas or subregions as upon widely scattered communities.[3] These included the traditional Atlantic ports of Saint John, Halifax, and Yarmouth; lumbering and shipbuilding towns, notably St. Stephen and New Glasgow; and newer railroad centres, such as Moncton and Amherst. The factors which produced this curious distribution of growth centres were human and historical rather than geographic. The one characteristic shared by them all was the existence in each of a group of entrepreneurs possessing the enterprise and the capital resources necessary to initiate the new industries. Strongly community-oriented, these entrepreneurs attempted, during the course of the 1880's, to create viable manufacturing enterprises in their local areas under the aegis of the protective tariff. Lacking the resources to survive the prolonged economic recessions of the period, and without a strong regional metropolis, they acquiesced in the 1890's to the industrial leadership of the Montreal business community. Only at the century's end, with the expansion of the consolidation movement, did a group of Halifax financiers join their Montreal counterparts in asserting an industrial metropolitanism over the communities of the eastern Maritimes. This paper is a study in that transition.

I

The Maritime business community in the 1870's was dominated by three groups: wholesale shippers, lumber and ship manufac-

TABLE 1

Industrial Development in Principal Maritime Centres 1880-1890

	Population	*Industrial Capital*	*Employees*	*Average Annual Wages*	*Output*	*Industry by Output (1891)*
Halifax/Dartmouth (1880)	39,886	$2,975,000	3,551	$303	$6,128,000	Sugar**
(1890)	43,132	6,346,000	4,654	280	8,235,000	Rope*
						Cotton
						Confectionary
						Paint
						Lamps
Saint John (1880)	41,353	2,143,000	2,690	278	4,123,000	Lumber**
(1890)	39,179	4,838,000	5,888	311	8,131,000	Machinery***
						Smelting
						Rope**
						Cottons
						Brass*
						Nails*
						Elect. Light**
New Glasgow (1880)	2,595	160,000	360	255	313,000	Primary Steel*
(1890)	3,777	1,050,000	1,117	355	1,512,000	Rolling Mills**
						Glass

St. Stephen/Milltown (1880)	4,002	136,000	447	314	573,000	Cottons
(1890)	4,826	1,702,000	1,197	320	1,494,000	Confectionary
						Fish Canning
						Soap
						Lumber
Moncton (1880)	5,032	530,000	603	418	1,719,000	Sugar
(1890)	8,765	1,134,000	948	333	1,973,000	Cottons
						Woollens
						Rolling Stock
Fredericton (1880)	7,218[a]	1,090,000[a]	911[a]	211[a]	1,031,000[a]	Cottons
Marysville (1890)	8,394	2,133,000	1,526	300	1,578,000	Lumber
						Foundry Product
Yarmouth (1880)	3,485	290,000	211	328	284,000	Cotton Yarn*
(1890)	6,089	783,000	930	312	1,234,000	Fish Canning
						Woollens
Amherst (1880)	2,274	81,000	288	281	283,000	Foundry Product
(1890)	3,781	457,000	683	293	724,000	Shoes
						Doors

[a] Estimates. Marysville was not an incorporated town in 1880, and totals for the date must be estimated from York County figures.
* Leading Canadian Producer; ** second; *** third.
SOURCE: Canada, *Census* (1891), III, Table 1; *ibid.*, (1901), III, Tables XX, XXI.

turers, and the small scale manufacturers of a variety of commodities for purely local consumption. As a group they were deeply divided on the question of whether the economic salvation of their various communities was to be found in the maintenance of an Atlantic mercantile system or in a program of continentalist-oriented industrial diversification. A wedding of the two alternatives appeared to be the ideal situation. While they had warily examined the proposed tariff of 1879, most leading businessmen accepted its philosophy and seriously attempted to adapt it to their community needs.[4]

For a variety of reasons the tariff held the promise of prosperity for the region's traditional commercial activities and, as well, offered the possibilities for the development of new manufacturing industry. For most Nova Scotian business leaders the West Indies market was vital to the successful functioning of the province's commercial economy. It was a major element in the region's carrying trade and also provided the principal market for the Nova Scotia fishing industry. These, in turn, were the foundations of the provincial shipbuilding industry. The successful prosecution of the West Indies trade, however, depended entirely upon the ability of the Nova Scotia merchants to dispose of the islands' sugar crop. The world depression in the 1870's had resulted in a dramatic decline in the price of refined sugar as French, German, British, and American refineries dumped their surplus production on a glutted world market. By 1877 more than nine-tenths of Canadian sugar was obtained from these sources,[5] a fact which threatened the Nova Scotia carrying trade with disaster. A significant tariff on foreign sugar, it was felt, would encourage the development of a Canadian refining industry which would acquire all of its raw sugar from the British West Indies. Through this means, most Nova Scotian wholesalers and shippers saw in the new policy an opportunity both to resuscitate the coastal shipping industry of the province and to restore their primacy in the West Indies.

Of the newer industries which the National Policy offered, the future for the Maritimes seemed to lie in textiles and iron and steel products. The optimism concerning the possibilities of the former appears to have emerged out of a hope of emulating the New England experience. This expectation was fostered by the willingness of British and American cotton mill machinery manufacturers to supply on easy terms the necessary duty-free equipment, and by the feeling of local businessmen that the market provided by the tariff and the low quality labour requirements of such an enterprise would guarantee that a profitable business could be erected and maintained by the efforts of a single community. Behind such reasoning lay the general assumption that, despite major transportation problems, the Maritimes, and notably Nova Scotia, would ultimately become the industrial centre of Canada. The assumption was not unfounded. The region contained the only commercially viable coal and iron deposits in the Dominion, and had the potential, under the tariff, of controlling most of the Montreal fuel sources. Under these circumstances the development of textiles and the expansion of most iron and steel industries in the Atlantic area were perhaps not surprising projects.

Despite a cautious enthusiasm for the possibilities offered by the new federal economic dispensation, there was considerable concern about the organizational and financial problems in creating a new industrial structure. The Maritimes was a region of small family firms with limited capital capabilities. Other than chartered banks, it lacked entirely the financial structure to support any large corporate industrial entity. Like the people of Massachusetts, Maritimers were traditionally given to placing their savings in government savings banks at a guaranteed 4 per cent interest than in investments on the open market.[6] Regional insurance, mortgage and loan, and private savings corporations were virtually unknown. The result was to throw the whole financial responsibility for undertaking most manufactories upon the resources of individual entrepreneurs.

Since most enterprises were envisioned as being of general benefit to the community at large, and since few businessmen possessed the necessary capital resources to single-handedly finance such an undertaking, most early industrial development occurred as the result of co-operative efforts by groups of community entrepreneurs. These in turn were drawn from a traditional business elite of wholesalers and lumbermen. In Halifax as early as May 1879 a committee was formed from among the leading West Indies shippers "to solicit capital, select a site and get a manufacturing expert" for the organization of a sugar refinery.[7] Under its leadership $500,000 was raised, in individual subscriptions of $10-20,000, from among members of the Halifax business community. This procedure was repeated during the formation of the Halifax Cotton Company in 1881; more than $300,000 was subscribed in less than two weeks, most of it by thirty-two individuals.[8]

The leadership in the development of these enterprises was taken by young members of traditional mercantile families. The moving spirit in both cases was Thomas Kenny. A graduate of the Jesuit Colleges at Stonyhurst (England) and St. Gervais (Belgium), Kenny had inherited from his father, the Hon. Sir Edward Kenny, MLC, one of the largest wholesale shipping firms in the region. In the early 1870's the younger Kenny had invested heavily in shipyards scattered throughout five counties of Nova Scotia and had even expanded into England with the establishment of a London branch for his firm. Following the opening of the refinery in 1881, he devoted an increasingly large portion of his time to management of that firm.[9] Kenny was supported in his efforts by a number of leading merchants including the Hon. Robert Boak, Scottish-born president of the Legislative Council, and John F. Stairs, manager of the Dartmouth Rope Works. Stairs, who had attended Dalhousie University, was a member of the executive council of Nova Scotia, the son of a legislative councillor, and a grandson of the founder of the shipping firm of William Stairs, Son and Morrow Limited.[10]

In contrast to Halifax, Saint John had always been much more a manufacturing community and rivalled Ottawa as the principal lumber manufacturing centre in the Dominion. Development in the New Brunswick city occurred as new growth on an existing industrial structure and centred on cotton cloth and iron and steel products. The New Brunswick Cotton Mill had been erected in 1861 by an Ulster-born Saint John shipper, William Parks, and his son, John H. Parks. The latter, who had been trained as a civil engineer under the tutelage of the chief engineer of the European and North American Railroad, assumed the sole proprietorship of the mill in 1870.[11] In 1881 he led the movement among the city's dry goods wholesalers to establish a second cotton mill, which was incorporated as the St. John Cotton Company.

The principal Saint John iron business was the firm of James Harris. Trained as a blacksmith, the Annapolis-born Harris had established a small machine shop in the city in 1828 and had expanded into the foundry business some twenty-three years later. In 1883, in consequence of the new tariff, he determined to develop a completely integrated secondary iron industry including a rolling mill and railway car plant. To provide the resources for the expansion, the firm was reorganized as a joint stock company with $300,000 capital, most of which was raised by Saint John businessmen. The New Brunswick Foundry, Rolling Mills and Car Works, with a plant covering some five acres of land, emerged as the largest industrial employer in the Maritimes.[12] The success of the Harris firm induced a group of wholesale hardware manufacturers under the leadership of the Hon. Isaac Burpee, a former member of the Mackenzie government, to re-establish the Coldbrook Rolling Mills near the city.

Yet, despite the development of sugar and cotton industries and the expansion of iron and rope manufactories, the participation of the Saint John and Halifax business communities in the industrial impulse which characterized the early 1880's can only be described as marginal. Each group played the role of participant within its locality but neither provided any positive leadership to its hinterland area. Even in terms of industrial expansion, the performance of many small town manufacturers was more impressive than that of their city counterparts.

At the little railway centre of Moncton nearly $1 million was raised under the leadership of John and Christopher Harris, John Humphrey, and Josiah Woods, to permit the construction of a sugar refinery, a cotton mill, a gas light and power plant, and several smaller iron and textile enterprises. The Harris brothers, sons of an Annapolis shipbuilder of Loyalist extraction, had established a shipbuilding and shipping firm at Moncton in 1856.[13] Under the aegis of their firm they organized the new enterprises with the assistance of their brother-in-law John Humphrey, scion of Yorkshire Methodist settlers of the Tantramar, longtime MLA for Westmorland, and proprietor of the Moncton flour and woollen mills. They were financially assisted in their efforts by Josiah Wood (later Senator) of nearby Sackville. The son of a Loyalist wholesaler, Wood first completed his degrees (B.A., M.A.) at Mount Allison, was later admitted to the New Brunswick bar, and finally entered his father's shipping and private banking business.[14] The leadership of the Moncton group was so effective that the owner of the *Monetary Times*, in a journey through the region in 1882, singled out the community for praise:

> Moncton has industrialized . . . business people only in moderate circumstances but have united their energies . . . persons who have always invested their surplus funds in mort-

gages are now cheerfully subscribing capital for the Moncton Cotton Co. Unfortunately for industrial progress, there are too many persons [in this region] who are quite content with receiving 5 or 6% for their money so long as they know it is safe, rather than risk it in manufactures, even supposing it yielded double the profit.[15]

At St. Stephen the septuagenarian lumber barons and bankers, James Murchie and Freeman Todd, joined the Annapolis-born shipbuilder, Zechariah Chipman, who was father-in-law to the Minister of Finance, Sir Leonard Tilley, in promoting an immense cotton concern, the St. Croix, second largest in the Dominion at the time. The son of a local farmer, Murchie, whose holdings included more than 200,000 acres of timber lands - half of it in Quebec - also developed a number of smaller local manufactories.[16] At the same time two young brothers, Gilbert and James Ganong, grandsons of a Loyalist farmer from the St. John Valley, began the expansion of their small confectionery firm,[17] and shortly initiated construction of a soap enterprise in the town.

At Yarmouth a group of shipbuilders and West Indies merchants led by the Hon. Loran Baker, MLC, a shipper and private banker, and John Lovitt, a shipbuilder and member of the Howland Syndicate, succeeded in promoting the Yarmouth Woollen Mill, the Yarmouth Cotton Manufacturing, the Yarmouth Duck Yarn Company, two major foundries, and a furniture enterprise.[18] The development was entirely an internal community effort - virtually all the leading business figures were third generation Nova Scotians of pre-Loyalist American origins. A similar development was discernible in the founding of the Windsor Cotton Company.[19]

A somewhat different pattern emerged at New Glasgow, the centre of the Nova Scotia coal industry. Attempts at the manufacture of primary iron and steel had been made with indifferent results ever since Confederation.[20] In 1872, a New Glasgow blacksmith, Graham Fraser, founded the Hope Iron Works with an initial capital of $160,000.[21] As the tariff on iron and steel products increased in the 1880's so did the vertical expansion of the firm. In 1889, when it was amalgamated with Fraser's other enterprise, the Nova Scotia Forge Company, more than two-thirds of the $280,000 capital stock of the resulting Nova Scotia Steel and Coal Company was held by the citizens of New Glasgow.[22] Fraser remained as president and managing director of the corporation unitl 1904,[23] during which time it produced most of the primary steel in the Dominion[24] and remained one of the largest industrial corporations in the country.[25]

Fraser was seconded in his industrial efforts by James Carmichael of New Glasgow and John F. Stairs of Halifax. Carmichael, son of a prominent New Glasgow merchant and a descendent of the Scottish founders of Pictou, had established one of the largest shipbuilding and shipping firms in the province.[26] Stairs' investment in the New Glasgow iron and steel enterprise represented one of the few examples of inter-community industrial activity in this period.

The most unusual pattern of manufacturing development in the region was that initiated at Fredericton by Alexander Gibson. Gibson's distinctiveness lay in his ability to impose the tradition and structure of an earlier semi-industrial society onto a changing pattern of development. A St. Stephen native and the son of Ulster immigrants, he had begun his career as a sawyer, and later operated a small lumber firm at Lepreau. In 1865 he bought from the Anti-Confederationist government of A. J. Smith extensive timber reserves on the headwaters of the Nashwaak River,[27] and at the mouth of that river, near Fredericton, built his own mill town of Marysville. Freed from stumpage fees by his fortunate purchase, the "lumber king of New Brunswick"was producing as much as 100 million feet of lumber annually by the 1880's - about one-third of the provincial output. His lumber exports at times comprised half the export commerce of the port of Saint John.[28]

One of the wealthiest industrial entrepreneurs in the Dominion, Gibson determined in 1883 to undertake the erection of a major cotton enterprise entirely under his own auspices.[29] He erected one of the largest brick-yards in the Dominion and personally supervised the construction of the plant, which was opened in 1885.[30] In that same year he employed nearly 2,000 people in his sundry enterprises.[31] By 1888 his sales of cotton cloth totalled nearly $500,000.[32] That same year the Gibson empire, comprising the cotton mill, timber lands, saw mills, lath mills, the town of Marysville, and the Northern and Western Railroad, was formed into a joint stock company, its $3 million capital controlled by Gibson, his brother, sons, and son-in-law.

Several common characteristics distinguished the men who initiated the industrial expansion of the 1880's. They were, on the whole, men of substance gained in traditional trades and staples.

They sought a substantial, more secure future for themselves within the framework of the traditional community through the instrumentality of the new industrial mercantilism. Averaging fifty-four years of age, they were old men to be embarking upon new careers.[33] Coupled with this factor of age was their ignorance of both the technical skills and the complexities of the financial and marketing structures involved in the new enterprises.

The problem of technical skill was overcome largely by the importation of management and skilled labour, mainly from England and Scotland.[34] The problem of finance was more serious. The resources of the community entrepreneurs were limited; the costs of the proposed industry were almost always far greater than had been anticipated. Moreover, most businessmen had only the vaguest idea of the quantity of capital required to operate a large manufacturing corporation. Promoters generally followed the normal mercantile practice and raised only sufficient capital to construct and equip the physical plant, preferring to finance operating costs through bank loans – a costly and inefficient process. The Halifax Sugar Refinery perhaps best illustrated these problems. When first proposed in 1879 it was to have been capitalized at $300,000. Before its completion in 1881 it was re-capitalized twice to a value of $500,000.[35] Even this figure left no operating capital, and the refinery management was forced to secure these funds by loans from the Merchants Bank of Halifax. At the end of its first year of operation the bank debt of the corporation totalled $460,000,[36] which immediately became a fixed charge on the revenues of the infant industry. Fearing bankruptcy, the stockholders increased their subscriptions and kept the business functioning until 1885 when they attempted a solution to the problem by issuing debenture stock to a value of $350,000 of which the bank was to receive $200,000 in stock and $50,000 cash in settlement of debts still owed to it.[37]

While many industries received their initial financing entirely from local capitalists, some projects proved to be such ambitious undertakings that aid had to be sought from other sources. The St. Croix Cotton Company at St. Stephen, for example, was forced to borrow $300,000 from Rhode Island interests to complete its huge plant.[38] Some industries came to rely so heavily on small community banks for perpetual loans for operating expenses that any general economic crisis toppled both the industries and the banks simultaneously. The financing of James Domville's enterprises, including the Coldbrook Rolling Mills, was a contributing factor in the temporary suspension of the Maritime Bank of St. John in 1880,[39] while such industrial loans ultimately brought down the Bank of Yarmouth in 1905.[40]

II

The problem of industrial finance was intricately tied to a whole crisis of confidence in the new order which began to develop as the first enthusiastic flush of industrial expansion paled in the face of the general business downturn which wracked the Canadian economy in the mid-1880's. At the heart of this problem were a gradual deterioration of the British lumber market and the continued shift from sea-borne to railroad commerce. Under the influence of an increasingly prohibitive tariff and an extended railroad building program a two-cycle interregional trading pattern was gradually emerging. The westward cycle, by rail into the St. Lawrence basin, left the region with a heavy trade imbalance as the central Canadians rapidly replaced British and American produce in the Maritime market with their own flour and manufactured materials.[41] In return, the region shipped to Montreal quantities of primary and primary manufactured products of both local and imported origins. The secretaries of the Montreal and Saint John boards of trade estimated the extent of this interregional commerce at about $15,711,000 in 1885, more than 70 per cent of which represented central Canadian exports to the Maritimes.[42] By contrast the external trade cycle moved in traditional fashion by ship from the principal Maritime ports to Great Britain and the West Indies. Heavily balanced in favour of the Maritimes, it consumed most of the output of the region's resource industries. The two cycles were crucially interdependent; the Maritime business community used the credits earned in the external cycle to meet the gaping deficits incurred in the central Canadian trade. The system worked as long as the equilibrium between the two could be maintained. Unfortunately, as the decade progressed, this balance was seriously threatened by a declining English lumber market.[43]

In the face of this increasingly serious trade imbalance, the Maritime business community became more and more critical of what they regarded as the subversion of the National Policy by central Canadian interests. Their argument was based upon two propositions. If Canadian transportation policy was dedicated to creating an all-Canadian commercial system, then this system should extend not from the Pacific to Montreal, but from the Pacific to the Atlantic. How, in all justice, could the Montreal interests insist on the construction, at a staggering cost, of an all-Canadian route west of that city and then demand the right to export through Portland or Boston rather than using the Maritime route? This argument was implicit in almost every resolution of the Halifax and Saint John boards of trade from 1880 onward.[44]

The second proposition maintained that, as vehicles of nationhood, the railways must be considered as a means of promoting national economic integration rather than as commercial institutions. The timing of this doctrine is significant. Before 1885 most Maritime manufacturers were competitive both with Canadian and foreign producers. Nails, confectionery, woollens, leather, glass, steel, and machinery manufactured in the Maritimes normally had large markets in both central Canada and the West.[45] The recession of 1885 reached a trough in 1886.[46] Diminishing demand coupled with over-production, particularly in the cotton cloth and sugar industries, resulted in falling prices, and made it increasingly difficult for many Maritime manufacturers to retain their central Canadian markets. The *bête noir* was seen as the relatively high freight rates charged by the Intercolonial Railway. The issue came to a head late in 1885 with the closing of the Moncton and the two Halifax sugar refineries. The response of the Halifax manufacturers was immediate and decisive. Writing to the Minister of Railways, John F. Stairs enunciated the Maritime interpretation of the National Policy:

> Four refineries have been set in operation in the Lower Provinces by the policy of the Government. This was right; but trade having changed so that it is now impossible for them to work prosperously it is the duty of the Government to accommodate its policy to the change. The reduction in freight rates asked for is necessary to this. . . . If in answer to this you plead that you must manage so that no loss occur running the I.C.R., we will reply, we do not, and will not accept this as a valid plea from the Government . . . and to it we say that the people of Nova Scotia, nor should those of Ontario and Quebec, for they are much interested, even admit it is essential to make both ends meet in the finance of the railroad, when it can only be done at the expense of inter-provincial trade, and the manufacturers of Nova Scotia. . . . How can the National Policy

succeed in Canada where such great distances exist between the provinces unless the Government who control the National Railway meet the requirements of trade. . . .[47]

At stake, as Stairs later pointed out in a confidential memorandum to Macdonald, was the whole West Indies trade of Nova Scotia.[48] Equally as important and also at stake was the entire industrial structure which had been created in the region under the aegis of the National Policy.

The Maritimes by 1885 provided a striking illustration of the success of that policy. With less than one-fifth of the population of the Dominion, the region contained: eight of the twenty-three Canadian cotton mills, including seven of the nineteen erected after 1879;[49] three of five sugar refineries; two of seven rope factories; one of three glass works; both of the Canadian steel mills; and six of the nation's twelve rolling mills.

Although Stairs succeeded in his efforts to have the I.C.R. sugar freight rates reduced,[50] the problem facing the Maritime entrepreneur was not one which could be solved simply by easier access to the larger central Canadian market; its cause was much more complex. In the cotton industry, for example, the Canadian business community had created industrial units with a production potential sufficient to supply the entire national market. In periods of recession many American cloth manufacturers were prepared to cut prices on exports to a level which vitiated the Canadian tariff; this enabled them to gain control of a considerable portion of the Canadian market. The problems of the cotton cloth manufacturers could have been solved by a further increase in the tariff (a politically undesirable answer), by control of railway rates, or by a regulated industrial output.

From a Maritime regional viewpoint the second of these alternatives appeared to be the most advantageous; the limitations of the tariff could then be accepted and, having attained geographic equality with Montreal throught a regulated freight rate, the more efficient Maritime mills would soon control the Montreal market. Such was the hope; there was little possibility of its realization. Such a general alteration in railway policy would have required subsidization of certain geographic areas – districts constituting political minorities – at the expense of the dominant political areas of the country, a prospect the business community of Montreal and environs could hardly be expected to view with equanimity. Apart from the political difficulties of the situation, most Maritime manufactories suffered from two major organizational problems: the continued difficulty faced by community corporations in securing financing in the frequent periods of marginal business activity,[51] and the fact that most firms depended upon Montreal wholesale houses to dispose of their extra-regional exports.[52] Short of a major shift in government railway or tariff policy, the only solution to the problem of markets which seemed to have any chance for success appeared to be the regulation of industrial production, a technique which was to bring into the Maritimes the Montreal interests, which already controlled the major part of the distributive function in eastern Canada.

III

The entry of Montreal into the Maritime region was not a new phenomenon. With the completion of the Intercolonial Railway and the imposition of coal duties in 1879, Montreal railway entrepreneurs moved to control both the major rail systems of New Brunswick and the Nova Scotia coal fields. A syndicate headed by George Stephen and Donald Smith had purchased the New Brunswick Railroad from Alexander Gibson and the Hon. Isaac Burpee in 1880,[53] with the intention of extending it to Rivière du Loup. This system was expanded two years later by the purchase of the New Brunswick and Canada Railroad with the ultimate view of making Saint John the winter port for Montreal.

In the same year, another Montreal group headed by John McDougall, David Morrice, and L.-A. Sénécal acquired from fifteen Saint John bondholders four-fifths of the bonds of the Springhill and Parrsboro Railroad and Mining Company,[54] and followed this up in 1883 with the purchase of the Springhill Mining Company, the largest coal producer in Canada.[55] The following year another syndicate acquired the International Mine at Sydney.[56] The coal mine takeovers were designed to control and expand the output of this fuel source, partially in an effort to free the Canadian Pacific Railways from dependence upon the strike-prone American coal industry. By contrast, the entry of Montreal interests into the manufacturing life of the Maritimes aimed to restrict output and limit expansion.

The first serious attempts to regulate production occurred in the cotton industry. Although informal meetings of manufacturers had been held throughout the mid-1880's, the business depression of 1886 and the threatened failure of several mills resulted in the organization of the first formal national trade association. Meeting in Montreal in the summer of 1886, representatives of sixteen mills, including four from the Maritimes, agreed to regulate production and to set standard minimum prices for commodities. The agreement was to be renegotiated yearly and each mill provided a bond as proof of good faith.[57] The arrangement at least stabilized the industry and the agreement was renewed in 1887.

The collapse of the association the following year was precipitated by a standing feud between the two largest Maritime mills, the St. Croix at St. Stephen and the Gibson at Marysville. Alexander Gibson had long been the maverick of the organization, having refused to subscribe to the agreement in 1886 and 1887. During this period he had severely injured his larger St. Stephen competitor in the Maritime market. By the time Gibson agreed to enter the association in 1888, the St. Croix mill, faced with bankruptcy, dropped out and reduced prices in an effort to dispose of its huge inventory. The Gibson mill followed suit. With two of the largest coloured cotton mills in the Dominion selling without regulation, the controlled market system dissolved into chaos, and the association, both coloured and grey sections, disintegrated.[58] The return to an unregulated market in the cotton industry continued for more than two years. A business upswing in 1889 mercifully saved the industry from what many manufacturers feared would be a general financial collapse. Even so, only the mills with the largest production potential, regardless of geographic location, escaped unscathed; most of the smaller plants were forced to close temporarily.

In the summer of 1890 a Montreal group headed by A. F. Gault and David Morrice prepared the second attempt to regulate the cotton market. The technique was to be the corporate monopoly. The Dominion Cotton Mills Company, with a $5 million authorized capital, was to bring all of the grey cotton producers under the control of a single directorate. In January 1891, David Morrice set out on a tour of Maritime cotton centres. On his first stop, at Halifax, he accepted transfer of the Nova Scotia Cotton Mill to the syndicate, the shareholders receiving $101,000 cash and $101,000 in bonds in the new corporation, a return of twenty-five cents on the dollar of their initial investment.[59] The following day Morrice proceeded to Windsor, "to consummate the transfer of the factory there,"[60] and from there moved on to repeat the performance at Moncton. Fearful of total bankruptcy and hopeful that this stronger organization would provide the stability that earlier efforts had failed to achieve, stockholders of the smaller community-oriented mills readily acquiesced to the new order. Although they lost heavily on their original investment, most owners accepted bonds in the new corporation in partial payment for their old stock.

The first determined opposition to the cotton consolidation movement appeared in Saint John. Here, John H. Parks, founder and operator of the thirty-year-old New Brunswick Cotton Mill, had bought the bankrupt St. John Cotton firm in 1886 and had proceeded to operate both mills. Despite the perennial problem of financing, the Parks Mills represented one of the most efficient industrial operations in the Dominion, one which had won an international reputation for the quality of its product. The company's major markets were found in western Ontario, a fact which made the continued independence of the firm a particular menace to the combination. The firm's major weakness was its financial structure. Dependent upon the Bank of Montreal for his operating capital, Parks had found it necessary to borrow more heavily than usual during the winter of 1889-90. By mid-1890 his debts totalled $122,000.[61]

At this point two events occurred almost simultaneously: Parks refused to consider sale of the St. John Mills to the new corporation, and the Bank of Montreal, having ascertained that the Montreal syndicate would buy the mills from any seller, demanded immediate payment in full of the outstanding debts of the company[62] – a most unusual procedure. Claiming a Montreal conspiracy to seize the company, Parks replied with an open letter to the dry goods merchants of greater Saint John.

> . . . I have made arrangements by which the mills of our company will be run to their fullest extent.
>
> These arrangements have been made in the face of the most determined efforts to have our business stopped, and our property sold out to the Montreal syndicate which is endeavouring to control the Cotton Trade of Canada. . . . I now propose to continue to keep our mills in operation as a St. John industry, free from all outside control. I would therefore ask you gentlemen, as far as your power, to support me in this undertaking–

> It remains with you to assist the Wholesale Houses in distributing the goods made in St. John in preference to those of outside manufacture so long as the quality and price of the home goods is satisfactory.
>
> The closing of our mills . . . would be a serious calamity to the community, and you, by your support can assist materially in preventing it. I believe you will.[63]

Parks' appeal to community loyalty saved his firm. When the bank foreclosed the mortgage which it held as security for its loans, Mr. Justice A. L. Palmer of the New Brunswick Supreme Court placed the firm in receivership under his control until the case was resolved. Over the strongest objections of the bank, and on one legal pretext after another, the judge kept the mill in receivership for nearly two years.[64] In the meantime he forced the bank to continue the provision of operating capital for the mill's operations, and in conjuction with the receiver, a young Fredericton lawyer, H. H. McLean, proceeded to run an efficient and highly profitable business. When the decision was finally rendered in December 1892, the firm was found to have cleared profits of $150,000 during the period of the receivership. Parks was able to use the funds to repay the bank debts and the mill continued under local control.[65]

The Saint John experience was unique. Gault and Morrice organized the Canadian Coloured Cotton Company, sister consolidation to the Dominion Cotton Mills, in 1891. The St. Croix Mill entered the new organization without protest early in 1892,[66] and even the Gibson Mill, while retaining its separate corporate structure, agreed to market its entire output through the new consolidation. By 1893 only the St. John Mills and the small Yarmouth plant remained in the hands of regional entrepreneurs.

The fate of the Maritime cotton mills are parallelled in the sugar industry. In 1890 a syndicate of Scottish merchants, incorporated under English laws as the Halifax Sugar Refinery Ltd., bought up the English-owned Woodside Refinery of Halifax.[67] The ultimate aim of the Scottish group was to consolidate the sugar industry into a single corporate entity similar to Dominion Cotton. Failing in this effort because of the parliamentary outcry against combines, they turned their efforts to regional consolidation. With the assistance of John F. Stairs, MP, they were able, in 1894, to secure an act of incorporation as the Acadia Sugar Refineries, which was to amalgamate the three Maritime firms.

Unlike the Cotton Union, the new consolidation worked in the interests of the regional entrepreneurs, the stockholders of all three refineries receiving full value for their holdings. Equally important, the management of the new concern remained in the hands of Thomas Kenny, MP.

The consolidation movement of the early 1890's swept most of the other major Maritime manufactories. In some cases local entrepreneurs managed to retain a voice in the direction of the new mergers – John Stairs, for example, played a prominent role on the directorate of the Consumers Cordage Company, which swept the Halifax and Saint John rope concerns into a new seven-company amalgamation in 1890.[68] On the other hand, the Nova Scotia Glass Company of New Glasgow disappeared entirely in the Diamond Glass consolidation of that same year.[69] On the whole, saving only the iron and steel products, the confectionery and the staple export industries, control of all mass consumption industries in the Maritimes had passed to outside interests by 1895. Thus, in large measure the community manufactory which had dominated the industrial growth of the 1880's ceased to exist in the 1890's. Given the nature of the market of the period, some degree of central control probably was inevitable. The only question at stake was whether it would be a control effected by political or financial means, and if the latter, from which centre it would emanate.

The failure of any Maritime metropolis to achieve this control was partly a result of geography and partly a failure of entrepreneurial leadership. The fear of being left on the fringes of a national marketing system had been amply illustrated by the frenetic efforts of the Saint John and Halifax business communities to promote political policies which would link the Canadian marketing system to an Atlantic structure with the Maritime ports serving as the connection points.[70]

The question of entrepreneurial failure is more difficult to document. In part the great burst of industrial activity which marked the early 1880's was the last flowering of an older generation of lumbermen and wholesale shippers. Having failed to achieve their position as the link between central Canada and Europe, and faced with the dominant marketing and financial apparatus of the Montreal community, they drew back and even participated in the transfer of control. This failure is understandable in the smaller communities; it is more difficult to explain in the larger. In the latter case it may well be attributable to the perennial failure of most Maritime communities to maintain a continuity of industrial elites. The manufacturing experience of most families was limited to a single generation: Thomas Kenny's father was a wholesale merchant, his son a stockbroker. John F. Stairs was the son of a merchant and the father of a lawyer. Even in such a distinguished industrial family as that of John Parks, a second generation manufacturer, the son attended the Royal Military College and then entered the Imperial service. Commerce and the professions provided a much more stable milieu, and while many participants in both of these activities were prepared to make the occasional excursion into manufacturing, usually as part of a dual role, few were willing to make a permanent and sole commitment to an industrial vocation.

IV

The lesson brought home to the Maritime entrepreneur by the industrial experience between 1879 and 1895 was that geography would defeat any attempt to compete at parity with a central Canadian enterprise. In response to this lesson, the truncated industrial community of the region turned increasingly to those resource industries in which geography gave them a natural advantage over their central Canadian counterparts. In the 1890's the thrust of Maritime industrial growth was directed toward the processing and manufacturing of primary steel and of iron and steel products. In part, since these enterprises constituted much of the industrial machinery remaining in the hands of regional entrepreneurs, there was little choice in this development. At the same time, Nova Scotia contained most of the active coal and iron deposits in the Dominion and had easy access to the rich iron ore deposits at Belle Isle. In any event, most competition in these industries came from western Ontario rather than Montreal, and the latter was thus a potential market.

Iron and steel development was not new to the region. Efforts at primary steel-making had been undertaken successfully at New Glasgow since 1882. Yet production there was limited and would continue so until a more favourable tariff policy guaranteed a stable market for potential output. Such a policy was begun in 1887 with the passage of the "iron" tariff. Generally labeled as a Nova Scotia tariff designed to make that province "the Pennsylvania of Canada"[71] and New Glasgow "the Birmingham of the country,"[72] the act provided an effective protection of $3.50 a ton for Canadian-made iron, and imposed heavy duties on a variety of iron and steel products.[73] Protection for the industry was completed in 1894 when the duty on scrap iron, considered a raw material by secondary iron manufacturers, was raised from $2 to $4 a ton, and most rolling mills were forced to use Nova Scotia-made bar iron rather than imported scrap.[74]

The growth of the New Glasgow industries parallelled this tariff development. In 1889 the Nova Scotia Steel Company was united with the Nova Scotia Forge Company to form a corporation capable of manufacturing both primary steel and iron and steel products. In the same year, to provide the community with its own source of pig iron, a group of Nova Scotia Steel shareholders organized the New Glasgow Iron, Coal and Railroad Company with a capital of $1 million.[75] Five years later, following the enactment of the scrap iron duty, New Glasgow acquired the rich Wabana iron ore deposits at Belle Isle – some eighty-three acres covered with ore deposits so thick they could be cut from the surface. This was followed the next year by the union of the Nova Scotia Steel and Forge and the New Glasgow Iron companies into a $2,060,000 corporation, the Nova Scotia Steel Company. Containing its own blast and open hearth furnaces, rolling mills, forges, foundries, and machine shops, the firm represented the most fully integrated industrial complex in the country. The process was completed in 1900 when the company acquired the Sydney Coal Mines on Cape Breton Island, developed new steel mills in that area, and reorganized as the Nova Scotia Steel and Coal Company with a $7 million capital.[76]

The development of the Nova Scotia Steel and Coal corporation had begun under the direction of a cabal of Pictou County Scottish Nova Scotians, a group which was later enlarged to include a few prominent Halifax businessmen. Aside from Graham Fraser, its leading members included James D. McGregor, James C. MacGregor, Colonel Thomas Cantley, and John F. Stairs. All four were third-generation Nova Scotians, the first three from New Glasgow. Saving only Cantley, all were members of old mercantile families. Senator McGregor, a merchant, was a grandson of the Rev. Dr. James McGregor, one of the founders of the Presbyterian Church in Nova Scotia; MacGregor was a partner in the large shipbuilding concern of Senator J. W. Carmichael, a prominent promoter of Nova Scotia Steel. Cantley was the only member of the group of proletarian origins. Like

Graham Fraser, he spent a lifetime in the active service of the company, having entered the newly established Nova Scotia Forge Company in 1873 at the age of sixteen. Promoted to sales manager of the amalgamated Nova Scotia Steel Company in 1885, he had been responsible for the introduction of Wabana ore into England and Germany. In 1902 he succeeded Graham Fraser as general manager of the corporation.[77]

Aside from its value to the New Glasgow area, the Nova Scotia Steel Company was of even greater significance as a supplier of iron and steel to a variety of foundries, car works, and machine mills in the region. Because of its unique ability to provide primary, secondary, and tertiary steel and iron manufactures, it was supplying most of the Maritime iron and steel needs by 1892.[78] In this respect, the industrial experience of the 1890's differed considerably from that of the previous decade. It was not characterized by the development of new industrial structures, but rather by the expansion of older firms which had served purely local markets for some time and expanded in response to the demand created by the tariff changes of the period.[79]

The centres of the movement were at New Glasgow, Amherst, and Saint John, all on the main lines of the Intercolonial or Canadian Pacific railroads. At New Glasgow, the forge and foundry facilities of the Nova Scotia Steel Company consumed half the company's iron and steel output. At Amherst, Nathaniel Curry (later Senator) and his brother-in-law, John Rhodes, continued the expansion of the small woodworking firm they had established in 1877, gradually adding a door factory, a rolling mill, a railroad car plant, and an axle factory, and in 1893 bought out the Harris Car Works and Foundry of Saint John.[80] At the time of its incorporation in 1902, Rhodes, Curry & Company was one of the largest secondary iron manufacturing complexes in the Dominion.[81] Curry's industrial neighbour at Amherst was David Robb. Son of an Amherst foundry owner, Robb had been trained in engineering at the Stevens Institute of New Jersey and then had entered his father's foundry. Specializing in the development of precision machinery, he expanded his activities into Massachusetts in the 1890's and finally merged his firm into the International Engineering Works of South Framingham, of which he remained managing director.[82]

If under the aegis of a protective government policy the iron and steel industry of the Maritimes was rapidly becoming a viable proposition for local entrepreneurs, it was also increasingly attracting the interest of both Boston and Montreal business interests. There was a growing feeling that, once a reciprocal coal agreement was made between Canada and the United States, Nova Scotia coal would replace the more expensive Pennsylvania product in the New England market. Added to this inducement was the fact that Nova Scotia provided the major fuel source on the Montreal market – the city actually consumed most of the coal produced in the Cape Breton fields.[83] With its almost unlimited access routes and its strategic water position midway between Boston and Montreal, Nova Scotia seemed an excellent area for investment.

In 1893 a syndicate headed by H. M. Whitney of Boston and composed of Boston, New York, and Montreal businessmen, including Donald Smith, W. C. Van Horne, and Hugh McLennan, negotiated a 119-year lease with the Nova Scotia government for most of the existing coal fields on Cape Breton Island.[84] The new Dominion Coal Company came into formal being in March of that year, with David MacKeen (later Senator) as director and general manager, and John S. McLennan (later Senator) as director and treasurer. The son of a Scottish-born mine owner and member of the legislative council, MacKeen had been an official and a principal stockholder in the Caledonia Coal Company, which had been absorbed in the new consolidation.[85] McLennan was the second son of Hugh McLennan of Montreal, a graduate of Trinity College, Cambridge, and one of the very few entrepreneurs who made the inter-regional transfer in this period.[86] The success of the Dominion Coal syndicate and the growing feeling that the Canadian government was determined to create a major Canadian primary steel industry led Whitney in 1899 to organize the Dominion Iron & Steel Company. The date was significant. Less than two years earlier the government had announced its intention to extend bounty payments to steel made from imported ores.[87] The $15 million capital of the new company was easily raised, largely on the Canadian stock market,[88] and by 1902 the company was employing 4,000 men in its four blast and ten steel furnace works.[89] Graham Fraser was induced to leave Nova Scotia Steel to become general manager of the new corporation,[90] and J. H. Plummer, assistant general manager of the Bank of Commerce, was brought from Toronto as president.

The primacy of American interests in both the Dominion Steel and Dominion Coal companies was rapidly replaced by those of Montreal and Toronto after 1900. The sale of stocks added a strong Toronto delegation to the directorate of the steel company in 1901.[91] In that same year James Ross, the Montreal street railway magnate, bought heavily into the coal corporation, reorganized its management, and retained control of the firm until 1910.[92]

V

The increasing reliance on the stock market as a technique for promoting and securing the necessary financial support to develop the massive Nova Scotia steel corporations emphasized the growing shift from industrial to financial capitalism. Centred on the Montreal stock market, the new movement brought to the control of industrial corporations men who had neither a communal nor a vocational interest in the concern.

In emulation of and possibly in reaction to the Montreal experience, a group within the Halifax business and professional communities scrambled to erect the financial structure necessary to this undertaking. The city already possessed some of the elements of this structure. The Halifax stock exchange had existed on an informal basis since before Confederation.[93] The city's four major banking institutions-the Nova Scotia, the Union, the Merchants (which subsequently became the Royal Bank of Canada), and the Peoples-were among the soundest in the Dominion. The development of Halifax as a major centre for industrial finance began in 1894, at the height of the first Montreal-based merger movement, when a syndicate headed by J. F. Stairs founded the Eastern Trust Company.[94] The membership of this group was indicative of the change that was occurring in the Halifax business elite. Although it contained representatives of the older mercantile group, such as Stairs, T. E. Kenny, and Adam Burns, it also included manufacturers and coalmen, notably J. W. Allison and David McKeen, a stockbroker, J. C. MacKintosh, and lawyers such as Robert L. Borden and Robert E. Harris.

Until his death in 1904, the personification of the new Halifax finance capitalism was John Stairs. It was Stairs who arranged the organization of Acadia Sugar in 1894, who initiated the merger of the Union Bank of Halifax with the Bank of Windsor in 1899, and who led the Halifax business community back into its traditional imperium in the Caribbean with the organization of the Trinidad Electric and Demerara Electric corporations.[95] After 1900, it was Stairs who demonstrated to this same group the possibilities for industrial finance existing within the Maritimes. With the assistance of his young secretary, Max Aitken, and through the medium of his own holding company, Royal Securities, he undertook the reorganization of a number of firms in the region, most notably the Alexander Gibson Railroad and Manufacturing Company, which was recapitalized at $6 million.[96] The scope of his interests and the changes which had been wrought in the Maritime business community in the previous twenty-five years were perhaps best illustrated in the six corporation presidencies which Stairs held in his lifetime, five of them at his death in 1904: Consumers Cordage, Nova Scotia Steel, Eastern Trust, Trinidad Electric, Royal Securities, and Dalhousie University.

Yet, while promotion of firms such as Stanfield's Woollens of Truro constituted a fertile field of endeavour,[97] the major industrial interest of the Halifax finance capitalists was the Nova Scotia Steel Company. In its search for additional capital resources after 1900, the entrepreneurial strength of this firm was rapidly broadened from its New Glasgow base. The principal new promoters of the company were Halifax men, notably James Allison, George Campbell, and Robert Harris. The New Brunswick-born nephew of the founder of Mount Allison University, Allison had entered the chocolate and spice manufactory of John Mott & Company of Halifax in 1871 and had eventually been admitted to a partnership in the firm. He had invested heavily in several Nova Scotia industries and sat on the directorates of Stanfield's Woollens, the Eastern Trust, and the Bank of Nova Scotia in addition to Nova Scotia Steel.[98] George Campbell, the son of a Scottish gentleman, had entered the service of a Halifax steamship agency as a young man and ultimately became its head. Like Allison he was deeply involved in a number of Nova Scotia firms, including Stanfield's, the Silliker Car of Amherst, the Eastern Trust, and the Bank of Nova Scotia.[99]

By far the most significant figure in the Nova Scotia Steel Corporation after Stairs' death was Mr. Justice Robert Harris. The Annapolis-born scion of a Loyalist family, Harris shared the same antecedents as the Moncton and Saint John entrepreneurs of the same name. After reading law with Sir John Thompson, he was called to the Nova Scotia bar in 1882 and rapidly became one of the leading legal figures in the province. In 1892 he moved his practice to Halifax and there became intimately involved in the corporate promotions of the period, ultimately serving on the directorates of thirteen major corporations, including Eastern Trust, Eastern Car, Bank of Nova Scotia, Maritime Telegraph and Telephone, Acadia Sugar, Robb Engineering, Brandram-Henderson Paint, and held the presidencies of Nova Scotia Steel, Eastern Trust, Demerara Electric, and Trinidad Electric.[100]

Despite the continuing need for additional capital, the Nova Scotia Steel Company found little difficulty obtaining most of this support from the Halifax business community.[101] In turn, the corporation remained one of the most efficiently organized industrial firms in the country. In striking contrast to the larger Dominion Steel enterprise, Nova Scotia Steel's financial position remained strong, its performance solid, and its earnings continuous. It was generally credited with being the only major steel company which could have maintained its dividend payments without the aid of federal bounties.[102]

As the first decade of the twentieth century wore to a close, the Halifax business elite appeared to have succeeded in establishing a financial hegemony in the industrial life of an area centred in eastern Nova Scotia and extending outward into both southern New Brunswick and peninsular Nova Scotia. Yet, increasingly, that hegemony was being challenged by the burgeoning consolidation movement emanating from Montreal. The most serious threat was posed in 1909 when Max Aitken, with Montreal now as the centre for his Royal Securities Corporation, arranged the amalgamation of the Rhodes, Curry Company of Amherst with the Canada Car and Dominion Car and Foundry companies of Montreal to form the Canadian Car and Foundry Company. The union marked a triumph as much for Nathaniel Curry as for Aitken – he emerged with the presidency and with nearly $3 million of the $8.5 million capital stock of the new corporation.[103] The move was a blow to the Halifax capitalists, however, as it placed the largest car manufactory in the country, an Amherst plant employing 1,300 men and annually producing $5 million in iron and steel products,[104] firmly in the Montreal orbit of the Drummonds and the Dominion Steel and Coal Corporation. Tension was heightened by the feeling that this manoeuvre was a prelude to the creation of a railroad car monopoly. The reaction was swift. To prevent the takeover of the other Amherst car works, the Silliker Company, a Halifax-based syndicate bought up most of the Silliker stock and organized a greatly expanded company, Nova Scotia Car Works, with $2,625,000 capital.[105] The following year Nova Scotia Steel organized its own $2 million car subsidiary, the Eastern Car Company.

The contest between Montreal and Halifax finance capitalism reached its climax at the annual meeting of the Nova Scotia Steel Company of New Glasgow in April 1910. Fresh from the triumph of the Dominion Coal and Steel merger, Montreal stockbrokers Rudolphe Forget and Max Aitken determined to extend the union to include the smaller steel firm, a proposal which the Scotia Steel president Robert Harris flatly refused to consider. Arguing that the firm was stagnating and that a more dynamic leadership in a reorganized corporation would yield greater returns, Forget launched a major effort to acquire proxies with a view to taking control from the Nova Scotia directors. Using the facilities of the Montreal Stock Exchange, he bought large quantities of Scotia stock at increasingly higher prices, an example followed by Robert Harris and his associates at Halifax. At the April meeting, Harris offered Forget a minority of the seats on the directorate; Forget refused. In the voting which followed, the Montreal interests were narrowly beaten. The *Monetary Times*, in a masterpiece of distortion, described this victory as the triumph of "the law . . . over the market place"[106] and a week later proclaimed that "New Glasgow prefers coal dust to that of the stock exchange floor."[107] In fact, it marked a victory, albeit a temporary one, for New Glasgow industrial capitalism and Halifax financial capitalism. More important, it marked the high point of a late-developing effort on the part of the Halifax business community to create an industrial region structured on that Atlantic metropolis. It was a short-lived triumph. By 1920 the Halifax group made common cause with their Montreal and London counterparts in the organization of the British Empire Steel Corporation, a gigantic consolidation containing both the Dominion and the Nova Scotia Steel companies. This event marked both the final nationalization of the region's major industrial potential and the failure of its entrepreneurs to maintain control of any significant element in the industrial section of the regional economy.

VI

The Maritimes had entered Canada very much as a foreign colony. As the least integrated part of the Canadian economy, it was the region most dependent upon and most influenced by those policies designated to create an integrated national state. The entrepreneurs of the 1880's were capable men, vividly aware of the problems involved in the transition from an Atlantic to a continental economy. The tragedy of the industrial experiment in the Maritimes was that the transportation lines which linked the region to its new metropolis altered the communal arrangement of the entire area; they did not merely establish a new external frame of reference, they recast the entire internal structure. The Maritimes had never been a single integrated organic unit; it was, in fact, not a "region" at all, but a number of British communities clustered on the Altantic fringe, each with its separate lines of communication and its several metropolises – lines that were water-borne, flexible, and changing. In this sense the railroad, with its implications of organic unity, its inflexibility, and its assumption that there was a metropolitan point at which it could end, provided an experience entirely alien to the Maritime tradition. The magnitude of this problem was demonstrated in the initial attempts at industrialization; they all occurred in traditional communities ideally located for the Atlantic market, but in the most disadvantaged positions possible for a continental one.

Central to the experience was the failure of a viable regional metropolis to arise to provide the financial leadership and market alternative. With its powerful mercantile interests and its impressive banking institutions Halifax could most easily have adopted to this role, but its merchants preferred, like their Boston counterparts, to invest their large fortunes in banks and American railroad stocks than to venture them on building a new order. Only later, with the advent of regional resource industries, did that city play the role of financial metropolis.

Lacking any strong regional economic centre, the Maritime entrepreneur inevitably sought political solutions to the structural problems created by the National Policy; he consistently looked to the federal government for aid against all external threats and to his local governments for aid against Canadians. Since the regional politician was more able to influence a hostile environment than was the regional businessman, the latter frequently became both. In many respects the National Policy simply represented to the entrepreneur a transfer from a British to a Canadian commercial empire. Inherent in most of his activities was the colonial assumption that he could not really control his own destiny; that, of necessity, he would be manipulated by forces beyond his control. Thus he produced cotton cloth for the central Canadian metropolis in precisely the same manner as he had produced timber and ships for the British. In so doing he demonstrated considerable initiative and considerable courage, for the truly surprising aspect of the whole performance was that he was able, using his limited community resources, to produce such a complex and diversified industrial potential during the last two decades of the nineteenth century. The inability of the Canadian market to consume his output was as much a failure of the system as of the entrepreneur; the spectacle of a metropolis which devoured its own children had been alien to the Maritime colonial experience. Ultimately, perhaps inevitably, the regional entrepreneur lost control to external forces which he could rarely comprehend, much less master.

NOTES

1. Nova Scotia's industrial output increased 66 per cent between 1880 and 1890; that of Ontario and Quebec by 51 per cent each. Canada, *Census* (1901), III, 272, 283. Bertram estimates that the per capita value of Nova Scotia's industrial output rose from 57.8 per cent to 68.9 per cent of the national average during the period. Gordon Bertram, "Historical Statistics on Growth and Structure of Manufacturing in Canada 1870-1957," Canadian Political Science Association Conference on Statistics 1962 and 1963, *Report,* 122.
2. Canada, *Census* (1901), III, 326-9. The increase between 1880 and 1890 was as follows:

	Saint John	*Hamilton*
Population	−3%	34%
Industrial Capital	125%	69%
Industrial Workers	118%	48%
Average Annual Wage	12%	2%
Value of Output	98%	71%

3. See Table 1.
4. For a sampling of business opinion on the National Policy, see K. P. Burn's reply to Peter Mitchell in the tariff debate of 1883, Canada, House of Commons, *Debates,* 1883, 551-2; the opinion of Josiah Wood, *ibid.,* 446-8; and the view of John F. Stairs, *ibid.,* 1885, 641-9.
5. Quoted by J. F. Stairs in the tariff debate of 1886, Canada, House of Commons, *Debates,* 1886, 775.

6. *Monetary Times,* 4 June, 6 September 1886. Forty-five of the fifty savings banks in the Dominion were located in the Maritimes.
7. *Ibid.,* 16 May 1879.
8. *Ibid.,* 20 May 1881.
9. George M. Rose, ed., *Cyclopedia of Canadian Biography* (Toronto, 1886-8), II, 729-31 (hereafter cited as *CCB*).
10. *Encyclopedia of Canadian Biography* (Montreal, 1904-7), I, 86; *CCB,* II, 155; W. J. Stairs, *History of Stairs Morrow* (Halifax, 1906), 5-6.
11. *Canadian Biographical Dictionary* (Montreal, 1880-1), II, 684-5 (hereafter cited as *CBD*); New Brunswick Museum, Parks Family Papers, F, 1.
12. *CBD,* II, 684-5; *Monetary Times,* 27 April 1883, 22 June 1888.
13. *CCB,* II, 186-7, 86.
14. *CCB,* II, 354-5; *CBD,* II, 693; Henry J. Morgan, ed., *Canadian Men and Women of the Time* (Toronto, 1898), 1000.
15. *Monetary Times,* 16 December 1882.
16. *CCB,* II, 221-2; *CBD,* II, 674-5; Harold Davis, *An International Community on the St. Croix (1604-1930)* (Orono, 1950), ch. 18; *Monetary Times,* 1 August 1890.
17. Canada, *Sessional Papers,* 1885, no. 37, 174-97.
18. *Monetary Times,* 11 December 1885; *Canadian Journal of Commerce,* 3 June 1881; *CBD,* II, 409-10, 510; Morgan, ed., *Canadian Men and Women* (1898), 44.
19. *Canadian Journal of Commerce,* 10 June 1881.
20. W. J. A. Donald, *The Canadian Iron and Steel Industry* (Boston, 1915), ch. 3.
21. *Monetary Times,* 28 April 1882.
22. *The Canadian Manufacturer and Industrial World,* 3 May 1889 (hereafter cited as *Canadian Manufacturer*).
23. Henry J. Morgan, ed., *Canadian Men and Women of the Time* (Toronto, 1912), 419; C. W. Parker, ed., *Who's Who and Why* (Vancouver, 1916), VI & VII, 259 (hereafter cited as *WWW*).
24. *Canadian Manufacturer,* 1 April 1892.
25. *Ibid.,* 7 March 1890.
26. *CBD,* II, 534-5.
27. A. G. Bailey, "The Basis and Persistence of Opposition to Confederation in New Brunswick," *CHR,* XXIII (1942), 394.
28. *Monetary Times,* 9 January 1885.
29. *Ibid.,* 11 May 1883.
30. *Our Dominion. Historical and Other Sketches of the Mercantile Interests of Fredericton, Marysville, Woodstock, Moncton, Yarmouth, etc.* (Toronto, 1889), 48-54.
31. Canada, *Sessional Papers,* 1885, no. 37, 174-97.
32. Canada, Royal Commission on the Relations between Labour and Capital (1889), *Evidence,* II, 448.

33. American industrial leaders of the same period averaged forty-five years. See W. F. Gregory and I. D. New, "The American Industrial Elite in the 1870's: Their Social Origins," in William Miller, ed., *Men of Business* (Cambridge, Mass., 1952), 197.
34. Canada, Royal Commission on the Relations between Labour and Capital, *Evidence,* II, 256, 458; III, 78, 238, 249; *Canadian Manufacturer,* 24 August 1883; *Monetary Times,* 17 June 1887.
35. *Monetary Times,* 18 March 1881.
36. *Ibid.,* 17 February 1882.
37. *Ibid.,* 19 March 1886.
38. *Canadian Journal of Commerce,* 26 October 1883.
39. *Monetary Times,* 18 October 1880.
40. *Ibid.,* 10 May 1905.
41. *Ibid.,* 8 January 1886.
42. *Ibid.,* 30 January 1885. Principal Maritime imports from central Canada included flour, shoes, clothing, textiles, alcoholic beverages, and hardware; exports to Quebec and Ontario centred on sugar, coal, cotton cloth, iron, and fish.
43. Exports of New Brunswick lumber declined from 404 million board feet in 1883 to 250 million feet in 1887. *Monetary Times,* 9 January 1885, 2 and 7 January 1887, 21 January 1898.
44. See particularly, *Proceedings of the Ninth Annual Meeting* of the Dominion Board of Trade (1879), 65-73; *Monetary Times,* 27 January 1882; New Brunswick Museum, Minute Book of the St. John Board of Trade (1879-87), 14 October 1887.
45. Canada, *Sessional Papers,* 1885, no. 34, 86-125.
46. Bertram, "Historical Sketches," 131.
47. PAC, Macdonald Papers, J. F. Stairs to J. M. Pope, 10 September 1885, 50080-5.
48. *Ibid.,* vol. 155, J. F. Stairs to Macdonald, 5 February 1886.
49. *Monetary Times,* 5 October 1888.
50. *Ibid.,* 12 February 1886.
51. See New Brunswick Museum, Parks Family Papers, F, for the problems faced by John Parks and the N.B. Cotton Mills.
52. Montreal *Herald,* 15 October 1883.
53. *Monetary Times,* 8 October 1880.
54. *Ibid.,* 15 December 1882.
55. *Ibid.,* 8 June 1883.
56. *Ibid.,* 16 November 1884.
57. *Ibid.,* 13 August 1886; *Canadian Manufacturer,* 20 August 1887.
58. *Canadian Journal of Commerce,* 7 September 1888.
59. Thomas Kenny in Canada, House of Commons, *Debates,* 1893, 2522.
60. *Monetary Times,* 16 January 1891.
61. St. John *Globe,* 1 May 1891.

62. PAC, Bank of Montreal, General Managers Letterbooks, vol. 8, E. S. Clouston to Jones, 25 April 1891.
63. New Brunswick Museum, Parks Family Papers, Scrapbook 2, 15 December 1890.
64. PAC, Bank of Montreal, General Managers Letterbooks, vol. 8, Clouston to Jones, 13, 22 April, 23 May 1891.
65. St. John *Sun,* 28 December 1892.
66. *Monetary Times,* 18 March 1892.
67. *Ibid.,* 24 October 1890.
68. *Canadian Journal of Commerce,* 22 March 1895.
69. *Monetary Times,* 24 October 1890.
70. *Ibid.,* 12 June 1885, 22 April 1887, 22 August 1902; New Brunswick Museum, Minute Book of the St. John Board of Trade (1879-87), 1 December 1879, 8 November 1886.
71. *Monetary Times,* 20 May 1887.
72. *Canadian Journal of Commerce,* 29 April 1887.
73. Canada, Statutes, 50-1 Victoria C.39.
74. Simon J. MacLean, *The Tariff History of Canada* (Toronto, 1895), 37.
75. *Nova Scotia's Industrial Centre: New Glasgow, Stellarton, Westville, Trenton. The Birthplace of Steel in Canada* (n.p., 1916), 45-6.
76. *Monetary Times,* 9 March 1900; *Industrial Canada,* 20 July 1901.
77. *WWW,* VI & VII, 927, 1075-6.
78. R. M. Guy, "Industrial Development and Urbanization of Pictou Co., N.S. to 1900" (M.A. thesis, Acadia University, 1962), 120-3.
79. *Canadian Manufacturer,* 20 April 1894.
80. *Monetary Times,* 30 June 1893.
81. *Industrial Canada,* March, 1910; Morgan, ed., *Canadian Men and Women* (1912), 290.
82. *CCB,* II, 183; *CBD,* II, 506-7; *WWW,* VI & VII, 997; Morgan, ed., *Canadian Men and Women* (1912), 947.
83. *Monetary Times,* 26 November 1896. The St. Lawrence ports imported 88,000 tons of British and American coal in 1896, and 706,000 tons of Nova Scotia coal. The transport of this commodity provided the basis for the Nova Scotia merchant marine of the period.
84. *Ibid.,* 3 February 1893.
85. Morgan, ed., *Canadian Men and Women* (1912), 698-9; *WWW,* VI & VII, 1118.
86. *WWW,* VI & VII, 1322.
87. Donald, however, argues that Whitney had been determined to go into steel production even if no bounty had been granted. See Donald, *The Canadian Iron and Steel Industry,* 203.
88. Partly, the *Canadian Journal of Commerce* (15 March 1901) sug-

gested, on the promise of the promoters that the company would receive bonuses of $8 million in its first six years of operation.

89. *Industrial Canada,* May, 1902.
90. University of Toronto Archives, Walker Papers, J. H. Plummer to B. E. Walker, 3 December 1903.
91. *Annual Financial Review,* 1 (1901), 92; 3 (1903), 158-60.
92. *Monetary Times,* 3 August 1907.
93. *Ibid.,* 17 April 1903.
94. *Ibid.,* 23 February 1894.
95. *Annual Financial Review,* 23 (1923), 682, 736.
96. *Monetary Times,* 5 December 1902.
97. *Ibid.,* 22 April 1911.
98. Morgan, ed., *Canadian Men and Women* (1912), 19; *WWW,* VI & VII, 762; *Annual Financial Review,* 3 (1903), 174-6.
99. Morgan, ed., *Canadian Men and Women* (1912), 192; *WWW,* VI & VII, 803.
100. Morgan, ed., *Canadian Men and Women* (1912), 505; *WWW,* VI & VII, 1107; *Annual Financial Review,* 3 (1903), 174-6.
101. Most of the stock in this concern was held by Nova Scotians who also bought up two-thirds of the $1.5 million bond the company put out in 1904. University of Toronto Archives, Walker Papers, L. M. Jones to B. E. Walker, 5 August 1904; *Monetary Times,* 15 August 1902.
102. *Monetary Times,* 9 March 1907.
103. *Ibid.,* 8 January 1910.
104. *Industrial Canada,* August, 1913.
105. *Monetary Times,* 29 October 1910.
106. *Ibid.,* 2 April 1910.
107. *Ibid.,* 9 April 1910.

II
Social Structure

Much recent social history has tried to go beyond the narration of events and instead has attempted to come to terms with the underlying structure of society. This has led historians to work in previously uncharted areas such as demography, inheritance patterns, the organization of landholdings, the structure of a community's wealth, and many others. David Gagan's article is a fine example of this new social history. Intensely quantitative, it uses statistical techniques to analyse masses of data previously unstudied by historians. When executed well, this results in useful insights into the regularities of life and how they changed over time. In this essay Gagan presents evidence regarding landholding, inheritance, and fertility to show how the farmers in one Ontario county adjusted to economic change. His conclusions provide an interesting insight into "the critical years" which led to 1867 and suggest reasons for the rural support of the central Canadian imperialist venture now known as Confederation.

These findings are a particularly good example of the utility of the new social history because Gagan uses his data to reflect on one of the crucial events of Canadian history. Much of the new history does not lend itself to such direct application to older questions in Canadian history and for that reason there is considerable skepticism about its usefulness. Clearly, at its best, it can tell us much about important issues and events.

FURTHER READING:
On Ontario agriculture, see Robert Jones, *History of Agriculture*

in Ontario, 1613-1880 (Toronto, 1946); and John McCallum, *Unequal Beginnings: Agriculture and Economic Development in Quebec and Ontario Until 1870* (Toronto, 1980). For a stimulating study of another Ontario county, see Leo Johnson, *History of the County of Ontario, 1615-1875* (Whitby, 1973). For other work on Peel, see David Gagan, "The Indivisibility of Land: A Microanalysis of the System of Inheritance in Nineteenth-Century Ontario," *Journal of Economic History*, 36 (1976), 126-41; Gagan, "Geographical and Social Mobility in Nineteenth Century Ontario: A Microstudy," *Canadian Review of Sociology and Anthropology*, 13 (1976), 152-64; Gagan, " 'Prose of Life': Literary Reflections of the Family, Individual Experience and Social Structure in Nineteenth-Century Canada," *Journal of Social History,* 9 (1976), 367-81; and Gagan, *Hopeful Travellers: Family, Land, and Social Change in Mid-Victorian Peel County, Canada West* (Toronto, 1981). For an urban study using many of the same types of data and a similar methodology, see Michael Katz, *The People of Hamilton, Canada West* (Cambridge, Mass., 1975). See also the recent heated controversy about this article: George Emery and José Igartua, "David Gagan's 'The Critical Years" in Rural Canada West': a critique of the Methodology and the Model" and Gagan, "Under the Lamp Post: a Reply to Emery and Igartua," *Canadian Historical Review,* LXII (1981), 186-96, 197-206.

David Gagan teaches history at McMaster University.

Land, Population, and Social Change: The "Critical Years" in Rural Canada West

by David Gagan

Confederation, with its promise of territorial expansion to create a field for agricultural immigration and commercial enterprise controlled by Ontario, emerged in the 1860's as the panacea for the doldrums of economic decline and demographic stagnation in Canada West. The history of Ontario's subsequent sense of "mission" in the West, which reached hysterical proportions in 1869-70, is well-documented.[1] We know somewhat less about the real nature and impact of the social crisis in Canada West, which evidently generated popular interest in confederation and its territorial objectives. During the debates on confederation in the provincial legislature, the spokesmen for the western section–George Brown, T. D. McConkey, J. S. Macdonald, Aquila Walsh, J. C. Aikins, J. H. Cameron, and others–agreed, even when they disagreed, on the apparent nature of the crisis in rural Upper Canada. The area was no longer a field for immigration; rural property values had plummetted; agrarian indebtedness had increased dramatically; sons could no longer afford to succeed their fathers in the family homestead; and there was a steady movement of population out of the province.[2] "I have no hesitation in declaring," said Aikins, "that there never was a period in the history of Canada when the people suffered more than they do at present."[3] Until we know more about the conditions and

Reprinted from *Canadian Historical Review,* LIX (1978), 293-318, by permission of the author and University of Toronto Press.

circumstances of ordinary life in rural Canadian society during these "critical years," however, it is difficult to assess how much of the impetus for confederation was provided by the attitudes of the people who experienced this crisis.[4]

There is evidence, for example, that by the time of union the Confederation generation in Canada West already had found more subtle means than territorial imperialism to mitigate the social, economic, and demographic crises which their society had confronted in the 1850's. But it is also apparent that the adjustments they were forced to make in the basic institutions of rural society, and in their expectations from rural life, represented a radical departure from a half century of tradition. Confederation, in short, was not the only solution to their problems; but a new farming frontier may have been the best line of resistance to the shock of social change dictated by forces the farmer could not control. In the West the Canadian farmer could hope to recapture Ontario's past and turn his back on the complexities of life in its future.

What follows is an analysis of some empirical data about the social, economic, and demographic history of the people of one rural community in pre-Confederation Canada West, Peel County. The data were derived from the census, real property, probate, and marriage records for the county and transposed into machine-readable form for the purposes of quantitative micro-analysis.[5] There are obvious hazards in generalizing from the experience of a single community. But insofar as Peel had emerged, by the 1850's, as a principal exporter of wheat to imperial and continental markets and consequently enjoyed a reputation as a prosperous, progressive community, it seems probable that the county is an acceptable surrogate for those country districts over which, according to one of their representatives, "a general gloom [hung] like a pall" by the 1860's.[6] In any case, micro-analysis affords the opportunity of examining closely the nature, the timing, and the impact of those social, economic, and demographic processes which shape the material expectations of individuals and inform their attitudes towards their environment. What is lost through exclusion may be regained in the ability to probe the reciprocal relationships among several factors fundamental to individual experience during a critical period of Canadian history.

A British visitor to Canada West in the 1860's remarked that "one of the great banes of the Canadian farmer consists in the occupancy of too much land."[7] Samuel Day was an unabashed snob whose astonishment at common yeomen occupying more than 100 acres was in character; but the comment nevertheless succinctly defined what had become one of the most persistent traits of farmers in Canada West in the 1850's and 1860's–land hunger. Peel's farmers were no exception. In 1850 a typical rural family in Peel County owned or occupied slightly less than 100 acres. Ten years later, their living space had increased more than thirty acres. By 1870 the average farmer occupied nearly 140 acres. In the breadbasket of Peel, Chinguacousy Township, the average holding of 250 of the township's most persistent farmers increased from less than ninety-seven acres in 1850 to nearly 160 acres in 1870. Table 1 summarizes this shifting pattern of landholding in a slightly different fashion, illustrating the disproportionate increase in the number of individuals occupying more than 100 acres (75 per cent) or less than ten acres (48 per cent) compared to the general rate of increase in the total number of occupiers (10 per cent) and the decline, both absolutely and proportionately, of small farmers (11-99 acres). Coincidentally, the ratio of adult males per 100 acres of occupied land, which had been climbing steadily for three decades, declined sharply in the 1860's, the greatest displacement taking place among men between the ages of thirty and sixty (Table 3). Taken together, these facts describe an agrarian society undergoing profound economic and demographic change characterized by competition among landholders to aggrandize their territory and the dislocation of population as the result of this competition for space.

This situation may have been aggravated by the continuing pressures of immigration and speculation which hastened the

TABLE 1

Percentage Distribution of Occupiers of Land by Amount of Land Occupied, Peel County, 1850-70

Date	*Number of occupiers*	*Under 10 acres (no. & %)*	*10-50*	*51-100*	*101-200*	*Over 200*
1851	2595	269	552	1361	357	56
		10.4	21.3	52.4	13.7	2.2
1861	2527	70	498	1365	497	97
		2.7	19.8	54.4	19.8	3.8
1871	2866	398	436	1302	494	136
		13.8	15.2	45.4	20.7	4.7

disappearance of Canada West's agricultural frontier in the 1850's.[8] But it is clear that the land and population crisis in Peel was generated internally, spawned by the traditional values and expectations of a rural society in which prosperity, security, and permanence were synonymous, after 1850 at least, with the occupation of as much land as a man reasonably could acquire. Originally, the unscientific, even wasteful practices of the immigrant farmer amid backwoods conditions had determined the land-intensive character of Upper-Canadian agriculture. The staples trade in wheat, one of the few sources of cash income for farmers, verified the equation of farm size and productivity, especially after 1845 when the demands of the imperial and American markets conspired to make Canada West the granary of two continents. In communities such as Peel, which ranked seventh among the wheat-producing counties of the United Province of Canada and second only to York among the south-central and eastern counties of Canada West, land-lots of land-was the prescription for prosperity and social status.[9]

Even after the collapse of the wheat trade in the late fifties and early sixties, and in spite of the advent of mechanization and the need to reorient production to the demands of more limited domestic markets, there still remained an argument for enhancing the size of the family farm. Its motive power in the 1840's and 1850's was provided by the farm family, especially children whose numbers and happy subordination to the economic and social goals of the family were limned by contemporary observers. Children, wrote one essayist, "the burden of our poor man in England . . . are in Canada his greatest blessing, and happy is that man who has a quiver full of them."[10] Among the farm population of Peel County between 1850 and 1870 a full quiver-a completed family-appears to have consisted of at least eight children.[11] Satisfying their legitimate, but competing, demands for compensation commensurate with their contribution to the family economy was an equally compelling reason to assemble property. There is considerable literary evidence that farmers indeed were anxious to guarantee the independence of their adult children, especially sons, as a reward for their long subordination to the family's common cause-improvement.[12] This, after all, was the fundamental promise of the Canadian backwoods, and the son could do with no less land than the father. Patrick Shirreff, for example, cites the case of a farmer who laboured in the 1830's to acquire a thousand acres of land so that he and his nine sons might be mutually independent.[13] One hundred acres of land for each son was a patrimony more easily acquired in the 1830's than in the fifties or sixties. Nevertheless, the culture of the farm family, informed by values and expectations instilled in successive generations of farm children and symbolized by the transmission of property from one generation to the next, was an equally important stimulus to expansion.

TABLE 2

Selected Summary Data for Agricultural Production, Peel County, 1850-70

	1851	*1861*	*1871*
% total acreage improved	50.7 (37.7)	64.8 (45.9)	72.7 (54.6)
% improved acreage in wheat	28.8 (20.2)	31.5 (22.9)	18.0 (15.5)
% total acreage cropped	29.9 (23.2)	49.0 (30.7)	59.6 (40.5)
% cropped acreage in wheat	48.9 (34.9)	41.7 (33.7)	21.9 (20.9)
% total acreage in wheat	14.6 (8.1)	20.4 (10.5)	16.6 (8.5)
Milch cow population	8,107	9,809	10,500
% increase		20.9 (52.0)	7.0 (41.4)
Butter production (lbs.)	491,882	741,100	728,720
% increase		50.7 (67.0)	(40.2)

Parenthetical data are for the Province of Canada West/Ontario.

SOURCES: *Census of the Canadas, 1851-52*, II (2 vols., Quebec, 1853), Table VI; *Census of the Canadas, 1860-61*, II (2 vols., Quebec, 1864), Table XI; *Census of Canada, 1870-71*, III (4 vols., Ottawa, 1873), Tables XIII, XI.

TABLE 3

Summary Data for the Distribution by Age Cohort of Adult Males, Peel County, 1838-71

	1838	*1851*	*1861*	*1871*
No. males over 15 yrs.	3,674	7,285	8,252	6,755*
Ratio of males over 15 to 100 acres occupied land	1.3	2.9	3.1	2.3
Ratio of males 15-30 to males 30-60		1,338	1,319	1,373
Males 15-30 as % of all males over 15		53.7	52.0	52.0
Males 30-60 as % of all males over 15		40.2	39.5	37.8
Males over 60 as % of all males over 15		6.1	8.5	10.3

*1871 data are estimates since two of Peel's townships were enumerated as part of Cardwell District.

SOURCE: *Census of the Canadas, 1851-52*, I, Table III; *Census of the Canadas, 1860-61*, I, Table VI; *Census of Canada, 1870-71*, II, Table VII.

Tables 1, 2, and 3 place these two sources of pressure on the community's most important commodity in perspective. The aggregation of land into larger economic units was essentially a phenomenon of the 1850's, but the process continued throughout the next decade as well (Table 1). It coincided, in the first instance, with the expansion of wheat cultivation in the county at a faster pace than was the case generally throughout the province, and also with the rapid diversification of newly cultivated land into crops other than wheat, particularly barley, oats, and pease. In short, territorial expansion reflected the vagaries of the wheat economy in the 1850's as farmers scrambled to increase wheat production in the best of times or to find profitable land-intensive substitutes in the worst of times. By 1860, however, the demise of the county's wheat economy was an ineluctable fact–hastened by a severe infestation of wheat midge in the 1860's–as the data for 1870 clearly indicate. But already the shift into other areas of agriculture, particularly dairying, had begun with a vengeance (Table 2) and the stage ought to have been set for a retreat from the compulsion to maintain man/land ratios characteristic of a staples economy.

Instead, over the decade Peel's man/land ratio declined dramatically (Table 3) until it was lower in 1870 than it had been for thirty years. This was accomplished primarily through the loss of (and failure to replace) approximately 20 per cent of the county's adult male population between the ages of fifteen and sixty, after 1860. Several factors may have been involved–for example, the end of a construction boom in Brampton, the transition from man to machine power in agriculture, and, of course, mortality. But as Table 3 suggests, this demographic revolution also took place within the context of a decided shift in the age structure of the adult male population. After 1860 the ratio of males 15-30 to males 30-60 increased, as did the proportion of elderly men in the community. Conversely, the ratio of middle-aged and late middle-aged men to younger men began to decline. This reversal of the trends apparent in the 1850's points to the emergence of a new generation of young, unestablished men whose aspirations evidently prolonged the competition among farm families for land. Clearly, many of them could not be accommodated. When they were, it may well have been at the expense of men in the next cohort whose ranks were being depleted faster than that of any other group.

Productivity and inheritance, then, appear to have been the

FIGURE 1

Trend line and three-year moving averages for cost of land per acre, Peel County, 1840-70

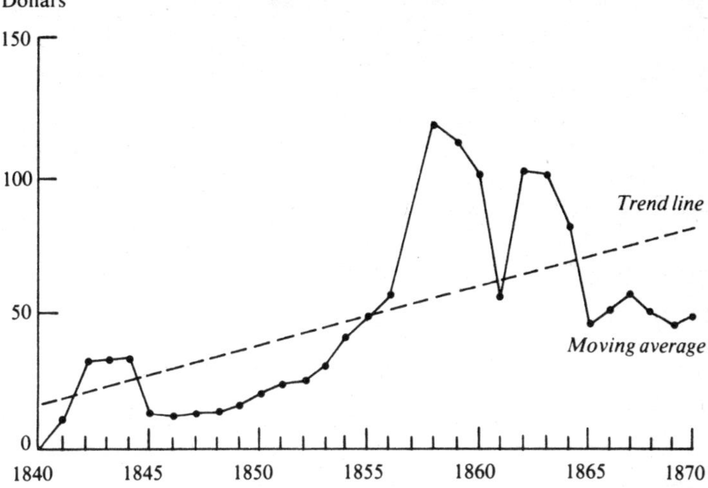

principal sources of the compulsive competition for land in Peel County between 1850 and 1870. The result was a crisis of major proportions in the 1860's, a crisis which would shape and condition the social, economic, demographic, even the cultural characteristics of the community for the next quarter century. The immediate effects of this competition for space are illustrated by Figure 1 (data for the graph are detailed in Appendix 1). The trend line from the time series analysis is the straight line, which best describes the long-term movement of land prices in the county. The trend is unrelentingly upward until the final value, for 1870, is more than quadruple the value for 1840. Inflation, devaluation, and variable conversion rates from sterling to decimal currency undoubtedly account for some of this startling appreciation, although it is difficult to know how much. Nevertheless, the trend of prices adequately testifies to the ever increasing pressure on land in this community as the result of competition. The situation benefited landowners in the long run, just as it was detrimental to poorer immigrants with agricultural proclivities, to tenants whose rents were calculated as 2-4 per cent of the market value of the farm, and to owners intent, for whatever reason, on enlarging their farms. But if the politicians are to be believed, the real concern among farmers lay in the short-term behaviour of land prices. ". . . [P]roperty, has depreciated in value within the last five years twenty, thirty, forty, ay, and even sixty per cent," complained the member for Cornwall in 1865.[14] The three-year moving average prices per acre (Figure 1) appear to underline his point. Average land values in 1865, higher than they had been a decade earlier, nevertheless had plunged headlong from the dizzy heights attained during the great recession of 1857-60. Not steadily appreciating values in the long term, but dramatic and unpredictable fluctuations in the short, were the real banes of the Canadian farmer determined to increase his holdings.

The implications of these fluctuations were devastating. Land purchased between 1855 and 1859 – as more than 12 per cent of all the proprietors of record in 1870 had done – had depreciated at least 60 per cent by 1865, representing a substantial loss to its owners. Land acquired before the scramble of the late fifties had appreciated in value, but had been robbed of its speculative promise, and the farmer was no less a speculator because he worked his investment. In either case proprietors had lost grounds, and many had paid a heavy penalty for their addiction to land as the record of mortgage indebtedness in the community seems to indicate (Table 4). In 1850 slightly more than 11 per cent of the county's acreage was mortgaged, representing a debt of approximately $1 borne by each acre of land in the community. Ten years later, nearly 40 per cent of all the land in the county was indentured and the dollar value of the debt had climbed 600 per cent to $70 per capita or $7 for each acre of land in several townships. In sum, the short-term effects of the crisis in Peel included a substantial increase in the need to borrow money, in the level of borrowing, and in the costs of borrowing. If the purpose of this activity was to finance the purchase of expensive land in order to increase productivity, then the collapse of the wheat market spelled disaster. If speculation was the objective of the mortgager, then the collapse of the land market equally spelled ruin. And if the purpose of expanding a farm and of going into debt to do so was to gratify the expectations of children, then perpetuating the traditional culture of the farm family had become an expensive, debt-prone proposition which threatened the very basis of the family's security.

TABLE 4

Mortgage Indebtedness, Peel County, 1850-70

	1850	*1860*	*1870*
% total country acreage mortgaged	11.3	38.0	16.2
$ value mortgages	228,708	1,915,029	812,271
Mean debt per mortgaged acre ($)	27.38	64.87	49.54
Debt/each acre county land (rounded)	1.00	7.00	3.00
Debt/per capita total population (rounded)	9.00	70.00	30.00
Avg. interest rate preceding decade	7%	8.3%	7.4%
Average term (years)	4	5	5

NOTE: This table is based on data for the four largest of the county's five townships.

The evidence suggests, in fact, that it was demographic pressure, more than the desire to increase productivity, which ultimately spawned this crisis. Land prices in Peel remained buoyant throughout the recession of 1857-9, bottomed out in 1860, perhaps reflecting panic among speculators, and then recovered significantly before finally levelling off at half the 1857 price. In other words, the effects of the commercial recession on the land market were dramatic, but short-lived. Other forces apparently conspired to drive the price of land upwards in spite of the commercial slump, and only brought it down permanently after the economy had recovered. The return to something like normality coincides with the reversal of population trends in the county. Between 1860 and 1870, after forty years of steady growth, the population of Peel declined almost 5 per cent. It kept on declining until the end of the century when changes in the focus of agricultural production brought about a redistribution of land into smaller units.[15] On the eve of Confederation, however, Peel had reached the limits of growth in terms of its ability to accommodate more farmers, as the result of the land hunger of its established farm families. They withdrew from the land market in the early sixties, reeling from the shock of inflated land prices, mounting debts, and uncertain commodity markets. How complete their withdrawal was can be seen in the mortgage data for 1870 (Table 4). Between 1860 and 1870 the ratio of mortgaged to unmortgaged land in the community declined nearly 60 per cent. The burden of debt borne by each mortgaged acre fell less than 25 per cent, however, and was still nearly double what it had been in 1850. All of this suggests a relatively inactive mortgage market catering to a small number of new proprietors with very little capital who bought out established owners almost wholly on credit.[16] Improving farmers were no longer willing or able to take the risks which continued competition among themselves for land entailed.

New technology and the demands of a developing domestic, urban market were already working to alleviate some of the pressures on farm land in Ontario by ending the land-intensive character of agriculture.[17] But the real source of the land and economic crisis of the 1850's and 1860's–demographic pressure emanating from within Ontario's farm families–was a less tractable problem because it involved human relationships and expectations defined by a half century of rural life in Upper Canada where, even in the 1860's, the dreams and aspirations of the immigrant backwoodsman continued to inform individual experience. Solving the problem of too many people competing for too little land in this social atmosphere would generate the ultimate crisis in rural pre-Confederation Canada West.

"It is certain," bemoaned Susannah Moodie in the 1850's, "that death is looked upon by many Canadians more as a matter of . . . a change of property into other hands, than as a real domestic calamity."[18] These were sentiments appropriate to a Victorian gentlewoman reflecting upon widowhood; but to children awaiting their patrimony, and to parents concerned for the future well-being of their dependents, the conditions and the consequences of inheritance, the transmission of property from one generation to the next, transcended the fleeting fact of mortality. Traditionally, the Canadian farmer had recourse to three methods of transferring his estate to his heirs. In the perfectly impartible system of inheritance, the estate was settled on a single heir to the exclusion of all other claimants. The perfectly partible system involved a more or less equitable division of the estate among all the legitimate heirs. A third system, identified some years ago by A. R. M. Lower as the "English-Canadian" system, appeared to Lower to have been the invention of the democratically inclined, land-rich, money-poor Upper-Canadian farmer.[19] In fact, the system originated in Europe amid similar demographic circumstances at least a century earlier. It involved devising landed property, either before or after death, upon a single heir, usually a son, who in return for his patrimony was then obligated to provide more or less equally for the man of property's other heirs and assigns. In this way the farmer avoided the alternative path of subdividing the land into units of decreasing economic viability, instead maintaining the family's capital investment and the source of its security intact by using the land's ability to sustain debt – and one heir's willingness to incur debt in return for a farm – in order to guarantee all of his heirs a share of his wealth.[20] Thus, a Peel County farmer who died in 1867 leaving his farm and a mere $54 in personal property instructed that one of his sons, James, was to inherit the 100-acre farm, its crops, stock, and implements providing that:

> 1st He shall find and furnish all the Flour, Pork and Butter and milk, potatoes and other vegetables with plenty of good firewood ready for use and . . . keep 1 horse [and buggy] . . . the above shall be found and supplied during . . . the life of . . . his mother.
> 2nd He shall pay . . . annually . . . the sum of $100 as part of [her] subsistence which payments shall be continued to the end of [her] natural [life].
> 3rd He shall pay . . . to his brother William . . . the sum of $1,200 . . . I give and bequeath to my daughter Jane . . . the sum of $200 which sum her brother James above mentioned shall pay . . . I give and bequeath to the [5] children of my late daughter Rachel . . . the sum of $200 . . . which sum shall be paid . . . by the said James . . . in equal sums when they severally attain their 20th year.
> And further the said James . . . shall pay all debts due by us . . . and defray all our funeral expenses.[21]

Under such a system the costs of inheritance to the principal heir could be substantial; and in fact the average debt incurred by Peel County heirs under this system in the last half of the nineteenth century was nearly $1,600 in cash settlements and more than $160 in annuities, distributed among three to five residual heirs. In the end, depending on the eventual cost of annuities and of borrowing capital to meet these obligations, the price of inheritance might indeed approach the value of the farm itself.

What is of vital importance, at any rate, is the relative preference which farmers showed for one or another of these systems of inheritance. Tables 5 and 6 summarize the results of a multiple classification analysis, which distinguishes among the characteristics of testators who resorted to one or another of the systems of inheritance employed in rural Ontario. The analysis assumes

TABLE 5

Summary Results From Multiple Classification Analysis of Systems of Inheritance by Selected Variables, Peel County, 1846-99

System employed	*Canadian*	*Impartible*	*Partible*
Variable		*Significance*	
Value personal property	0.02	0.04	0.75
No. properties mentioned	0.01	0.03	0.08
Year will written	0.01	0.30	0.11
No. children mentioned	0.01	0.01	0.18
Occupational classification	0.25	0.83	0.08
Overall significance (F)	0.01	0.01	0.01
R^2	0.179	0.112	0.074
Multiple R	0.423	0.334	0.273
Rank order of variables			
Value personal property	4	2	5
No. properties mentioned	2	3	4
Year will written	3	4	2
No. children mentioned	1	1	1
Occupational classification	5	5	3

NOTE: Multiple classification analysis (MCA) reports the significance of each independent variable and of all the variables collectively in contributing to the explanation of variation in the dependent variable. It also ranks the independent variables in order of importance and reports (Multiple R) how much of the variation is explained by the independent variables employed – in this case 52% (.423), 33% (.334), and 27% (.273), respectively. In short, what prompted men to distribute wealth equally is much less certain. Finally, MCA predicts how the population in any category of a variable ought to behave, comparatively, once the confounding effects of other variables have been removed (Table 6). Thus, in Table 6 73% of all testators wrote "Canadian" type wills; all things being equal, 56% of the men who wrote wills between 1846 and 1855 ought to have written "Canadian" wills, 75% of those who wrote will between 1856 and 1865 ought to have written such wills, and so forth.

that the decedent had to make a choice between at least two contending claimants. A significant level of .01 in Table 5 indicates a particularly strong explanatory variable. In Table 6 the adjusted mean percentages indicate the percentage of the observations in any variable category which ought to behave in a particular way once the effects of all the other variables have been eliminated. Four generalizations implicit in the tables are of particular interest. First, Table 5 suggests that the year in which the testator devised his will – that is, the circumstances which informed his judgement – is especially significant in explaining why he resorted to the "Canadian" system. As Table 6 indicates, the "Canadian" system was adopted wholesale by testators in Peel County during the crisis years 1856-65, was only slightly less popular during the more optimistic years surrounding Confederation, and then established itself as the principal means of transferring wealth with the advent of a new crisis after 1873. Second, within this context, transmitting wealth in this fashion was clearly related to family size. The more children a man had, the more likely he was to adopt the "Canadian" system or, alternatively, to throw up his hands and simply adopt the rule of perfect impartibility since the end result was virtually the same.[22] Third, the wealthier the man, the more likely he was to pass on his substance undivided. Those with the least personal property, men with little or no real property, and the unskilled were more likely to divide their estates equally among their surviving children. In this way, the poor became poorer and the rich richer. Finally, among the people of Peel County, farmers, retired farmers, and men with the assets of farmers (stage owners, livery stable owners, teamsters, and conveyors) were more likely after 1850 to resort to the "Canadian" system of inheritance than any other group.

The implications of these data seem fairly obvious in the light of the land and economic crises of the 1850's. By 1860 it had become clear to this rural society that its ability to occupy more social and economic space had been severely constrained. As events conspired to thwart the expectations of two generations of farmers by threatening the social objectives of one and the economic aspirations of the other, established farmers reconciled themselves to a system of inheritance which would at least preserve that best of all possible worlds – the large farm – undivided for one member of the next generation. The extent of his property, and its time-tested productive capacity, might in turn compensate his brothers for their lost future and give them a start in some other capacity or in some other place.

As elegant as this adjustment to the culture of the farm family was, however, it merely obviated an immediate problem by creating others, and in any case left the principal issue unresolved. In short, continued economic stability had been purchased at the expense of the legitimate, and traditional, expectations of the majority of Peel's younger generation, many more of whom would now join the army of migrants who passed through the county every year.[23] The real challenge in the long term was to solve the problem of those overpopulated rural households which

TABLE 6

Adjusted Mean Percentage for Categories of Selected Variables By System of Inheritance Employed, Peel County, 1846-99 (from MCA)

System employed	*Canadian*	*Impartible*	*Partible*
Grand mean	*73%*	*13%*	*12%*
Variable			
VALUE PERSONAL PROPERTY			
0	67	8	13
Less than $1,000	68	18	13
$1,000-2,999	74	14	13
3,000-6,999	80	12	8
7,000-14,999	86	4	11
15,000 through highest	93	3	6
NO. OF PROPERTIES			
0	61	17	18
1	69	16	12
2	78	11	9
3+	82	7	10
YEAR WILL WRITTEN			
1846-55	56	24	25
1856-65	75	16	15
1866-73	67	12	12
1874-99	78	9	10
NO. OF CHILDREN			
0	66	21	12
1	51	34	10
2	65	9	20
3	66	18	13
4	80	11	9
5	79	10	9
6	74	7	14
7	72	7	16
8	95	2	4
9	94	5	3
10	87	6	8
11	83	5	12
12	68	21	16

OCCUPATIONAL CLASS			
Farmer	74	13	11
Manufacturer	62	17	24
Construction	65	0	27
Unskilled	52	12	35
Commerce	67	15	19
Transportation	74	13	14
Professional	49	24	27
Retired	75	12	12

had once depended for their standard of living on the labour of many children but could no longer compensate them adequately for their contribution and even victimized them in the interests of social security and stability. Fewer children, on the other hand, would ease the pressure on the family/land ratio, improve or at least maintain standards of living in a changing and uncertain economy by reducing the number of consumers of wealth, anticipate the shift in the role of children from producers to consumers, and promote the farmer's real and sentimental commitments to gratify, as equitably as possible, the social expectations of all of his children. Thus, in the wake of the crisis of the 1850's the younger generation of farm families in this rural community began to adjust their behaviour to the new realities of their environment just as farmers had done, and were doing, elsewhere in response to similar circumstances.[24]

Tables 7 and 8 present data on the fertility of married women in Peel County, 1851-71. In broadest outline they can be summarized as follows. Between 1851 and 1871 the percentage of married women who had given birth to more than one child before their twenty-fifth birthday declined from 60.9 to 41.2 per cent. The percentage of married women in the same age group who had no children or who had only one living child increased from 40 per cent in 1851 to nearly 60 per cent in 1871. On the other hand, changes which took place in the childbearing patterns of women in the 25-29 cohort were minimal from one decade to the next. The inescapable conclusion is that the youngest group of married women in the community in 1871 experienced a significant change in the timing of their first conception compared with a similar group of women starting their families in the late forties. The change is all the more significant because delaying conception in the years of highest fertility

TABLE 7

Percentage Distribution of Married Rural Women by Age Cohort and Number of Children, Peel County, 1851-71

	1851	*1861*	*1871*
Women 15-24 (*N*)	(607)	(397)	(407)
% with no children	28.8	31.2	34.2
% with one child only	10.2	15.9	24.6
% with more than one child	60.9	52.9	41.2
Women 25-29 (*N*)	(452)	(515)	(602)
% with no children	22.3	18.4	21.1
% with one child only	5.9	5.8	7.5
% with more than one child	71.7	75.7	71.4

results in a disproportionately large decrease in completed family size. How dramatic this decline in marital fertility was can be seen in Table 8, which also illustrates the difference in the relative decline of marital fertility among farm wives compared to other women in the community. It also raises the question of how family limitation was accomplished, since it is almost certain that this rural society was a perfectly natural demographic regime in which women without the benefit of contraceptive devices or information produced children at regular intervals of thirty months, more or less, from marriage to menopause. This was the ordeal of marriage which made young wives "old women at the age of thirty."[25]

The necessary reduction in farm family size was accomplished in Peel, as it was elsewhere, through homeostatic adjustments which had nothing to do with physiology and everything to do with the impulse toward equilibrium within society itself. Delaying the creation of new family units in times of stress, a decision subject to the influence of a wider array of forces than the interests of the principals involved in matrimony, was the essential medium of family limitation in pre-industrial societies where conception normally took place only within the context of marriage.[26] Figure 2 and Appendix 2 document the pattern of age at marriage among 474 Peel County women who married between 1840 and 1870. The three-year moving averages suggest regular fluctuations with the peaks occurring shortly after periods of severe social or economic distress (1837-8, 1848-9, 1857-9). The trend values and the trend line, however, confirm the slow but continuous upward movement of mean ages at marriage for women over the thirty-year period until, by 1870, the trend value is almost two-and-a-half years greater than it was for 1840. Aggregate census data substantiate this evidence. In 1850 approximately half of the women in the 16-30 age cohort had ever been married. Twenty years later, less than 40 per cent (38.7) of the same age group were married or widowed. There is some evi-

TABLE 8

Marital Fertility Ratios (Number of Children Under 10 Years of Age Per Thousand Married Women) by Age Cohort of Wife, Peel County, 1851-71

Age Group		**15-19**	
	1851	*1861*	*1871*
All Wives	1,462	500	452
Farm Wives	1,585	533	385
Per cent Decline: all wives	−69.1		
Per cent Decline: farm wives	−75.7		

Age Group		**20-24**	
	1851	*1861*	*1871*
All Wives	1,762	1,494	1,302
Farm Wives	1,879	1,405	1,124
Per cent Decline: all wives	−26.1		
Per cent Decline: farm wives	−40.2		

Age Group		**25-29**	
	1851	*1861*	*1871*
All Wives	2,402	2,356	2,333
Farm Wives	2,492	2,558	2,222
Per cent Decline: all wives	−2.9		
Per cent Decline: farm wives	−10.9		

dence that this constraint on fertility was not the only form of family limitation within the community. For example, completed family size was lower among second generation Upper Canadians (6.5 children) than among immigrant families (8.5); and the fact that Upper-Canadian women tended, on the average, to complete their childbearing in their thirty-fifth year while immigrant women continued to produce children through their fortieth year is evidence of decision-making as opposed to natural constraints.[27]

Nevertheless, the advancement of the age at which women married and started to bear children appears to have been the principal cause of the decline in fertility in Peel after 1860, and it is clear that this phenomenon was related directly to the changing opportunities for marriage in the community. As Table 9 illustrates, between 1850 and 1870 sex ratios in the two age cohorts 10-15, 15-20, and across the larger age group 10-30, gradually reversed until young women outnumbered their male peers. Undoubtedly the imbalance resulted from the outmigration of both single young men and of the families of middle-aged men; and it

FIGURE 2

Trend Line and Three-Year Moving Averages for Age at Marriage, Women Under 35, Peel County, 1840-70

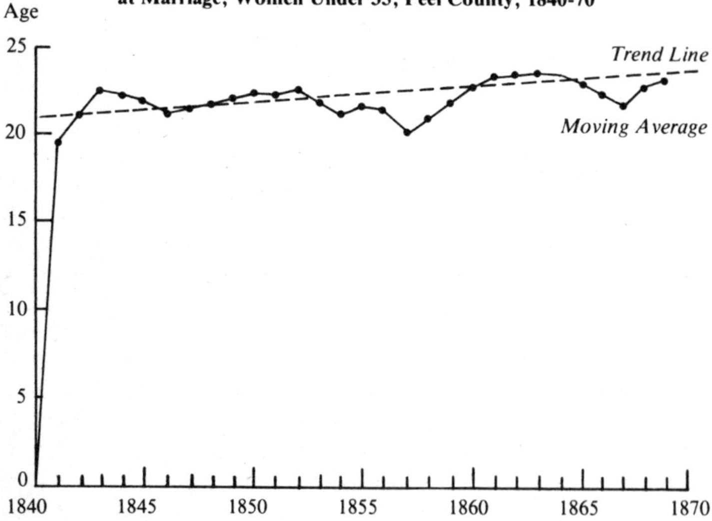

was compounded by the trend toward later ages of marriage among the single men who remained in the community awaiting their inheritance. Their behaviour follows the trend described in Figure 2, but the trend value for the male age at marriage increases from 23.9 years to 26.4 years.[28] This implies a prolonged stage of dependence for young men who, in earlier times, would have been heads of their own households.

TABLE 9

Ratio of Males Per Thousand Females by Age Cohorts, Peel, County, 1830-70

	1836	*1851*	*1861*	*1871*
Under 16 yrs.	1,047			
Over 16 yrs.	1,330			
Ages 10-15		1,090	1,081	913
Ages 16-20		1,102	957	984
Ages 21-30		1,216	1,160	1,072
Ages 10-30		1,145	1,077	997

SOURCES: George Walton, *Directory of Toronto and the Home District* (Toronto, 1937); *Census of the Canadas*, 1851-52, I, Table III; *Census of the Canadas*, 1860-61, I, Table VI; *Census of Canada*, 1870-71, II, Table VII.

Marital fertility, family size, and youthful independence in this community, then, were functions of the age at which marriage was permissible, or possible, in a rapidly changing economic and demographic environment. Indeed, by 1870 Peel County had begun to exhibit at least some of the demographic characteristics – a preponderance of females, later ages of marriage, declining fertility, and smaller families – associated with the ever-lengthening shadow of the metropolis which gradually enveloped its nearest, more primitive, clients.[29] It would take time for these, and other, adjustments to alter the contours of life in Peel permanently; but on the eve of Confederation the process was well under way as the generation of families coming into existence took, or were compelled to take, drastic action to mitigate the crises of the critical years in Canada West.

It is instructive to ask what it meant, then, to be a farmer in Peel County on the morrow of Confederation compared with earlier, perhaps better, times. Table 10 displays the results of a multiple classification analysis of the characteristics of farmers in the community in 1851, 1861, and 1871. From it some important generalizations emerge. First, the society which in 1851 associated more or less equally all ethnic groups among its farming community, except Irish Catholics, was by 1871 fast becoming the preserve of native-born Protestants. Peel was no longer a field for European immigration. Second, as a result of the land crisis of the 1850's, farmers, who had been greatly over-represented among owners of rural land in 1851, were no longer especially favoured and in fact were nearly as likely to be renters. Similarly, in 1851 farmers were more likely to be over-represented among the most mobile groups in society than they were in 1871. The disappearance of cheap land nearby, presumably, had restricted the customary mobility of men who had been taught that "tying [themselves] down to a locality" was inconsistent with the economic opportunities afforded by the limitless spaces of the continent.[30] Finally, in 1851 and 1861 farmers were over-represented among the older generation of male householders and under-represented among younger men. Twenty years later the gap had narrowed considerably as one generation of farmers died off and was replaced by the next.

This generation had already put in a long period of dependence waiting for their land, and the real costs of inheriting it had been substantial, if indeed these young farmers owned their land at all. In either case their future, from the vantage point of 1867, must have seemed less certain than the halcyon days of their fathers' youth. Then, cheap or free land, unrestricted mobility, the labour of a young, large, and vigorous family, and a buoyant wheat market were the essential ingredients of success in an open agrarian society. By 1867 the adjustments to rural life and to men's expectations from it in a closed society had long since been set in motion.

The necessity of Canada West expanding its frontiers after 1850 was an important factor in the drive to unite the British North American provinces. The resistance movement to the expansion of the new Dominion, subsequently mounted at Red River, produced what was by any name an armed invasion of the West fired by the rhetoric of nationalism but fed by the thwarted imperialism of Ontario. When the first invasion was followed by a second–of emigrant Ontario farmers–with the enactment of the Dominion Lands Act of 1872, which created a new frontier of cheap land, the circle of events was complete.

The intriguing aspect of this process is that by 1870 rural society in Ontario had already dealt decisively and effectively with

TABLE 10

Adjusted Category Means and Tests of Significance From Multiple Classification Analysis of Farming as a Vocation, Peel County, 1851-71

	1851	*1861*	*1871*
A. Significance (F) of Variables			
Ethnicity	0.01(4)*	0.01(3)	0.01(1)
Land tenure	0.01(1)	0.01(1)	0.01(3)
Mobility	0.01(3)	0.01(4)	0.01(2)
Stage of life	0.01(2)	0.01(2)	0.01(4)
Overall significance	0.01	0.01	0.01
R^2	0.176	0.230	0.066
Multiple R	0.419	0.479	0.256
B. Grand Means	64%	61%	59%
C. Adjusted Category Means			
Ethnicity:			
Irish Catholic	55	51	46
other Catholic	67	73	59
native protestant	67	68	67
other protestant	65	59	54
Land Tenure:			
owner	80	82	64
renter	54	43	51
Mobility:			
stayer	73	66	69
mover	59	56	54
Stage of life:			
15-34 years	54	55	58
35-49 years	63	59	56
50-65 years	76	70	63
over 65	80	68	64

* Numbers in parentheses indicate rank order of variables.

NOTE: MCA is concerned with the variable behaviour of subpopulations in comparison with the characteristics of the whole population. The adjusted means are means derived after the effects of all other variables have been removed. Thus, the table can be read as follows. "In 1851, 64 per cent of all male heads of household are farmers. In comparison, all things being equal, 55 per cent of Irish Catholic heads of household will be farmers, 67 per cent of native-born heads of household will be farmers" and so forth. Significance lies in the amount of variability of the category mean above or below the grand mean.

the crisis that had threatened its future. By means of a dramatic shift in customary patterns of inheritance and consequently the displacement of surplus population through the exercise of social controls over the formation of new farm families and by limiting the offspring of new partnerships, the community had taken steps to protect the integrity of the traditional economic space from which the farm family derived its security and to maintain the standard of living–the rewards of its labour–historically associated with rural prosperity. In short, radical but nevertheless thoroughly pragmatic adjustments to the size, the structure, and the culture of the farm family by 1867 had begun to mitigate the effects of the crisis in rural Canada West. What stake, then, did the farmers of Ontario have in the territorial objectives of Confederation as they were advertised in the newspapers and the political arena?

The question must properly be left in the realm of speculation. As an aid to speculation, however, it may be useful to consider the experience of William Taylor, a farmer who resided in 1871 at Lot 8 Concession 4 in Chinguacousy Township. Aged thirty-five, born in England, with a wife and five children, Taylor rented 100 acres of land, seventy-five of it improved of which eleven acres were devoted to wheat. In June 1874 Taylor emigrated to Manitoba and settled in the Woodlands area where he homesteaded 160 acres and held a pre-emption on 160 more. He planned to sow it mainly in wheat.[31] Much to his surprise Taylor found that most of his neighbours were also from Chinguacousy, and many more would be. There was Noah Chant, fifty-nine, also born in England, a farmer who had owned seventy acres in Peel and had rented 150 more, only twelve of them devoted to wheat in 1871. Another, George Lipsett, was an Ulsterman who had owned fifty acres in Chinguacousy, seven of them sown in wheat. At the age of fifty he, too, had decided to move his wife and five children to Manitoba. A younger farmer, Josiah Hunter, thirty-one, abandoned a 200-acre farm in Peel, where he had grown wheat on only nineteen of his 130 improved acres, and took up a homestead in Woodlands. Finally, there was James Anderson, like Taylor an English-born tenant farmer, who had worked 105 acres in Peel, twenty-one of them producing wheat in 1871.[32]

Each of these men had been an established farmer in Chinguacousy Township where their improved acreage, once devoted to wheat, by 1871 had been turned over to oats, barley, forage, and root crops. In Manitoba, according to Taylor, in spite of lower prices for wheat delivered at Winnipeg or Prince Arthur's Landing, the cost of buying or pre-empting land meant that the Ontario farmer could continue to do what he did best and maintain his standard of living. "There are thousands of bushels of wheat in the country now," he reported in 1878. "Last Fall we got .75¢ a bushel for 1st class wheat . . . and . . . buyers would be in a position to even raise on that, if they had a good way of getting it out of the country through our own territory. Notwithstanding this drawback we are better off than Ontario farmers. . . ."[33] The new frontier, then, held out the promise of returning to the tradition of land-intensive, staples-based agriculture for experienced farmers who were unwilling to cope with the changing nature of farming and rural life in Ontario. And indeed they wanted no part of the generation of young men who "left their hearts with their mothers" when they came to have a look at Manitoba and went away muttering that "[t]he country . . . is nothing but wilderness, and settlers are all frauds."[34] The best farms for them, advised Taylor, were in Ontario.

The United States consul in Sarnia reported a related phenomenon in describing emigration from Ontario in the 1870's. "The farmer whose farm of one hundred acres was at one time sufficient to yield a comfortable living for himself and family now finds himself surrounded by grown up sons for whom he feels it incumbent upon himself to provide . . . and proceeds to Michigan, or some other western state or territory . . . to buy land sufficient for himself and his boys."[35] Cheap land and father-son relationships more appropriate to Canadian rural society in the 1840's–in a word, tradition–once again seemed responsible for dislocating well-established Ontario farm families. The lure of the frontier was the ability to recapture Ontario's rural past and to escape a future compromised by the necessity to change in order to survive. These escapees, like the men of Woodlands, had experienced both worlds and readily chose the uncertainties of life on the American frontier over the predictable regularities of life amid the neat farmsteads of post-Confederation Ontario in order to regain what they had lost.

These are isolated examples of individual motivation; but together with the statistical evidence they suggest that for the farmers of Ontario, territorial expansion after 1867 and the creation of a new agricultural frontier may have been the key to a resistance movement launched in Ontario but fought in some other place. Much of the gloom that hung like a pall over rural

Canada West in the 1860's was undoubtedly the product of the crisis in land specifically, and more generally, in the rural economy. The community's self-imposed solution to this crisis underlies the severity of the situation. But the solution must itself have taken on critical proportions spawning a social and psychological crisis of equally appalling applications for a society with a panglossian faith in the ability of backwoods Ontario to sustain a traditional way of life.

The adjustments were made, but the upshot was a crisis of confidence in the future of this society on the part of essentially conservative men who could not, or would not, accommodate themselves to the implications of a necessary and vital transition in the nature of human experience in a familiar environment. Confederation was only one solution to their problems; but by 1870 territorial expansion must have seemed the simplest route of escape for the individual caught between the millstones of tradition and change in rural Ontario.

NOTES

This essay is based on research undertaken by the Peel County History Project with the support of the Canada Council, the Ontario Historical Studies series, and McMaster University, whose support I gratefully acknowledge. Rosemary Gagan provided valuable assistance with the printed primary sources, and the manuscript has benefited from a continued dialogue with Peter George, Gérard Bouchard, and R. M. McInnis.

1. W. L. Morton, *The Critical Years: The Union of British North America* (Toronto, 1964), 232-44; P. B. Waite, *The Life and Times of Confederation* (Toronto, 1962), esp. ch. 17; Carl Berger, *The Sense of Power* (Toronto, 1970), 56-9; David Gagan, "The Relevance of 'Canada First,' " *Journal of Canadian Studies,* 5 (November, 1970), 36-44.
2. Province of Canada, Legislature, *Parliamentary Debates on the Subject of Confederation of the British North American Provinces* (reprint, Ottawa, 1951), Aikins, 10 February 1865, 158; J. S. Macdonald, 7 March 1865, 788-91; Walsh, 8 March 1865, 808; McConkey, 9 March 1865, 892 (hereafter cited as *Debates*).
3. *Ibid.,* 10 February 1865, 158.
4. Waite, *Confederation,* 4.
5. See David Gagan and Herbert Mays, "Historical Demography and Canadian Social History: Families and Land in Peel County, Ontario," *CHR,* LIV (1973), 27-47. The sources of data employed here

are: PAO, United Counties of York and Peel, Probate Court, Wills, 1820-67; Peel County, Surrogate Court, Wills, 1867-90, Genealogical Society Microfilm; Peel County (Twps. of Albion, Caledon, Chinguacousy, Toronto, and Toronto Gore), Abstracts of Deeds and Copy Books of Deeds, 1820-90, Genealogical Society Microfilm; PAC, Manuscript Census of Canada West for Peel, 1851-2 and 1861, and for Peel and Cardwell, 1871; Marriage Register, Brampton United Presbyterian Church, 1858-85, Genealogical Society Microfilm; Brampton Marriage Register, 1858-85, Genealogical Society Microfilm; Parish Register, Christ Church, Brampton. Marriage data were derived, more generally, from the decennial entries in the manuscript census returns, particularly the return for 1861 in which some misinformed enumerators recorded the date of marriage for every married couple in their enumeration districts.

6. *Debates,* T. D. McConkey, 9 March 1865, 182; and see W. H. Smith, *Canada: Past, Present and Future* . . . (Toronto, 1852), II, 277-83.
7. Samuel P. Day, *English America: or, Pictures of Canadian Places and People* (London, 1864), II, 193.
8. C. P. Traill, *The Backwoods of Canada* . . . (London, 1856), 179; J. S. Hogan, *Canada: An Essay* (Montreal, 1855), 67; Thomas Conant, *Upper Canada Sketches* (Toronto, 1895), 187.
9. M. H. Watkins, "A Staple Theory of Economic Growth," in W. T. Easterbrook and M. H. Watkins, eds., *Approaches to Canadian Economic History* (Toronto, 1967), 53, 61; Robert L. Jones, *History of Agriculture in Ontario 1613-1880* (Toronto, 1966), 189-203; Conant, *Sketches,* 186-7; *Census of the Canadas, 1851-1852* (Montreal, 1856), xxix.
10. Harvey J. Philpot, *Guide Book to the Canadian Dominion Containing Full Information for the Emigrant, the Tourist, the Sportsman and the Small Capitalist* (London, 1871), 119.
11. This figure is derived from longitudinal reconstruction of 160 of the most permanent families in the county from 1851, 1861, and 1871 manuscript census returns. Cross-sectional analysis yields a misleading completed family size of about five children. Taking the highest number reported for each persistent family over three enumerations raises the mean to about seven children. Manual reconstruction, which identifies children who die or leave home or return home between enumerations, raises the average completed family to between eight and nine children, higher for immigrant couples than for native-born parents.
12. Anna Jameson, *Winter Studies and Summer Rambles,* eds. J. J. Talman and E. M. Murray (Toronto, 1943) 53; Patrick Shirreff, *A Tour Through North America Together with a Comprehensive View of Canada and the United States* . . . (Edinburgh, 1835), 170;

William Catermole, *Emigration: The Advantages of Emigration to Canada* (London, 1831), 166; Conant, *Sketches,* 177. I discuss this issue, as it appeared to contemporaries, in " 'The Prose of Life': Literary Reflections of the Family, Individual Experience and Social Structure in Nineteenth-Century Canada," *Journal of Social History,* 9 (January, 1976), 369-71.

13. Shirreff, *Tour,* 170.
14. *Debates,* Aikins, 10 February 1865, 158.
15. S. A. Cudmore, "Rural Depopulation in Southern Ontario," *Transactions of the Royal Canadian Institute,* 9 (1913), 261-7.
16. This conclusion confirms an earlier inference drawn from a more detailed analysis of mortgage indentures in the community; see David Gagan, "The Security of Land: Mortgaging in Toronto Gore Township, 1835-1895," in F. H. Armstrong *et al.,* eds., *Aspects of Nineteenth Century Ontario* (Toronto, 1974), 141.
17. D. A. Lawr, "The Development of Farming in Ontario, 1870-1914: Patterns of Growth and Change," *OH,* 64 (1972), 240-51.
18. Susannah Moodie, *Life in the Clearings Versus the Bush* (New York, 1853), 138.
19. A. R. M. Lower, *Canadians in the Making* (Toronto, 1958), 366.
20. See David Gagan, "The Indivisibility of Land: A Microanalysis of the System of Inheritance in Nineteenth-Century Ontario," *Journal of Economic History,* 36 (1976), 126-41.
21. Peel County, Surrogate Court, Wills, vol. 1, 1867, Will of J. V.
22. J. P. Cooper makes the point that any number of inheritance systems can "produce the same result as primogeniture." See Cooper, "Patterns of Inheritance and Settlement by Great Landowners From the Fifteenth to the Eighteenth Centuries," in J. Goody and J. Thirsk, eds., *Family and Inheritance* (Cambridge, 1976), 197.
23. See David Gagan, "Geographical and Social Mobility in Nineteenth Century Ontario: A Microstudy," *Canadian Review of Sociology and Anthropology,* 13 (1976), 156.
24. H. J. Habbakuk, "Family Structure and Economic Change in Nineteenth Century Europe," *Journal of Economic History,* 15 (1955), 1-12; Kenneth Lockridge, "Land, Population and the Evolution of New England Society," *Past and Present,* 39 (1968), 62-80; Philip Greven, Jr., *Four Generations: Population, Land and Family in Colonial Andover, Massachusetts* (Ithaca, N.Y., 1970), esp. 222-58. The inheritance motive and the demographic behaviour of Canadian farmers is discussed in Marvin McInnis, "Childbearing and Land Availability: Some Evidence from Individual Household Data," Behavioural Models in Historical Demography Conference, Philadelphia, 1974 (mimeo).
25. Thomas Radcliff, *Authentic Letters From Upper Canada,* ed. J. J. Talman (Toronto, 1967), 58.

26. E. A. Wrigley, *Population and History* (Toronto, 1969), 116-18.
27. The data for age at last birth are from the family reconstitution procedures described in note 11 above. The aggregate data for women ever married by age cohort are from the census sources cited for Table 9.
28. The age at marriage analyses excluded individuals who married past the age of thirty. This was done to minimize the effects of extraordinarily late or second marriages.
29. This theme has been explored most recently by Sam Bass Warner, Jr., and Sylvia Fleisch, "The Past of Today's Present: A Social History of America's Metropolises, 1860-1960," *Journal of Urban History,* 3 (November, 1976), 3-65.
30. John Rowan, *The Emigrant and Sportsman in Canada: Some Experiences of an Old Country Settler* (London, 1876), 34: Samuel Strickland, *Twenty-Seven Years in Canada West* (reprint, Edmonton, 1970), 265-6.
31. William Taylor to Editor, Brampton *Times,* 29 August 1874 (transcript). I am indebted to Professor George Richardson of Queen's University for providing me with transcripts of his relative's letters dated 29 August 1874, December 1874, 10 February 1875, 9 April 1875, 5 June 1875, 8 February 1878.
32. These data are from nominal entries in Schedules 1, 2, 3, and 4 of the 1871 manuscript census of Peel and Cardwell.
33. William Taylor to Brampton *Times,* 29 August 1874, 8 February 1878.
34. *Ibid.,* 8 February 1878.
35. U.S. Department of State, Consular Reports, RG 59, Reel T488-2, Trade and Commerce Report for Sarnia, 17 July 1879.

APPENDIX 1

Means, Trend Values, and Three-Year Weighted Averages for Cost of Land Per Acre, Peel County, CW, 1840-70

Date	*Mean* (Y) *$*	*Units* (N)	X	X^2	XY	*Trend value $*	*Three-year moving average*
1840	8.30	0	15	225	-124.50	13.99	
1	8.00	1	14	196	-112.00	16.18	9.15
2	11.15	2	13	169	-144.95	18.37	28.45
3	66.19	3	12	144	-794.28	20.56	30.82
4	15.13	4	11	121	-166.43	22.75	31.03
5	11.79	5	10	100	-117.90	24.94	12.31
6	10.02	6	9	81	- 90.18	27.13	12.40
7	15.40	7	8	64	-123.20	29.32	12.98
8	13.53	8	7	49	- 94.71	31.51	12.80
9	9.49	9	6	36	- 56.94	33.70	15.45
1850	23.34	10	5	25	-116.70	35.89	19.06
1	24.34	11	4	16	- 97.36	38.08	22.75
2	20.56	12	3	9	- 61.68	40.27	24.84
3	29.61	13	2	4	- 59.22	42.46	29.82
4	29.90	14	1	1	- 39.90	44.65	37.25
5	42.85	15	0	0	0	46.84	46.04
6	55.38	16	1	1	55.38	49.03	56.87
7	72.27	17	2	4	144.54	51.22	121.86
8	237.94	18	3	9	713.82	53.41	115.36
9	35.88	19	4	16	143.52	55.60	104.72
1860	40.35	20	5	25	201.75	57.79	57.29
1	95.64	21	6	36	573.84	59.98	106.33
2	183.02	22	7	49	1281.14	62.17	102.69
3	29.42	23	8	64	235.36	64.36	82.04
4	33.69	24	9	81	303.21	66.55	45.18
5	72.44	25	10	100	724.40	68.74	50.86
6	46.45	26	11	121	510.95	70.93	56.90
7	51.82	27	12	144	621.84	73.12	48.02
8	45.79	28	13	169	595.27	75.31	45.96
9	40.28	29	14	196	563.92	77.50	49.42
1870	62.19	30	15	225	932.85	79.69	
	1452.16	**31**		**2468**	+7601.79		
					-2199.35		
					5402.44		

$Y_1 = 46.84 + 2.19X_1$

N = 1916

NOTE: The *mean* is the average value of an acre of land purchased in a given year. The trend *values* locate the straight line which best describes the long-term trend of land prices. The *three-year moving average* is the average of the values for a given year, the year preceding it, and the year following it. It is designed to smooth out anomalous irregularities in the curve.

APPENDIX 2

Means, Trend Values, and Three-Year Weighted Averages for Age at Marriage, Women Under Thirty-Five, Peel County, CW, 1840-70

Date	Yearly average age at marriage	Units (N)	X	X^2	XY	Trend value	Moving average
1840	18.0	0	15	225	−270.0	20.79	
1	20.5	1	14	196	−288.4	20.87	19.4
2	19.8	2	13	169	−257.4	20.95	21.1
3	23.0	3	12	144	−276.0	21.03	22.4
4	24.5	4	11	121	−269.5	21.11	22.4
5	20.7	5	10	100	−207.0	21.19	22.2
6	21.3	6	9	81	−191.7	21.27	21.1
7	21.2	7	8	64	−169.6	21.35	21.3
8	21.3	8	7	46	−149.1	21.43	21.4
9	21.6	9	6	36	−129.6	21.51	21.8
1850	22.4	10	5	25	−112.0	21.59	22.2
1	22.7	11	4	16	− 90.8	21.67	22.1
2	21.6	12	3	9	− 64.8	21.75	22.3
3	22.6	13	2	4	− 45.2	21.83	21.4
4	20.2	14	1	1	− 20.2	21.91	20.9
5	19.9	15	0	0	0	21.99	21.2
6	23.7	16	1	1	23.7	22.07	21.3
7	20.3	17	2	4	40.6	22.15	20.0
8	20.7	18	3	9	62.1	22.23	20.8
9	26.0	19	4	16	104.0	22.31	21.4
1860	22.6	20	5	25	113.0	22.39	22.4
1	22.9	21	6	36	137.4	22.47	22.6
2	21.8	22	7	49	152.6	22.55	22.9
3	24.0	23	8	64	192.0	22.63	23.0
4	23.2	24	9	81	208.8	22.71	23.1
5	22.2	25	10	100	222.0	22.78	22.4
6	21.9	26	11	121	240.9	22.87	22.1
7	22.2	27	12	144	266.4	22.95	21.4
8	20.2	28	13	169	262.6	23.03	22.4
9	24.9	29	14	196	348.6	23.11	22.9
1870	23.7	30	15	225	355.5	23.19	
	681.6	**31**		**2468**	+2730.2		
					−2541.3		
					188.9		

$Y_1 = 21.99 + 0.08X_1$

$N = 474$

III
The Working Class

In this excerpt from his *A Culture in Conflict: Skilled Workers and Industrial Capitalism in Hamilton, Ontario, 1860-1914*, Bryan Palmer looks to the point of production, the shop floor, to discover insights into the nature of working-class life in the nineteenth century. Artisan, craftsman, or skilled worker, it was these men - moulders, machinists, cigarmakers, printers, carpenters, etc. - who provided the early working-class movement with its leadership. The control they exercised over their work was initially based on their unique skill and knowledge - the "mysteries" of the craft - but, as industrial capitalism developed, their control increasingly depended more on their unions than on their skills. Turning to their unions to defend their traditional methods of work, craftsmen increasingly came into frequent battles with their employers whose new notions of efficiency and profit maximization often conflicted with older ideas of independence, pride in craftsmanship, and notions of "a fair day's work for a fair day's wage." The shop-floor struggle for control was the major battleground for late nineteenth-century Canadian workers, and their frequent victories often surprise modern historians. In the early years of the twentieth century the rise of scientific management and of other similar managerial schemes was the effective ideological and technological response of a new phase of capitalist development, monopoly capitalism. In this battle craft unionism was to prove a less effective weapon to defend the workers' interests.

The role skilled workers played in the labour movement has

always been controversial. While some scholars view their contribution to the working-class movement as positive, others raise questions about divisions within the working class itself between skilled and unskilled. In this latter argument skilled workers are often seen as a conservative influence owing to their relative success, their respectability, and their sense of craft exclusiveness. This is a classic debate in working-class history which remains unresolved.

FURTHER READING:
On other groups of skilled workers, see Gregory S. Kealey, *Toronto Workers Respond to Industrial Capitalism* (Toronto, 1980), chs. 3-6; and also, the rest of Palmer's *A Culture in Conflict* (Montreal, 1979). For short overviews of working-class development in the nineteenth century, see Eugene A. Forsey, *The Canadian Labor Movement: The First Ninety Years* (Ottawa, 1977); and Stephen Langdon, *The Emergence of the Canadian Working-Class Movement, 1845-1875* (Toronto, 1975). For articles which suggest a different emphasis in viewing skilled workers, see Ian McKay, "Capital and Labour in the Halifax Baking and Confectionery Industry During the Last Half of the Nineteenth Century," *Labour/Le Travailleur,* 3 (1978), 63-108; and Craig Heron, "The Crisis of the Craftsman: Hamilton's Metal Workers in the Early Twentieth Century," *Labour/Le Travailleur,* 6 (1980), 7-48. This latter article follows some of Palmer's craftsmen into the crises of their crafts in the twentieth century and will be reprinted in volume 4 of this series.

Bryan D. Palmer teaches history at Simon Fraser University and has published widely on the nineteenth-century Canadian working class.

The Culture of Control

by Bryan D. Palmer

The mechanic who built all creation,
Who spanned earth and sea with his arch,
Gave the 'plumb-line' and square to
  Trades Unions,
And sent progress with them on the march;
It was he made the craftsman a noble
Before even Kingdoms were born;
God gave to Trade Unions his warrant
This globe to enrich and adorn.

Iron Molders' International Journal
(September 1884)

The notion of workers' control did not enter the vocabulary of the international working-class movement until the World War I years, a period of escalating syndicalist struggle which saw British shop stewards and western Canadian miners articulate radical demands for national, democratic, working-class control of basic industries and services. Yet, despite the dating of this phenomenon, workers' control had a long history, constituting a fundamental feature of the shop-floor experience of nineteenth-

Reprinted with permission of the author and publisher from *A Culture in Conflict: Skilled Workers and Industrial Capitalism in Hamilton, Ontario, 1860-1914* by Bryan D. Palmer, ch. 3 (Montreal: McGill-Queen's University Press, 1979), 71-95.

century skilled craftsmen. A British shop steward hinted at the long-standing existence of certain forms of workers' control when he told Carter Goodrich: "People talk as if the demand for control was something that had to be created among the workers by a slow process, but it's there already!"[1] Even the most cursory glance at nineteenth-century work relationships suggests strongly that both skilled workers and their employers considered control of the shop floor to be of vital importance. Moreover, while such a glance reveals the drawing of firm battle lines, it *does not* suggest that employers necessarily controlled the workplace.[2]

The *Brockville Daily Times*, commenting on an 1884 strike at the James Smart Manufacturing Company's foundry, asserted: "The question at issue is simply one of 'control'. It is a fact, however humiliating, the acknowledgement that during the past three years of the company's existence, the business has been practically controlled by the Moulder's Union." Robert Gill, manager of the concern, concurred: "If the conditions are such that 'control' cannot be gained by the proprietors, then Brockville will lose the industry which we are trying to carry."[3] A Montreal founder seemed to agree with Gill, discharging all of his moulders in 1883 for "dictating to him how he should conduct his establishment."[4] *John Swinton's Paper*, in discussing a prominent trade dispute, called attention to the importance of control and its relation to union strength: "The fact that the manufacturers hope to crush the Troy Union shows that the Union is not as strong and firm as it ought to be. If it were, they would not indulge in their hopes. The employers of Pittsburgh entertain no hope of breaking up the Amalgamated Association of Iron and Steel Workers, to which they have just surrendered. It is too strong for them. It controls the trade, as the Window Glass Workers' Association controls that trade." Swinton continued, in a later issue of the paper, to extol the virtues of workers' control: "It was even said of Pittsburgh by the old iron masters, that Trade Unions have such a grip upon their industries that they are crippled."[5] Thorold, Ontario, stonecutters apparently exercised an equally forceful control, for their contractors reacted with vigour in the depression years of the late 1870's, locking them out of work. "The reason for this," wrote H. J. O'Neil of the union, "was distinctly stated by the contractors to be that they could get the work done in winter time for much less money, and they were not going to be dictated to by the union, that the stonecutters had been bosses long enough, and the contractors were going to try it for a while." After a long and hard battle, in which they were sustained by their International Union, the Thorold cutters returned to work on their own terms.[6] A Toronto boss painter decided against such tactics of resistance, acquiescing in the pernicious control his own men practised:

> Paint pots empty – brushes dry,
> Jobs unfinished – and for why?
> Men dictate – then I kick,
> I'm the cheese – I'm a brick.[7]

Organization, of course, was usually the preliminary stage in the realization of this limited form of workers' control. "The first step for wage-earners," wrote "Imogene" in Hamilton's *Palladium of Labor*, "is to organize every industry, and thus obtain control of their wages."[8] Workplace confrontations, arising out of this struggle over organization, fed directly into labour's political consciousness by bringing the issue of control to the forefront. Potters in East Liverpool, Ohio, for instance, clashed with their employers over their affiliation with the Knights of Labor. "We desire to be clearly understood by all citizens of the United States that this is not a strike or lock-out on account of any dispute about wages," they noted. "It is a stand taken by us in support of the principle of liberty, that was achieved by our fathers in the Revolution and by ourselves in the Rebellion. We are not slaves, to be prohibited by our employers from joining any organization we see fit to become members of, whether religious, political, or for mutual protection. Grant our employers the right to dictate to us in this point," the potters concluded, "and they can with equal justice dictate to us how we should vote, or worship God."[9] From this kind of perspective it was but a short step to a more explicit argument.

Speaking for most trade unions, the Cigar Makers' International posed the question, "Have the Unions A Right to Control The Shops?," answering it with an emphatic yes:

> Every time a union is formed the employers say it is an attempt on the part of the workingmen to control the shops. . . . They believe in hiring whom they please; they believe in private contracts and will suffer no dictation from the union. . . . Dictatorship must exist either in the employer or the man, and the organization of the men is only an attempt to restrict the ab-

> solute dictatorship of the boss. He has not the right to do as he pleases in his shop or business affairs, for every act he does has an influence on his fellow men, and if his self-interest is not foiled by the counter self-interest of the men, he would soon have them in a condition where human beings would be lower than beasts.

"Human rights," concluded the *Official Journal*, "are more sacred than the rights conferred on dead matter, on property. Therefore men organized in unions have a right to control the shops and interfere in business affairs, . . . the right to a voice in management."[10]

Hamilton cigarmakers found these words particularly attractive, and among the city's other tradesmen – moulders, glass-blowers, tailors, machinists, building trades' workers, engineers, blacksmiths, iron and steel workers, and shoeworkers – the argument was no less appealing. The *Hamilton Spectator* saw the essential feature of work relationships as a conflict between capital and labour, each camp struggling for control: "This is the war between capital and labor: Capital continually withdrawing itself from healthful work because it is afraid of losing its price, continually at difference with its one friend, without whom it must perish; Labor striking, demanding shorter time, more wages, dictating imperious rules about piece-work and apprentices, quarreling with its one friend, without whom it must die or seek the poor house. To adjust these difficulties is the problem of the day."[11] For the skilled worker the "problem" was easily overcome, Hamilton's *Palladium of Labor* proposing a blunt solution:

> Monopoly must not control,
> The Labor Market heart and soul.[12]

The *Palladium of Labor*'s predecessor, the *Labor Union*, also saw the issue of control as an important aspect of the solution of the "problem of the day." It noted that a "revolutionary agitation" had been initiated, and that everywhere "the claims of labor to control production are being debated by knots of workmen."[13]

The *Labor Union* had correctly identified workers' control as a central concern of masses of skilled workers, but it had erred in suggesting that their attachment to control was revolutionary.

Rather, in its nineteenth-century variants, workers' control meant adherence to commonplace practices and workplace customs. Thus, in the summer of 1883 a fireman on the *Southern Belle*, James Foren, was brought before the police court on a charge of mutiny. Foren had been ordered to "trim coal" at another man's boiler and had agreed to do so provided he was to have the customary fee of fifty cents extra, a long-standing practice on the ship. The *Southern Belle's* owners, however, had chosen this moment to break the tradition of extra payment, and ordered Foren to proceed without compensation. He staunchly refused, and for his resistance received a sentence of three weeks in the common jail and a fine of one dollar. "Custom doth breed a habit in a man," concluded the *Palladium of Labor*.[14]

Other workers, however, succeeded in preserving their customary workplace rights. In such trades as nailmaking, glassblowing, and moulding, for instance, no employer could exercise dictatorial power over skilled hands whose craft knowledge was the only assurance of an acceptable product. Technology itself had made few inroads on these crafts prior to 1890 and employers often had to settle for workmen whose desultory work habits they deplored, but whose skills they needed. Coremakers who added molasses to sand in the creation of moulds judged their recipe according to "taste"; glass bottle blowers relied on their "sure touch" to turn "the smouldering brew of glass and soda" recently extracted from the "glory hole" into a container. Craftsmen like these could not be driven to produce, and their skill, a recognized and valued commodity, assured them of a measure of control over their work.[15] In this sense, workers' control was nothing more than the functional autonomy of the skilled worker, a workplace practice flowing out of the craft worker's knowledge of the production process.[16]

Workers' control, however, was much more than a mere technological phenomenon, for in trades where mechanization did make inroads, craft unions often proved capable of "controlling" the machine, successfully demanding that only union labour be allowed to operate the new "labour-saving" devices. Printers perhaps best exemplify the case, although glass bottle blowers after 1896 (when the blowing machines were introduced into the trade) were also reasonably successful.[17] "Labour must control the tools," declared Toronto's *Labor Advocate* in 1890, endorsing the International Typographical Union's policy of manning all typesetting machines with union printers. Other crafts would follow suit.[18]

The essence of nineteenth-century workers' control lay in the restrictive powers exercised by the trade union over the employer. Carter Goodrich long ago recognized three types of workers' control: restrictive control, shop control, and control of an entire industry. The last-named came to prominence only with the emergence of ostensibly revolutionary movements, such as the British shop stewards or the One Big Union of the Canadian West. Restrictive and shop control, however, thrived in the late nineteenth century in the rules and regulations of the trades.[19] Limitations on the number of apprentices per shop and institutionalized restriction of output were important features of workplace life in both Canada and the United States; they formed the key components of restrictive control.[20] Shop control was a more complex practice, involving the use of union foremen in some trades and shop committees in others; both mechanisms controlled hiring and firing, secured adherence to trade regulations, parcelled out work to members of the craft, and set prices and negotiated agreements with employers.[21] While both restrictive and shop control would and could be practised by workers outside the pale of trade unionism, skilled as well as unskilled,[22] the real bastion of workers' control was the craft union. Indeed, among Hamilton's craft unionists, workers' control thrived as something of a culture of the shop floor.

As a culture of the shop floor, control was bred within the context of industrial capitalist development. Unlike the continuous culture of the community, which exhibited the persistence of many cultural forms and traditions with roots in precapitalist times, control was an essentially new phenomenon. It manifested itself most blatantly in moments of conflict, when the workingman's conception of control clashed sharply with his employer's views of work relations. Control was, essentially, the skilled workers' response to the realities of workplace organization within a society transformed by industrial capitalism. Against industrial capitalist work discipline, the skilled worker posed the rules and regulations of his trade.

Glass workers, for instance, exemplified the case of nineteenth-century workers' control. Virtually every international craft union praised their record of achievement. John Swinton's laudatory appraisal of the glassblowers of Pittsburgh knew no bounds. His enthusiasm for their restriction of output (each man's weekly labour was limited to forty-eight boxes of glass), their adherence to limited hours of labour, and their summer stop rule, by which the union dictated that from July 1 to September 1 each year the fires in North American glass works be extinguished to give the men a well-deserved rest, was striking. "Control is a bitter word to the manufacturer," concluded Swinton.[23] In Hamilton, where glass workers were associated with the Amalgamated Flint Glass Blowers' Union No. 13 and Branch No. 45 of the United Green Glass Workers' Association, the summer stop rule and institutionalized restriction of output were honoured practices in the trade.[24] As day workers, few Hamilton glass men laboured more than seven or eight hours a day during a six-day week.[25] So complete was their control of the trade that Hamilton glass workers were rarely challenged by their employers and virtually never found themselves involved in strikes or lockouts. To the *Palladium of Labor* this was a record of achievement worthy of emulation. "What is possible in one trade," it noted, "is presumably so in another."[26]

Few trades would develop the art of control to the level attained by the glass workers, but all crafts exercised some form of restrictive or shop control. M. A. Pigott, a Hamilton contractor, wrote to the city's Member of Parliament, Adam Brown, prior to the release of the 1887 Royal Commission on the Relations of Labour and Capital findings. The contractor's theme was the negative impact of the restrictive practices of Hamilton's skilled workers. He first attacked the system of apprenticeship regulation:

> The apprentice restrictions *practically prohibits* boys from learning trades, for instance I may have 25 or 30 masons & bricklayers, the union will only allow *one apprentice in three years* to each employer regardless of the number of men he employs. *Moulders* one apprentice to every 8 men in four years. *Stonecutters* same as masons. The object is, since they cannot boom the demand, they can by the above restrictions reduce the supply.

Then, to conclude, he railed against restriction of output:

> Another matter regulated by the unions that must soon become injurious to trade is the reducing of the standard quantity of work per day in the matter of daily paid employees for instance, you may have a number of workmen engaged on a similar class or kind of work, among the gang be one or two slow coaches, it then becomes the duty of the faster men to

> adapt themselves to the slower motion of their slow companions, to save them from reprimand and possible discharge & also to provide against a scarcity of work by not pushing on, it helps to keep good the supply of work, which assists them in obtaining their increased demands.

Pigott's own stonecutters, in fact, had blocked work on the city's Custom House in late 1883 over the enforcement of their union rule limiting the daily output of trade members. While the *Hamilton Times* found the situation deplorable, the *Palladium of Labor* again came to the men's defence.[27]

Judging the disdain with which Hamilton's skilled workers regarded workingmen who "rushed," "hogged," or "speeded up," Pigott's charges were rooted in the real practices of craft unionists.[28] Indeed, contempt for the "hog" who ignored collective control of daily output was, as David Montgomery has suggested, one badge of the craftsman's "manliness," a concept that connoted independence, respectability, and a cultivated sense of self-worth. "A hog union man," wrote the editor of the *Industrial Banner*, "is a thing that takes union wages and spits tobacco juice over a scab pair of shoes, and a scab suit of clothes."[29] "Junius Junior" wrote of three workers in a Hamilton factory, caught in the midst of a rush order from their foreman:

> They worked like demons once the rush started; came back nights, and piled up a wages bill that fairly made their eyes bulge out when they got the money. In their haste to push along the good thing, they shortened the noon meal hour to fifteen minutes, and 'beat the clock' at the starting hour in the morning. By dint of these efforts they managed to nearly double their output. That was all right, while the rush lasted. After it was over they were rewarded by a 50 per cent cut in the price. They protested and the cut was reduced to 40 per cent.

"And they blamed the boss," noted "Junius Junior." "I don't," he countered.[30] The *Palladium of Labor* voiced a similar sentiment: "It is to the fact of the existence of hoggish workmen more than any other cause that nearly all wage differences are brought about, and trouble between employee and employer occasioned. On men guilty of such actions a heavy fine should be imposed by each union for every offence; two or three doses of which would probably bring most of them to their senses. If this failed to convince them they should be fired out of the union altogether."[31]

But the real conflict over the question of control was not the craft workers' disapproval of the "hog," for the aberrant "rusher" was merely the exception proving the rule of craft solidarity. Conflict over control, in its restrictive and shop realms, was almost exclusively a clash involving craft workers and their employers. Moulders, building trades' workers, and cigarmakers, for instance, were often drawn into struggles turning on the question of apprentice regulations. On rare occasions mechanization would pose a threat to skilled craftsmen, and in an attempt to preserve their control mechanisms workers would strike rather than succumb to the machine. More common were control struggles waged against the dismissal of union foremen or workmen, or the hiring of workers who had defied union authority, either by acting as strikebreakers or by failing to fulfil their craft obligations. Finally, in many union shops, where control was related to the "standard rate," and its enforcement by shop committees, employers' attempts to stifle union power by wage reductions led to violent strikes and lockouts that went well beyond the limited question of wages.[32] It was within these broad parameters that Hamilton's skilled workingmen and their employers became locked into a struggle for control.

One of the first recorded instances of a control struggle occurred in 1856, when the mechanics of the Great Western Railway yards struck work in protest over the dismissal of a shopmate. While the company claimed the man "had been drunk while on duty," the workers contended that "a capable workman had been abruptly dismissed to make a job for a friend" of one of the superintendents. Over 500 workers turned out, demanding the reinstatement of the worker and the discharge of the supervisor. "A valued principle had been violated," they claimed. At a time when strikes were a relatively new and exceptional phenomenon, the men's action spoke of a deeply entrenched solidarity. In the face of potential legal prosecution for violation of the conspiracy laws, the mechanics instituted negotiations with their employer. A few days later the dispute was settled, and the discharged man was back at his place in the company's yards. Although the strikers did not secure the superintendent's dismissal, an early victory had been won.[33]

By 1864 a number of craft unions had surfaced in the city, and, led by the Iron Molders' International Union No. 26, they banded together to form a Trades Assembly, the first of its kind in Canada.[34] This body apparently had wide-ranging local powers. When the city's carpenters and joiners struck work in the late spring of 1864, they first sought the approval of the Trades Assembly, receiving the assurance of a "rate . . . to provide for the maintenance of those who may be compelled to remain on strike."[35] At this early date craft workers had institutionalized mechanisms to support their control struggles, mechanisms which crossed craft lines, binding one trade to the cause of another.

These were also years which saw the beginnings of conflict between the founders and moulders. As early as December 15, 1864, Copp's foundry was the scene of a confrontation over the apprentice question.[36] By February 1866 the rift had widened, developing into an escalating struggle between the employers and the union. The founders' tactic, as one moulder recounted, was to break the union and secure, once and for all, control of the shops:

> Most of the foundry-men of Hamilton, as well as of other places in Canada, sometime since formed themselves into a union for mutual protection against the encroachments of labour, and in the plentitute of their power, they enacted a law to be enforced by penalty, that no member was to hire a moulder who had of his own accord left the employment of another member, no matter what the cause of his leaving or under what conditions. To leave voluntarily was to make himself within the jurisdiction of the boss' union a proscribed man, thus depriving the working man of that personal liberty which is the necessary consequence of living in this free country; and Mr. Editor, that law has been enforced in Hamilton at least three different times during the present winter. Sir, would you believe it possible for a committee of three gentlemen to drive gaily down in a sleigh to hound a poor man from his employment.

Faced with this kind of opposition, the moulders struck work, only to see the founders flood the community with "men from the United States." For the moulders it was a battle against "slave law."[37]

Less than a month later, Hamilton's founders had made common cause with their American counterparts. Many Canadian foundrymen, undoubtedly more than a few from Hamilton, helped to draft the preamble of the *Proceedings of the National Convention of Iron Founders*, a statement which left no doubts as to the founders' views on workers' control:

> Whereas the Iron Moulders in different sections of the country are seeking, by concert of action and union amongst themselves, to change the relations which exist naturally between employer and employee, assuming arbitrarily to dictate the prices which shall be paid by the employer, and to direct the government of the workshop and the management of the business of their employers . . . [we resolve] to proceed to introduce into our shops all the apprentices or helpers we deem advisable, and that we will not allow any Union committees in our shops, and that we will, in every possible way, free our shops from all dictation or interference on the part of our employees.

Among the iron moulders' most offensive rules and practices, the founders listed: (1) the apprentice restriction of one apprentice to every ten moulders; (2) the closed shop, allowing no nonunionists to work in the foundries; (3) the presence of shop committees at each foundry to set prices on work and enforce the rules and regulations of the trade; (4) the moulders' "control" of the labour market, the shop committees "giving all necessary information to applicants for work, and whether their services are required, and if so, whether it be proper for such applicant to apply either to the employer or his foreman for employment"; (5) the prevalence of strikes resulting from the founders' inability to live with such restrictions.[38] Troy became the centre of the founders' offensive, but the unionists there stood firm, registering impressive victories over their employers.[39]

In Hamilton the moulders won no such victory in 1866, their fight carrying on into the autumn months. Well after the May settlement in Troy, Hamilton moulders continued to face the resistance of their employers, who demanded the right to introduce as many apprentices as they thought appropriate. While the "obnoxious" rules of the founders were eventually withdrawn from many iron works, and the apprentice ratios of the union re-established, the pages of the *Iron Molders' International Journal* indicated that the price for these concessions had been high. "Scabs" abounded in two city shops, and reports from the Hamilton local to the international union indicated that the closed shop had been dealt a strong blow. Not until January 1867 was the dispute in Hamilton settled, and then only with the intervention of William Sylvis, president of the International Union.[40] Many Hamilton moulders had grown dissatisfied with their shop committee, and sometime after the settlement of the protracted contest of 1866, Hamilton's Molders' Union retreated into obscurity, contenting itself with activities such as balls and picnics, apparently lacking the confidence to test its employers again.[41]

By the winter and spring months of 1872 the Molders' Union had revitalized itself, playing an important role in the strike wave aimed at securing the nine-hour day.[42] The union had begun to rid the shops of the many non-unionists who had originally flooded the city in the late 1860's.[43] Then, too, the organized moulders re-established their control over the labour market, all travelling moulders being instructed to apply for work at the Clyde Hotel, whose proprietor John Miller was an honorary member of the union.[44] Recovery, however, was far from complete; moreover, it was to be stifled by the economic downturn of 1873-74 and by the flooding of the Hamilton shops with unemployed moulders from the United States. "There are too many molders here at present," wailed Fred Walters, and the pages of the *International Journal* bristled with an exchange of letters debating the "Invasion of Canada."[45] With the labour market glutted and the economy moving toward recession, the founders imposed a 10 per cent wage reduction in December 1873.[46] By March 1874 Hamilton's union was informing moulders from many North American cities to stay away from the foundries "as we expect trouble."[47]

Even the moulders' limited attempts to secure a measure of control over their work spurred the foundrymen to action. When the union asked for a resumption of their former wages-the abandonment of the 1873 reduction-in the summer of 1874, the employees reacted forcefully. At the Burrow, Stewart and Milne foundry the moulders received a terse reply: "While regretting any serious consequences such as a strike, from our refusal, we can only say if such is resorted to in either of the two shops you have made the demand from, or any other, there is not an iron foundry in Hamilton that will not be instantly closed thereafter." To add force to this pledge, the Hamilton founders issued a complementary communication, signed by D. Moore and Company, Burrow, Stewart and Milne, A. Laidlaw and Company, Copp Brothers, James Stewart and Company, E. & C. Gurney, and L. D. Sawyer and Company.[48]

With the battle lines drawn, the conflict commenced. After two brief strikes, the employers turned to a general lockout. Led by the Gurney brothers, whose shop employed only non-unionists, and backed by the Canadian Founders' Association, presided over by the Hamilton founder James Stewart, the foundrymen presented a formidable front. But the union also stood firm. "The fight is forced on us. Let us meet it like men," declared the *International Journal*. From late August 1874 through the early winter months of 1875 the struggle raged. For both the employers and the unionists the conflict turned on the open shop.[49]

Edward and Charles Gurney posed the issue clearly, demanding that all employees sign an "Iron clad" contract:

> I, the said ______, in consideration of the said Messrs. E. and C. Gurney hiring and employing me, as they hereby do, upon the terms hereinafter mentioned, covenant and agree to serve the said Messrs. E. & C. Gurney, as a molder, at such work, and in such manner, as they, or their foremen for the time being, shall assign or direct me, for the period of one year from this date, at the current rate of wages, for such work payable from week to week during such year, and faithfully and diligently, to the best of my ability, and without interruption, other than by sickness, bodily injury, or such like accident; and that during said year I will wholly abstain from being a member of, and being in any way connected with, and from any manner, or to any extent, contributing to or toward the funds of, or any object of, or any connection with any Molders' Union, or any such like combination or association of persons; and in any case of any breach or breaches by me of this agreement, or for any other cause as to them may seem just, said Messrs. E. & C. Gurney and their foremen, for the time being, and any of them, are hereby employed to discharge me immediately, or whenever they see fit, and also after discharging me, or without so discharging, to take such proceedings against me under this agreement, as to them may be advised.

J. Campbell, president of the Hamilton Iron Molders' Union, commented on the Gurney agreement: "The agreement is worthy of the veriest tyrant, and the men who would sign it would degrade themselves below the standing of a Chinese coolie or African slave." The *International Journal* concluded that "wages are not the only thing a man looks to or for in a foundry; but the poor cowardly things that sign such an agreement put themselves at the mercy of an employer's idea of justice, and we hope they may get it."[50]

The outcome of the 1874-75 lockout was ambiguous, but it seemed that once again some of the shops remained under union control, while others were run with non-union labour. Victory rested securely with neither employers nor union. With the onslaught of depression, however, the employers were given the upper hand and, for the moulders at least, the struggle for control would be submerged. Tailors also engaged in a brief skirmish with their employers over the trade's bill of prices, but they likewise foundered in the context of economic downturn.[51] The struggle for control was temporarily halted, as craft unions faced the disruptive impact of depression. The economic recovery of the early 1880's, however, was around the corner, and with it came an impressive assertion of the craftsman's penchant for control.

Leading the craft workers back into the struggle for control were the "bottomers" of the MacPherson and Company's shoe works, who struck work in the fall of 1879, protesting against the employment of a painter who had never "served his full time at the boot and shoe trade."[52] By the summer of 1881 Hamilton craftsmen had used the relative prosperity of the early 1880's to re-establish positions of strength. Bricklayers extended a fine net of control over their trade, refusing to work for contractors who remained unfair to union workers.[53] Hamilton tailors secured a new and more favourable price list, averting a strike.[54] Shoemakers managed to gain a 15 per cent wage increase.[55] Iron moulders, who had been granted an advance of 10 per cent in 1879, struck for a further 10 per cent in April 1881, all the shops eventually giving in to the men's demands.[56] Three months later the Molders' Union felt sufficiently strong to strike the Stewart foundry, demanding the removal of two non-union men.[57] Similarly, in July 1881 bricklayers and masons struck work against the contractor D. & C. Cripps, protesting the contractors' employment of their brother, an incompetent non-unionist.[58] The upheaval drew even the unskilled into battle with their employers: coal heavers struck work for higher wages and, when police arrived to protect a new force of men, routed the constables as well as the strikebreakers;[59] municipal labourers employed on the water mains left work, demanding $1.50 a day;[60] teamsters on the Grant Western Railway took job actions to secure a raise of $2 a month.[61] "The effect of the labour movement is already making itself felt in a general rise in everything," concluded the *Hamilton Spectator*.[62]

Relations between skilled workingmen and their employers were perhaps exemplified in the cigarmaking trade. Hamilton's Cigar Makers' International Union No. 55 determined to demand an advance of $1 per thousand cigars, on hand work, with a proportionate increase on "fancy brands." On May 28, 1881, the union issued a communication to the manufacturers:

> Gentlemen: In view of the present advance in the cost of living and rents, we conclude it is but justice to ourselves and families to present to you a bill of prices, which has a tendency to equalize cigar-makers' wages with mechanics and other artists of the Dominion of Canada and the United States. We most respectfully hope you will give the subject your most careful consideration. All we ask is compensation for our labour. Please do us the kindness to inform the shop committee man of your conclusion.

The manufacturers replied in kind: "We beg to acknowledge receipt of your favor of May 28, accompanied by the list of prices adopted by your board. In reply we are willing to meet your views; provided it is to be provincial and strictly carried out in every shop in the city." In times of economic recovery employers were evidently prepared to acquiesce in shop control of the union, and the strike wave of 1881 attested to the craft workers' quickness in judging a moment ripe for the reintroduction of control mechanisms, securing the union shop and the standard rate.[63]

March of 1882 saw the continuation of the 1881 spring offensive. The moulders once again secured a 10 per cent wage increase, their third such hike in three years. Their employers, however, were beginning to balk. Burrow, Stewart and Milne acceded to the 10 per cent, "but no more." Laidlaw, Bowes, and

Company made it clear that this was the last increase they would tolerate. "We want to get a little of the profits," said the company spokesman. And at E. & C. Gurney's foundry the manager granted the 10 per cent advance, "but no more, no matter what the consequence would be." When some employers refused the increase, the moulders simply sought work elsewhere and, in order to keep men in the shops, the Hamilton employers eventually gave in. It had been a significant show of strength on the part of the International Union.[64]

Tailors and nailers, following in the wake of the moulders, instituted similar demands.[65] The custom shoemakers' shop committee presented their employers with a new price list, which was quickly accepted.[66] The early spring of 1882 also saw conflicts involving lathers, painters, bakers, and carpenters.[67] At the Ontario Rolling Mills 150 men sent a note to their foremen stating that they were walking off the job. They demanded the reinstatement of a discharged employee, and won their request four days later.[68]

Two brief months after this first settlement at the Ontario Rolling Mills, members of the Amalgamated Iron and Steel Workers' Association again struck work. The union's major grievance was the superintendent, a Mr. Whitehead, whom they claimed was dedicated to "overthrow[ing] the union." Among Whitehead's transgressions had been the firing of union workmen, the hiring of non-unionists, and the assignment of union men as helpers to non-union labour. All of these acts violated the "rules of the organization." Words ensued between Whitehead and Lloyd, the chairman of the mills committee, and the workers' representative was discharged for verbally abusing the overseer. A strike resulted. Whitehead then terminated the employment of the president of the Workers' Association. Eventually the dispute was settled, Lloyd securing work elsewhere and agreeing not to press the matter. All of the other unionists returned to their places.[69]

Amidst this kind of strike activity, both workers and employers sought institutionalized means of protection. The Trades Assembly, active in the mid-1860's and in the 1872 upheaval, was reborn in late March 1882 when delegates from various unions and labour organizations met to form "a trades and labor assembly, whereby all branches of labor could act unitedly on all questions which affected any one branch of labor in this or any other locality." Hamilton's workingmen were thus building bridges linking them to other centres of working-class agitation; moreover, the interests of skilled and unskilled had been united in one organization.[70] Employers, too, were on the move. When the builders and contractors met to form "a union both offensive and defensive," they turned aside a resolution urging that they not "combine against the workmen." Their associations, it seemed, were also born with the aim of control in mind.[71]

With the emergence of the Knights of Labor in Hamilton in 1882 much of the story of workers' control is transferred to the context of the Order's development.[72] But skilled workers continued to resist the encroachments on their shop-floor power, struggling to retain control mechanisms. In April 1883 members of the Hat Finishers' Union and the Dominion Hat Factory became embroiled in a controversy involving apprentice ratios in the shop.[73] The following month the bricklayers and the Master Builders' Association were at odds, the bricklayers demanding $3 a day and the contractors complaining of the union's arbitrary rules. Most offensive to the building contractors were the union's refusals to allow injured men to work at reduced rates, the union's practice of allowing bricklayers to take independent contracts up to $100, and the craft's apprenticeship regulations, which restricted the master to one apprentice, regardless of the number of journeymen employed. By the end of May, after considerable negotiation, the bricklayers emerged victorious, their rules intact and the $3 a day standard rate secured.[74]

By the closing months of 1883 the economic boom of the early 1880's was clearly waning. In December the moulders were forced to accept a 20 per cent reduction.[75] The Ontario Rolling Mills became the site of a hotly contested control struggle in January 1885, one that would see the destruction of the Amalgamated Iron and Steel Workers' Association. Iron workers objected to changes in the method of work, changes which reduced earnings severely and forced men to work with poor quality scrap iron. A shop committee approached the company's manager, but when no satisfaction could be gained the men struck work. With rolling mills across North America idle and workers in the trade desperate for employment, the company easily won the day and filled the strikers' places immediately. Craft control in the Ontario Rolling Mills had succumbed to managerial authority.[76]

Seth J. Whitehead, manager of the rolling mills, saw the strike of 1885 as the consequence of his offensive strategy:

Q. Do you have any trouble with strikes?
A. No.
Q. None?
A. We had in the Ontario Rolling Mill. We had a union in connection with the Amalgamated Association in the United States, but it became necessary to upset it. The management bore it as long as they could, but the men acted very foolishly; we thought they began to dominate, and the gentlemen who run the place concluded that they would be better off without it, and they just sat upon it and squelched it out.

The employer's aggressive retaliation, however, was not directed against the union's wage policy, but against customary workplace practices, against the irksome presence of routine aspects of workers' control:

Q. Was the difficulty for an increase of wages or shortening of hours?
A. No; it was not. It was for matters that didn't amount to anything. In fact, a great part of the trouble was that they would get drunk and try to run things their own way, and shut us down and go on just as it suited them.

But even in the aftermath of the employer's victory, Whitehead recognized that the penchant for control died hard:

Q. Did any of the men object to the association being wiped out?
A. Well, they did and they didn't. There is a sort of terrorism in connection with that thing that a man does not dare to speak.[77]

Nor were the iron workers the only "defeated" craft still harbouring memories of their lost control and the "manly" stand accompanying it. Coopers at the Ontario Nail Works, a craft displaced by mechanization and devoid of organization, refused a 12 per cent reduction and bluntly told their employer they would not countenance the year-long contracts contemptuously forced upon them.[78] Shoemakers, who had faced the disruptive impact of technological innovation throughout the 1860's and

1870's,[79] could still mount offensives in the 1880's, securing significant control over workplace settings. At the Hamilton factory of MacPherson and Company, shoe workers affiliated with the Knights of Labor launched "a determined stand" against an imported non-unionist and apprentice. Although their employer agreed to pay the two recent arrivals the regular scale of prices, "the shop committee called a meeting of workmen on Monday evening, at which they took these facts into consideration, and refused to go to work with them." The shoemakers apparently exercised considerable power, for they received a polite reply from their employer the next day: "Gentlemen: Having no other course to pursue, we are obliged to accept your terms, as our samples must not be delayed." A shoemaker's lament of the depression-ridden years of the mid-1870's,

> Whats our trade a coming to
> for I am used up how are you
> I hav little work and Less money
> to live on that is very funny,
> for shoes are cheaper than the leather
> and it still remains a query whether
> they'ell be any alteration
> in this our stagnate Nation,

had been replaced by a more positive refrain.[80]

Organized craft workers affiliated with international unions, however, continued to lead the way. A strike wave in March 1888, involving the building trades, indicated just how securely many trades retained their control mechanisms and how staunchly they would defend them from attack. Carpenters initiated the upheaval, demanding that their employers hire only union men and that all foremen be affiliated with one of the two carpenters' unions in the city.[81] On March 9, 1888, a conflict developed at Hancock's stone quarry, where the Bricklayers' and Masons' Union objected to the use of non-union labourers, the long hours imposed on the men, and the practice of importing stonecutters to work on the stone to be used in the construction of the new city hall on Ontario Street.[82] Ten days later union labourers at the construction site of the city hall quit work, declaring that they would not work with stone drawn from a quarry employing non-unionists; masons on the same job followed suit. The contractors, members of the Builders' Exchange, attributed the trouble to agitators, particularly condemning the unions' policy of controlling foremen on all jobs, and expressing irritation at the restrictions imposed on all contractors by trade regulations. "Many of these restrictions are so arbitrary," claimed the *Hamilton Spectator*, "that the bosses find themselves completely in the hands of the men, and they decidedly object to the men running their business."[83]

On March 28, 1888, the contractors, led by the quarryman Hancock, took the offensive, informing the building trades' unions:

> Whereas, certain labour organizations or unions in connection with the building trades have in the past and are now using the power they have acquired by combining together for unjust and arbitrary purpose, having no reference whatever to wages; and, whereas, serious loss must result to the employer and the building trade generally by the abuse of power . . . the Builders' Contractors, and Dealers' Exchange . . . resolve that on and after March 28, all known union men of every branch in the employ of members of the Exchange shall be and remain suspended from work until the satisfactory removal of the difficulty between the Laborers' and Bricklayers' Unions and the Master Builders' Association, when work will be resumed.

Replying to the Builders' Exchange, the Amalgamated Association of Carpenters and Joiners condemned the notice as, "one of the most unjust and arbitrary actions ever perpetrated in the city of Hamilton, in that without any warning previous to Tuesday they discharged their old and faithful hands for the crime of belonging to a society banded together for mutual improvement and beneficial purposes. It is well known to us that they have combined for the purpose of crushing all the trade societies of this city if they can."[84] By the end of March 1888 over 700 men were locked out of work, and a Council of Building Trades – composed of delegates from two carpenters' unions, a plasterers' union, a stonecutters' union, a teamsters' union, and a building labourers' union – had convened and censured the Builders' Exchange.[85]

Dragging on well into April 1888, the stalemate revolved around union restrictions and the crafts' support for one another. Hancock, president of the Builders' Exchange, explained that all trades had been locked out because of their shared demand that union foremen be hired. Moreover, he added, the Exchange resented the conspiratorial thrust of the unanimous trade union support for the Bricklayers' and Masons' Union. Finally, he stressed the cumbersome rules of each craft, restrictions which had even been adopted by the unskilled members of the Builders' Laborers' Union. In that category of work, for instance, a man was not to carry more than fourteen bricks in a hod; a man carrying bricks was not to carry mortar; a man carrying mortar was not to carry bricks; and none were to carry sills, planks, or anything other than what they were particularly engaged in handling.[86]

By early May 1888 some trades had settled with their employers, but other crafts remained out. M. A. Pigott, a contractor whom we have seen to be a rabid opponent of craft restrictions, became involved in a conflict with the Stonecutters' Union on April 25, 1888. Pigott claimed that he had "a decided objection to have the union run his work and propose[d] to show them that he [could] be independent."[87] The struggle took a turn in another direction shortly after the stonecutters' run-in with Pigott. As contractors filled job sites with non-union men, antagonism built between the organized and unorganized workers. To protect their interests, the non-unionists formed an Independent Workingmen's Association, open to all non-union building trades workers. Its first meeting was physically disrupted by craft workers affiliated with the union, although the strikebreakers promised to continue their "organizational" efforts.[88] Three members of the Bricklayers' and Masons' Union – William Mitchell, William Littlejohns, and David Gibson – were charged with conspiracy in the context of their union's efforts to boycott a job site where a non-unionist was employed. On June 21, 1888, they were convicted. Even in the midst of these setbacks, however, the building tradesmen stood firm, gaining their point in many cases.[89] By mid-August the conflict continued to excite the passions of union men, but only M. A. Pigott's city hall construction site still employed non-union labour.[90]

Outside of the building trades, the late 1880's and early 1890's saw similar struggles. Nailmakers struck work July 5, 1888, objecting to a change in the work process.[91] In the spring of 1891 brickmakers fought a losing battle against the mechanization of their trade.[92] And in 1892 and 1895 Hamilton's cigarmakers opposed their employers over the union price list and the apprentice ratios in a major city cigar manufactory.[93] But once again the struggle for control was sharpest in the city's foundries.

Hamilton moulders had utilized the relative prosperity of the late 1880's to re-establish their prominence in the city's foundries. Engaging in almost ritualized yearly confrontations with their employers, the moulders had won wage advances in 1887 and 1888. By the spring of 1888 the union's shop committee controlled the labour market, and all applicants for work reported directly to it.[94] Things remained relatively peaceful until 1892, when the employers struck back with a vengeance.[95]

In early January 1892 the Molders' Union was notified that the founders intended to reduce wages 10 per cent on all piece and day work. Complaining that they could not compete with the open shops of London, Brantford, and Toronto (where Hamilton's Charles Gurney owned and operated a foundry on non-union principles), the employers contended that "Hamilton [was] the only place governed by the union." Over 350 union men were thus faced with lay-offs following the traditional Christmas break, for the foundrymen claimed that they would run their shops with non-union men if the moulders resisted the reduction. By the end of January the clash appeared inevitable. Union moulders resolved to oppose the reductions, preserving their commitment to the union shop as their *only* protection. The foundries dedicated themselves to the realization of the open shop and further wage cuts.[96]

A local founder saw the cause of the dispute as the union's policy of "dictat[ing] terms to the Hamilton manufacturers"; he outlined the new manner in which the shops would be run:

> What the stove firms intend to do is run their shops on new principles. Instead of paying wages according to a fixed scale, we will pay each workman according to his work, the good workman and the poor workman will not be paid alike, as in the case under union principles, but good workmen will be paid more than the poor workman. . . . Another change will be that we will be able to distribute work in such a manner as to secure better results, to give fine jobs to good workmen, and coarse jobs to those who are unskilled. Heretofore we have not been allowed to distribute the various aspects of work: that is done by the men themselves and the results are often unsatisfactory. Another change will be in the direction of specializing the work–that is, keeping certain men at certain pieces and nothing else, thus ensuring a greater average skill and rapidity of workmanship in the total results. I anticipate a

> long struggle, and a bitter one. But the foundrymen realize the gravity of the issue involved in it, and they will not yield any longer to the dictation of the union.[97]

The founder's statement left no doubt that the conflict hinged on the restrictive powers of the craft unionists.[98]

By mid-February 1892 the struggle was well under way. Many Hamilton moulders left the city, securing employment in Detroit and London shops. Others stayed behind to "welcome" the influx of "scab" workmen from Salem, Ohio, and Toronto, and to deride the efforts of incompetent apprentices and "botch" workers who manned the foundries. While the founders refused to pay union men more than $2 a day, they contracted with non-unionists, promising them $2.50-$3 for the duration of the year. Despite these lucrative terms, the union was often able to induce the non-unionists to leave town, and the city's foundries appeared to be stifled by the conflict.[99]

The union continued to persuade moulders to leave the city, coaxing them with cash (as much as $30-$50 a strikebreaker), whiskey, threatening letters, and, in more than one case, physical violence. To replenish their diminishing stock of non-unionists, the foundrymen secured the services of Joseph Payette, a Gurney moulder who acted as the founders' agent in Montreal, delivering French-Canadian moulders to the Hamilton shops. Ironclad agreements, driven from the moulding trade in the 1880's, reappeared. Crowds of workingmen, numbering over 500, gathered each evening outside D. Moore and Company's foundry and followed the non-union workmen to their boardinghouses, hooting, jeering, and yelling all the while. Burrow, Stewart and Milne rented a frame house next to their shop to house their labourers, fearing that it "won't be long before there will be mobs around our foundry as there have been at Moore's." Arsonists succeeded in igniting a small fire at the Moore foundry. Assault cases involving non-unionists and craft workers–moulders as well as other skilled workers–were frequently tried in the city courts. Boardinghouse owners often refused to rent accommodation to strikebreakers. Street fights became an everyday happening. By early May 1892 the community stood polarized, but neither union nor employer had given way.[100]

For the unionists, indeed, the struggle for control had been transformed into a struggle for existence. John Jennings, secretary of the Molders' strike committee, wrote to the Peterborough Molders' Union, explaining the desperate situation No. 26 found itself in:

> In answering to how we are getting along I might say there are four shop runing with scab labor & Boys Gurney shop as about forty boys and twenty five scabs Burrows eleven french canadians and Boys Copps 8 men and boys Moore shop 4 french men and boys and the other as not started as yet – we have sent away about 46 scabs since we began and still they come they are a hard class to deal with they tell you straight they are going to stay here and them that wants to go we cannot touch them for they want the earth the main thing is to keep our employers Just were they are but it takes money to do it we have to get it somewhere or we are going to loose which means crushing the Banner Union of this Dominion of ours or otherwise Unionism in Canada Trusting you will still continue to help us for its money against money[101]

Jennings's argument was restated in a North American circular, "Labor Against Capital," issued by the Hamilton Union:

> This trouble of ours has been gradually coming on for the last four or five years. The Manufacturers' Combine have closed down, on an average, from twelve to fourteen weeks each winter, and have been doing their best to limit the production and starve us into submission. . . . We are the BANNER UNION of Canada, and second to none in America as competent workmen. . . . They are determined, as we said before, to wipe us out of existence. In order to fight them successfully, *we must have money*, we therefore appeal to every union molder throughout the length and breadth of the land, to give us a helping hand, and to do it *as soon as possible*. No time should be lost, as our very existence is involved in this issue.[102]

In August 1892 the two parties remained locked in a stalemate. James A. Laidlaw, owner of a local foundry, consented to hire union moulders, but only if they abandoned the restrictions of their organization. "We have made an agreement with our foreman, Hugh Sweeney," said Laidlaw, "by which he is to employ the moulders and get so much a ton. If he fulfills his agreement the men can't be union men. We have no objection to the union men, but we want to control our shop." Three days later the union moulders walked out of Laidlaw's foundry, refusing to work with non-unionists.[103] But a week later union men were in control, the closed shop apparently in effect.[104]

The crack in the wall of employer resistance exhibited at Laidlaw's did not widen, however, and the struggle between the foundrymen and the moulders dragged on into 1893. By mid-February, with only twenty-eight union moulders employed in the locked-out shops, the unionists had been out for over one year, and the International had expended $30,000 in their cause. Time proved to be on the founders' side. The 1892-93 conflict would be something less than a victory for IMIU No. 26, and the drift into economic recession would ensure that union control of Hamilton's stove foundries would not be established in the immediate future. But neither had the union given in, and its quest to re-establish control would surface again.[105]

Control, then, formed an essential component of nineteenth-century work relationships. Its importance was revealed most dramatically in conflict situations, when employer and craftsman confronted one another over the question of workplace hegemony. That many of these conflicts revolved around seemingly "economistic" issues – the standard rate, price lists, and wage reductions or increases – should not obscure the essential context in which struggle evolved. Opposition to reductions, demands for wage increases, and the enforcement of union price lists all tested the strength of the craft union and its shop committee. To be defeated by an employer on such bread-and-butter issues spelled the demise of craft control just as surely as a contractor's circumvention of apprenticeship regulations or a founder's attack on restriction of output. Restrictive and shop controls thus knew few boundaries, forming the essential context of shop-floor life in nineteenth-century Hamilton. Workingmen struggled to preserve these forms of control, and strikes therefore serve as the prism through which the historian can best observe the process. At the same time, it must be stressed that, as a culture of the shop floor, control thrived on a daily basis in the routine and mundane practices of the working day. Control, won in the context of class conflict, extended well beyond the episodic.

When Hamilton mechanics read labour and reform newspapers aloud to one another at the workplace, exchanging issues among themselves, for instance, they exhibited a degree of autonomy from their employers.[106] Iron rollers and heaters regularly punctuated their day's work with a smoke and a glass of beer, having twenty minutes between heats "to go where they have a mind." At Hamilton's Duncan Lithographing Company, Robert T. Armstrong recalled the boisterous atmosphere of the turn-of-the-century workplace, where supervision seemed non-existent:

> All Bronze work was done by hand also dusting. Many a fight was started by the men and boys by firing bronze at each other. . . . What times we did have. Remember a fight between George Webb and Jim Gray and everybody stopped work to see it to a finish. And again a fight between the fireman and Joe Best. Of course, in those days Jack McCarthy had to be in on every fight. And the booze question!! What a time. There were three hotels on one alley and two on the other, and then we saw the result of drink. It was a common thing on Monday to be short of help. It is to smile when I think of going out the back door, and buying fresh doughnuts for 5¢ a dozen.

Another printer, "Red Ink," recalled the camaraderie of the shop, where young workers constantly aided their workmates, and "sojering" was the norm.[107]

As men who often hired their own helpers, Great Western Railway boilermakers, glassblowers at the Burlington Glass Works, nailers at the Ontario Rolling Mils, and cigarmakers at Tuckett's factory exercised direct control over much of the work process.[108] Other crafts, like the iron moulders, asserted their power against employer demands that unionists work with helpers, contemptuously referred to as "bucks" or "berkshires."[109] Thus in 1892 the Hamilton moulders refused any compromise involving "the system of 'brick-shares'."[110] The point is that craft unionists could exercise their workplace discretion in many directions, controlling their helpers by hiring them themselves, or refusing to work with helpers altogether.[111]

Control was also intimately related to pride in craftsmanship, an aspect of working life that thrived in times of peace as well as in times of trouble. Restriction of output often involved much more than simple job security. Against the accelerating pace of work the true craftsmen posed the issue of a quality product, always contingent upon the skilled workers' autonomy:

> The 'hurrah' and 'rush' of American practice in the workshop or on American buildings, is surely destroying skillful

> workmanship. To do good work requires time, and no man can make a good honest piece of work with the lash of the foreman pressing him on to 'hurry up', 'hurry up.' The writer of this has known of more than one case where first class workmen have been elbowed out of existence by men who did not know half as much, but who have the fatal knack of always appearing to be in a hurry. In these days – in the building trades at all events – there seems to be in most instances no incentive to become a good workman. It is not the quality but the quantity of work a man can do that gives him value in the eyes of his employer. All this has a tendency to make indifferent workmen and to fill up the ranks of the building trades with half-trained men, botches and pretenders.

"It is hurried workmanship which overtasks the strength of the workman," argued the *Palladium of Labor*. The Hamilton labour paper then defended restricting output, claiming that a union rule against "undue haste [was] directly favourable to improvement in the quality of work."[112] Indeed, each trade had its derogatory term for incompetent workmen: telegraphers dubbed poor operatives "pegs" after the metal implements dividing the switches on the keyboard; printers and jewellers referred to clumsy craftsmen as "blacksmiths"; and tailors labelled incompetent workers "shoemakers," indicative of their inability to work with cloth. Likewise each trade had a specific epithet for the strikebreaker.[113]

The basis of quality work lay in the craftsman's early years of apprenticeship training. Apprentice regulations were far more than a restrictive mechanism aimed at preserving a job security. Ratios were also intimately connected with the craft's realization that for skill to be properly cultivated an appropriate balance of journeymen to apprentices needed to be maintained. It was in this context that many Hamilton trades preserved their apprenticeship conditions during the late nineteenth century, despite persistent employer opposition.[114] Then, too, apprenticeship was an intense cultural experience, and one that conditioned solidarity as well as workmanship:

> We knew he had overcome difficulties, often had he been disheartened and dismayed, often he had heard the mocking jest or coarse laugh of his companions, at his imperfect workmanship, often heard the angry words over goods or tools

> spoiled through his ignorance or carelessness. He had risen on dark mornings when his neighbours, lads his own age were snugly sleeping; he had toiled on glorious summer days when his indolent companions were resting under green trees, or plunging into the cool waters; he had done the rough work because he was 'the boy'. Yes, but there is another side to the picture. With courage renewed, with eyes and fingers becoming more and more accustomed to the handicrafts of the trade, every month found him progressing, till tonight, as the still bell tells us, he has overcome. His companions gather round him with boisterous mirth, and the 'older hands' feel a certain pride in him, as wringing his hand they know he ranks among themselves, the means of an honest living at his disposal, one of God's great army of working men.[115]

Youths reared in this context often found it easier to oppose their masters than their future shopmates when conflict situations arose.[116]

As a final indication of the craft worker's attachment to control, and all that it symbolized, one need only consider the question of co-operation.[117] Co-operation was first seriously embraced by local craftsmen in the fall of 1862, when the Molders' Union of Canada West met in the city to discuss the prospects of establishing co-operative ventures on the model of the Rochdale Equitable Pioneers Society. A union moulder wrote to *Fincher's Trade Review*, outlining the stimulus behind the co-operative movement: "Our present organization does not accomplish what we want. That is to take us from under the hand of our employers and place us on equal footing."[118]

By November 1864 the Hamilton Trades Assembly was holding meetings of the "friends of co-operation among the workingmen of Hamilton."[119] A month later Hamilton's Co-operative Association was formed, sustained by 160 subscribers, pledging $5 each towards the establishment of a co-operative grocery store. "The objects of this association," declared the constitution, "are to carry out the principles of co-operation between seller and purchaser in the buying and selling of food, clothing, and other necessities, with the view of ameliorating the condition of the working classes, and, in furtherance thereof, to begin with the establishment of a co-operative grocery store."[120] Throughout the 1860's the association prospered, growing to 300 members by 1867. But financial stability did not assure social success, and the founders of the association were disappointed in the response of the working-class community. Led by the proprietor stratum of the "producing classes," this early co-operative venture attracted few actual workingmen, and by the early 1870's had foundered.[121]

Despite this failure, the working-class community persistently raised the spectre of a more militant co-operation before the eyes of its employers, often in times of conflict. A co-operative bakery, for instance, was often seen to be the solution to the exorbitant prices charged by the master bakers.[122] Hamilton moulders sought to intimidate the founders in the midst of the 1872 nine-hour lockouts by starting a co-operative moulding shop.[123] In the opening months of the 1892 conflict in the stove shops, four union moulders – W. J. Kerr and his son W. H. Kerr, George Coombs, and William Coombs – began their own business, running the shop on union principles.[124] The Hamilton Painters' Union established co-operative businesses in 1882, as did cigarmakers embroiled in apprenticeship struggles with their employers in 1883 and 1885.[125] Their craft assaulted by non-union labour throughout the 1880's, the United Hatters of North America founded the Eureka Hat Works in Hamilton in 1889, informing the Trades and Labor Council: "Our capital is very limited and unless the labor organizations of the city make a more decided stand for union made goods, the Hat Industry will be completely dead in about another year and we will have had to succumb long before that."[126] Bricklayers regularly turned to co-operation, employing the tactic in the middle of the 1883 and 1888 spring strike waves.[127] For the city's Knights of Labor, co-operation was a widely touted panacea for the evils of monopoly and corporate greed.[128] It was not the success or failure of these efforts that deserves commentary, for none lasted beyond the moment of crisis. What is important is the deeply embedded commitment to workers' autonomy that active involvement in co-operative ventures articulated.

By the end of the nineteenth century the skilled workingman and the employer had repeatedly tested one another. The question of control had loomed large. In the words of the Royal Commission on the Relations of Labour and Capital, trade unions had done much "in promoting a spirit of self-control." With their development had grown "a spirit of independence and self-reliance." Rather than look to government legislation, the unions preferred "to better their condition by united action."[129]

Frederick Winslow Taylor's close associate, Henry Gantt, saw a similar process at work, noting, "There is in every workroom a fashion, a habit of work, and the new worker follows that, for it isn't respectable not to."[130] The mechanical superintendent of the Ontario Rolling Mills chose harsher terms to describe the phenomenon. "There is a sort of terrorism in connection with that thing," he said, "that a man does not dare to speak." All of these authorities had come to know the culture of control intimately.

NOTES

1. See, for instance, James Hinton, *The First Shop Stewards' Movement* (London, 1973); Branko Pribicevic, *The Shop Stewards' Movement and Workers' Control, 1910-1922* (Oxford, 1959); Arthur Gleason, "The Shop Stewards and Their Significance," *Survey,* 41 (4 January 1919), 417-22; Gleason, "British Labor Breaks the Truce," *Survey,* 40 (27 July 1918), 467-72; Peter Warrian, "The Challenge of the One Big Union Movement in Canada, 1919-1921" (M.A. thesis, University of Waterloo, 1971), 52-60. Cf. the important discussion of the situation in the United States in David Montgomery, "The 'New Unionism' and the Transformation of Workers' Consciousness, 1909-1922," *Journal of Social History,* 7 (1974), 509-22. The quote is from Carter Goodrich, *The Frontier of Control: A Study of British Workshop Practices* (New York, 1920), 31.
2. See the recent studies: David Montgomery, "Workers' Control of Machine Production in the Nineteenth Century," *Labor History,* 17 (1976), 485-509: Gregory S. Kealey, "The 'Honest Workingman' and Workers' Control: The Experience of Toronto Skilled Workers, 1860-1892," *Labour/Le Travailleur,* 1 (1976), 32-68; Bob Gilding, *The Journeymen Coopers of East London: Workers' Control in an Old London Trade* (Oxford, 1972).
3. Quoted in Dale Chisamore *et al., Brockville: A Social History, 1890-1930* (Brockville, Ont., n.d.), 87.
4. *Hamilton Spectator* (hereafter cited as *HS*), 5 May 1883.
5. *John Swinton's Paper,* 8 and 15 June 1884.
6. *Workingman's Advocate,* 25 March 1876.
7. *Trades Union Advocate,* 4 May 1882.
8. *Palladium of Labor* (hereafter cited as *POL*), 17 November 1883.
9. *Labor Union,* 10 March 1883.
10. *Cigar Makers' Official Journal,* 15 October 1882.
11. *HS,* 18 May 1876.
12. *POL,* 1 May 1886.

13. *Labor Union,* 27 January 1883.
14. *POL,* 25 August 1883.
15. See the accounts of the Hamilton glass factory and the work process in glassblowing in *HS,* 12 September 1864, 29 March, 24 June 1867, 29 August 1871, 15 April 1874. On nailmaking in the Hamilton rolling mill, see *HS,* 27 September 1879. On moulding at the Gartshore foundry, see *The National,* 17 October 1878. On hand cigarmaking, prior to the introduction of the mould, see *Workingman's Advocate,* 11 May 1872. On the limitations of technological innovation in some important trades, see Daniel J. Walkowitz, "Worker City, Company Town: Adaptation and Protest Within the Troy Iron Worker and Cohoes Cotton Worker Communities, 1855-1884" (typescript, Rutgers, 1976), ch. 2; Lee W. Minton, *Flame and Heart: A History of the Glass Bottle Blowers Association of the United States and Canada* (New York, 1961), 3, 23-4; Margaret Loomis Stecker, "The Founders, The Molders and the Molding Machine," in John R. Commons, ed., *Trade Unionism and Labor Problems,* 2nd ser. (New York, 1921), 433-57; Wayne Roberts, "Metal Workers and the Second Industrial Revolution: Toronto, 1896-1914" (typescript, University of Toronto, 1976), esp. 5, n. 3.
16. See the excellent discussion in Benson Soffer, "A Theory of Trade Union Development: The Role of the 'Autonomous' Workman," *Labor History,* 1 (1960), 141-63.
17. See George Barnett, "The Printers: A Study in American Trade Unionism," *American Economic Association Quarterly,* 3rd ser., 10, no. 3 (1909), 182-208, 243-56; Barnett, *Chapters on Machinery and Labor* (Carbondale, Ill., 1969); Wayne Roberts, "The Last Artisans: Toronto Printers, 1896-1914," in Gregory S. Kealey and Peter Warrian, eds., *Essays in Canadian Working Class History* (Toronto, 1976), 125-42; *Proceedings of the 24th Annual Session, Glass Bottle Blowers Association of the United States and Canada, Detroit, 9-16 July 1900* (Camden, N.J., 1900), 40-1; *Proceedings of 26th Session, Glass Blowers Association, 1902* (Camden, N.J., 1902), 51; Minton, *Flame and Heart,* 19-22, 30; *The Craftsman,* 29 October 1887.
18. *Labor Advocate,* 5 December 1890. See the early statements on controlling the machine in *The Socialist,* 6 May 1876; *Iron Molders' International Journal,* 10 October 1875.
19. Carter L. Goodrich, "Problems of Workers' Control," *Locomotive Engineers' Journal,* 57 (May, 1923): 356-65, 415; Goodrich, *The Frontier of Control,* 41-2, 137-8, 264-5.
20. On Canada, see *Report of the Royal Commission on the Relations of Labour and Capital in Canada,* Quebec Evidence, III (Ottawa, 1889), 55, 457; Quebec Evidence, IV, 900; New Brunswick Evidence, V, 131; Nova Scotia Evidence, VI, 61, 371, 401, 411. On

the United States practices, see the monumental Carrol D. Wright *et al.*, "Regulation and Restriction of Output," *Eleventh Special Report of the Commissioner of Labor* (Washington, 1904); and the abbreviated discussion in Wright, "The Restriction of Output," *North American Review,* 183 (2 November 1906), 887-96.

21. On the foreman, see Benson Soffer, "The Role of Union Foremen in the Evolution of the International Typographical Union," *Labor History,* 2 (Winter, 1961), 62-81; *Canadian Labor Reformer,* 16 October 1886. On shop committees, see the discussions in Kealey, "Honest Workingman," 40-2; Frank T. Stockton, *The International Iron Molders' Union of North America* (Baltimore, 1921), 40; Iron Molders' International Journal, 10 December 1875.
22. *POL,* 19 July 1884, reported an interesting case of restriction of output by a gang of labourers: "A gang of Italian labourers near Saratoga was recently cut down ten cents a day. Instead of striking they cut an inch off their shovel blades at night. The boss asked what it meant and one of the men replied: 'Not so much pay, not so much dirt left; all right, job last the more long. Italian no fool like Irishman; he no strike.' " On the persistence of output restriction in unorganized trades, see S. B. Mathewson, *Restriction of Output Among Unorganized Workers* (Carbondale, Ill., 1969).
23. "What One Trade Has Done," *John Swinton's Paper,* 23 March 1884; Montgomery, "Workers' Control," 493-4; Irwin Yellowitz, *Industrialization and the American Labor Movement, 1850-1900* (Port Washington, N.Y., 1977), 59. Other assessments of glass workers' power are found in *HS,* 6 and 9 January 1879; *Relations of Labour and Capital,* Nova Scotia Evidence, VI, 371; *Proceedings of the U.G.G. Workers' Association of the United States and Canada, Composed of Glass Bottle Makers, 18th Annual Session, Atlantic City, 9-19 July 1894* (Lockport, N.Y., 1894), 90-3: *Proceedings of the National Trade Assembly of No. 143, Knights of Labor of America, Composed of Glass Bottle Workers in the United States and Canada, 15th Annual Session, St. Louis, 13-24 July 1891* (Lockport, N.Y., 1891) 367-9; *The Carpenter,* March 1884; *POL,* 10 January 1885. Cf. the discussion of French glass workers' strength prior to 1895 in Joan Wallach Scott, *The Glassworkers of Carmaux: French Craftsmen and Political Action in a Nineteenth Century City* (Cambridge, Mass., 1974), 19-52.
24. See *HS,* 24 June 1867; *POL,* 16 August 1884, 5 and 22 August, 1885, 16 October 1886. On the esteem in which glass workers were held, see the coverage of the 1886 convention, and the reception afforded a group of Steubenville glass blowers, camping at Burlington Beach over one summer stop, in *HS,* 15 July 1886, 10 and 17 July, 5 August 1890; *POL*, 17 July 1886.
25. *HS*, 8 April 1886.
26. Exceptional conflicts are mentioned in *HS,* 5 and 7 May, 1881;

Minute Book of the Trades and Labor Council, 1888-1896, 28, Hamilton Trades and Labor Council. Note the endorsement of the Pittsburgh glass workers' 48-box limit in *POL,* 19 April 1884.

27. PAC, MG 26 A, vol. 155, Macdonald Papers, M.A. Pigott to Adam Brown, MP, 8 May 1888, 63160-4; "Combinations Restricting the Amount of Work," *POL,* 22 December 1883.
28. On depreciation of the "hog," see *Relations of Labour and Capital,* Ontario Evidence, II, 821-22; *POL,* 12 April 1884, 7 February, 25 July 1885, 10 April 1886. Attacks on "rushing" were widespread. See *The Carpenter,* November 1885, 15 January 1889; *Iron Molders' International Journal,* 31 October 1870, 10 September 1875, April 1884, November 1885, December 1885; Wright, *Eleventh Special Report,* "Regulation and Restriction of Output," 18, 26-30. Note the religious critique in *POL,* 27 March 1886.
29. Montgomery, "Workers' Control," 491; Kealey, "Honest Workingman," 37; *Iron Molders' International Journal,* November 1887; *Workingman's Advocate,* 5 November 1864; *POL,* 26 January, 20 September 1884. The quotation is from *Industrial Banner,* September 1908.
30. *Industrial Banner,* December 1899.
31. *POL,* 9 October 1886. On union discipline, see Iron Molders' International Collecton, Box 1, Archives of Labor History and Urban Affairs, Wayne State University, *Minute Book, Molders' Union of New York, 1860-1868,* 26; International Iron Molders' Union No. 191 (Peterborough), *Minute Book, 1882-1892,* 4 September 1882, Gainey Collection, Trent University Archives. Cf. Solomon Blum, "Trade Union Rules in the Building Trades," in Jacob H. Hollander and George C. Barnett, eds., *Studies in American Trade Unionism* (New York, 1907), 295-319.
32. The most detailed study of the standard rate is David A. McCabe, *The Standard Rate in American Trade Unions* (Baltimore, 1912). Cf. Stockton, *International Molders' Union,* 137-58.
33. The strike is mentioned in "Hamilton Early Stronghold in Organized Labor Cause," *HS,* 15 July 1946; *The Hamilton and District Trades and Labor Council, 60th Anniversary, Diamond Jubilee, 1888-1848* (Hamilton, 1948), 3. Both of these sources, however, mistakenly date the conflict in 1859. Contemporary accounts are found in *HS,* 8 November 1856; *Windsor Herald,* 7 and 14 November 1856.
34. PAC, MG 28 I 103, vol. 249, Canadian Labour Congress Collection, Lloyd Atkinson and Eugene Forsey, "The Labour Movement in Hamilton, 1827-1888," typescript, 4.
35. *Hamilton Times* (hereafter cited as *HT*), 1 June 1864; *HS*, 31 May 1864.
36. *Iron Molders' International Journal*, 15 December 1864; *HS*, 13 December 1864.

37. *HT*, 23 February 1866.
38. *Ibid.*, 23 March 1866.
39. On the Troy moulders' struggle, see Walkowitz, "Worker City, Company Town," chs. 1-2; *Iron Molders' International Journal*, April 1866, May 1866; *HT*, 5 May 1866; *Workingman's Advocate*, 21 April 1866.
40. *HT*, 5 May 1866; *Iron Molders' International Journal*, May 1866, June 1866, July 1866, August 1866, October 1866, January 1867; Charles Brian Williams, "Canadian American Trade Union Relations-A Study of the Development of Binational Unionism" (Ph.D. thesis, Cornell University, 1964), 122.
41. Atkinson and Forsey, "Hamilton Labor Movement," 7. Hamilton's Molders' Union was organizationally inactive for some of the period. See *Iron Molders' International Journal*, 31 October 1871.
42. Williams, "Canadian American Trade Union Relations," 126-7; *Ontario Workman*, 23 May 1872; *Dumfries Reformer*, 22 May 1872. For detail on the moulders and the 1872 upheaval, see Bryan Palmer, *A Culture in Conflict: Skilled Workers and Industrial Capitalism in Hamilton, Ontario, 1860-1914* (Montreal, 1979), ch. 5. On the reorganization of IMIU No. 26, see *Iron Molders' International Journal*, January 1872.
43. *Iron Molders' International Journal*, October 1872.
44. *Ibid.*, December 1872.
45. Williams, "Canadian American Trade Union Relations," 131-40; *Iron Molders' International Journal*, 30 June 1873, October 1873, February 1874, 30 April 1874.
46. *Iron Molders' International Journal*, 10 September 1874; Robert H. Storey, "Industrialization in Canada: The Emergence of the Hamilton Working Class, 1850-1870s" (M.A. thesis, Dalhousie University, 1975), 179-80.
47. *Iron Molders' International Journal*, April 1874.
48. *HS*, 27 August 1874.
49. On the beginnings of the struggle, see *HS*, 27 and 28 August, 4 and 11 September 1874; *Iron Molders' International Journal*, 10 September, 10 October, 10 December 1874; Storey, "Industrialization in Canada," 179-80; PAC, *Minutes of the Proceedings of the Toronto Trades Assembly, 1871-1878*, typescript, p. 211. This period was one of a general assault on the moulders. See *Iron Molders' International Journal*, 10 October 1875; Kealey, "Honest Workingman," 43-4.
50. *Iron Molders' International Journal*, 10 February 1875.
51. On the tailors' struggle see *HS*, 15 and 19 August, 24 and 30 October 1873; *Ontario Workman*, 21 August, 30 October 1873.
52. *HS*, 21 November 1879.
53. *Ibid.*, 17 and 19 February 1881.
54. *Ibid.*, 21 and 25 April 1881.

55. *Ibid.*, 6 and 9 May 1881.
56. *Ibid.*, 5 May 1879, 25-30 April 1881.
57. *Ibid.*, 9 July 1881.
58. *Ibid.*, 9 and 13 July 1881.
59. *Ibid.*, 2, 5, and 6 May 1881.
60. *Ibid.*, 5 May 1881.
61. *Ibid.*, 10 May 1881.
62. *Ibid.*, 7 May 1881. Note the editorial in *ibid.*, 9 May 1881.
63. *Ibid.*, 27 May, 1 and 2 June 1881.
64. *Ibid.*, 4, 6, and 16 March 1882.
65. *Ibid.*, 9 March - 3 April 1882.
66. *Ibid.*, 28 and 29 March 1882.
67. *Ibid.*, 10 and 14 April 1882.
68. *Ibid.*, 5 April - 1 June 1882.
69. *Ibid.*, 8, 10, 12, and 17 June 1882.
70. *Ibid.*, 27 March, 10 and 15 April 1882; Eugene Forsey, "The Canadian Labour Movement, 1812-1902," Canadian Historical Association, *Historical Booklet No. 27* (1974), 9.
71. *HS*, 15 April 1882.
72. For detail, see Palmer, *A Culture in Conflict*, ch. 6.
73. *HS*, 18 and 20 April, 1 and 5 May 1883.
74. *Ibid.*, 1-26 May 1883.
75. *Relations of Labour and Capital*, Ontario Evidence, II, 795; *HS*, 4, 10, and 13 December 1883; *POL*, 15 December 1883.
76. *HS*, 12, 13, 17, and 20 January 1885; *The Craftsman*, 21 March 1885; *POL*, 17 January, 2 May 1885.
77. *Relations of Labour and Capital*, Ontario Evidence, II, 790-1.
78. *POL*, 4 and 11 April 1885. On the coopers' demise, see Kealey, "Honest Workingman," 34-40.
79. On the shoemakers' experience, see Gregory S. Kealey, "Artisans Respond to Industrialism: Shoemakers, Shoe Factories and the Knights of St. Crispin in Toronto," Canadian Historical Association, *Historical Papers* (1973), 137-57.
80. *POL*, 7 November 1885. The poem, from an 1875 issue of *The National*, is quoted in N. Brian Davis, *The Poetry of the Canadian People, 1720-1920: Two hundred years of hard work* (Toronto, 1976), 148.
81. *HS*, 5 March 1888.
82. *Ibid.*, 23, 24, and 26 March 1888.
83. *Ibid.*, 26 March 1888. For Hamilton bricklayers' apprenticeship regulations, see *The Carpenter*, March 1887.
84. *HS*, 28 March 1888.
85. *Ibid.*, 30 March 1888.
86. *Ibid.*, 2 April 1888.
87. *Ibid.*, 25 April 1888.

88. *Ibid.*, 27 April, 1 and 8 May 1888.
89. *Ibid.*, 30 April, 21 June, 28 November 1888, 5 and 6 February, 10 May 1889.
90. *Ibid.*, 20 and 16 August 1888. Cf. clippings in PAC, Macdonald Papers, vol. 332, R. R. Elliot to Macdonald, 11 March 1889, 150045-6.
91. *HS*, 5 July 1888.
92. *Ibid.*, 6 April, 21 May 1891; *Labor Advocate*, 10 April, 29 May 1891.
93. *HS*, 5 July 1892, 20 and 27 September, 7 and 10 October 1895.
94. *Relations of Labour and Capital*, Ontario Evidence, II, 796; *HS*, 4, 6, 8, and 9 June, 18, 19, and 27 July 1887, 21 and 22 February, 12 and 13 March 1888: *Iron Molders' International Journal*, June 1887, July 1887. On the moulders and control, see *POL*, 6 February 1886.
95. Between 1888 and 1892 only one brief skirmish occurred. See *Iron Molders' International Journal*, November 1890, on a strike in one foundry.
96. *HS*, 11-29 January 1892; *Iron Molders' International Journal*, January 1892, February 1892.
97. *HS*, 1 February 1892.
98. Similar conflicts had been precipitated in Toronto in 1891 and in Kingston, Ontario, in 1892. See Kealey, "Honest Workingman," 46; *HS*, 6 February 1892.
99. *HS*, 5-10 February 1892.
100. On the progress of the strike and the increasing use of violence, see *HS*, 11 February-11 May 1892.
101. Trent University Archives, Gainey Collection, vol. 10, file 3, Iron Molders' International Union No. 191, "Canadian Correspondence," John Jennings to Mr. Parkes, Hamilton, 20 March 1892. Cf. *ibid.*, M. Basquil and Fred Walters to No. 191, Hamilton, 8 February 1892; *Minute Book, Hamilton Trades and Labor Council, 1888-1896*, 224.
102. Trent University Archives, Gainey Collection, vol. 10, file 6, Iron Molders' International Union No. 191, "Miscellaneous," "Labor Struggle Against Capital."
103. *HS*, 1 and 3 August 1892.
104. *Ibid.*, 5 and 10 August 1892.
105. *Ibid.*, 17 and 27 February 1893, and *Iron Molders' International Journal*, March 1893, document the continuing struggle.
106. On this practice in Hamilton, see *HS*, 25 April 1879, 14 June 1882. The phenomenon was common among skilled workers. See *Labor Standard*, 2 September 1877; *Workingman's Advocate*, 11 May 1872; *Toronto Tribune*, 23 September 1905; Samuel Gompers, *Seventy Years of Life and Labor: An Autobiography* (New York,

1925), 80-1; Herbert G. Gutman, "Work, Culture, and Society in Industrializing America, 1815-1919," *American Historical Review*, 78 (1973), 558.

107. *Relations of Labour and Capital*, Ontario Evidence, II, 791; Robert T. Armstrong, "Memoir of Duncan Lithographing Company, 1882-1978," n.p. John Weaver provided a xerox of this interesting document, currently in the archives of the Duncan Lithographing Company of Hamilton. "Red Ink's" recollections are in *'Pi': A Compilation of Odds and Ends Relating to Workers in Sanctum and Newsroom, Culled From the Scrap-Book of a Compositor* (Hamilton, 1890), 5-7, 186, drawing upon an article by Bob Burdett and a poem by Jimmy Platt.
108. Hamilton Public Library, Hamilton Collection, files 1-18 and 19-22, GWR Pay List, Locomotive Department, 18-31 January, 1-14 February 1863; *HS*, 22 February 1881, 23 February 1882; *Relations of Labour and Capital,* Ontario Evidence, II, 743-4, 761.
109. On the moulders' opposition to "bucks," see *Iron Molders' International Journal,* October 1873, 10 November 1875, December 1866; Stockton, *Molders' International Union*, 170-85; Joseph A. Barford, "Reminiscences of the Early Days of Stove Plate Molding and the Union," *International Molders' and Foundry Workers' Journal*, 94 (July, 1958): 8-12; Kealey, "Honest Workingman," 45-6; *Labour Leaf*, 16 June 1886.
110. *HS*, 29 February 1892.
111. The question of helpers is discussed in Montgomery, "Workers' Control," 488; John H. Ashworth, *The Helper and the American Trade Unions* (Baltimore, 1915).
112. *The Carpenter*, November 1885; *POL*, 22 December 1883.
113. *Iron Molders' International Journal*, October 1883.
114. On Hamilton apprenticeship conditions and their importance to the crafts, see *POL*, 20 September 1884; *Relations of Labour and Capital*, Ontario Evidence, II, 296, 797.
115. Harriet Annie Wilkins, *Victor Roy: A Masonic Poem* (Hamilton, 1882), 99-100. Cf. *Journal of the Board of Arts and Manufactures for Upper Canada*, 5 (1864), 305.
116. See Kealey, "Honest Workingman," 43-4; *HS*, 20 September 1892, 12 April 1893; Craig Heron and Bryan D. Palmer, "Through the Prism of the Strike: Industrial Conflict in Southern Ontario, 1901-1914," *CHR*, LVIII (1977), 423-58.
117. As an introduction to nineteenth-century co-operation, see John F. C. Harrison, *Quest for the New Moral World: Robert Owen and the Owenites in Britain and America* (London, 1969); Sidney Pollard, "Nineteenth Century Co-operation: From Community Building to Shopkeeping," in Asa Briggs and John Saville, eds., *Essays in Labour History* (London, 1960), 74-112. The relationship between co-operation and control is outlined in Kealey, "Honest Workingman," 58-61.

118. *Fincher's Trade Review*, 15 August 1863. My thanks to Gregory S. Kealey for making this source available to me.
119. *HT*, 26 November 1864.
120. *Constitution and By-Laws of the Hamilton Co-operative Association, Constituted December 1864* (Hamilton, 1864), 3. Cf. *HS*, 5 and 13 December 1864.
121. On the rise and fall of the association, see *HS*, 17 January, 18 April, 16 August, 22 October 1867, 16 January 1868, 9 March, 28 October 1870; *HT*, 5 July, 28 December 1865, 18 January, 9 February, 4 April, 20 July 1866, 29 May 1867.
122. *HS*, 29 November, 12 December 1865, 26 and 29 June 1878; *Labour Union*, 10 February 1883.
123. *Workingman's Advocate*, 25 May 1872.
124. *HS*, 13 February 1892.
125. *Ibid.*, 14 April 1882, 13 April 1883; *POL*, 20 June 1885.
126. Minute Book, *Hamilton Trades and Labor Council, 1888-1896*, 28.
127. *HS*, 10 and 16 May, 4 and 7 April 1888.
127. *HS*, 10 and 16 May, 4 and 7 April 1888.
128. See Palmer, *A Culture in Conflict*, ch.6.
129. *Relations of Labour and Capital*, Report, I, 112.
130. Henry L. Gantt, *Work, Wages and Profits* (New York, 1913), 186.

IV
Violence and Protest

Desmond Morton examines here the pervasive popular mythology of the peaceful and orderly Canadian West – patrolled by the efficient North West Mounted Police (NWMP) and relatively benevolent to the native peoples. A closer examination suggests that the historical reality provides far less ground for Canadian pride and self-congratulation. The Canadian West, which did witness two major uprisings, was spared bloody warfare more by the timing of western expansion than any other factor. By the time Canadians began to people their West, the Indians were "looking for terms not triumphs." Subsequent Canadian treatment of the native peoples differed little from the United States case. As the new nation marched westward to fulfil the central Canadian expansionist dream, the previous inhabitants of the Canadian West were regarded as little more than an unfortunate impediment to progress. A force to minimize their "regressive" impact was found in the creation of the NWMP.

The history of the native peoples of Canada is only beginning to be written. The best work to date has focused on the early fur trade and especially on French-Indian relations before the Conquest. The later periods are covered sporadically at best and receive most attention, such as during the two Riel rebellions, when they interrupt the newcomers' nation-building and western expansion. To the native peoples the NWMP must have looked quite different from the way they appear in most Canadian histories.

FURTHER READING:
On the Rebellions, see Joseph Kinsey Howard, *Strange Empire* (Toronto, 1965); and G. F. G. Stanley, *The Birth of Western Canada* (Toronto, 1961). On Riel, the most recent work is Thomas Flanagan, *Strange Prophet* (Toronto, 1979). On the suppression of protest by the state, see Desmond Morton, "Aid to the Civil Power: the Canadian Militia in Support of Social Order, 1867-1914," *Canadian Historical Review*, LI (1970), 407-25. Other types of violent behaviour are described in G. F. G. Stanley, "The Caraquet Riots of 1875," *Acadiensis*, 2 (1972), 21-38; and Patricia Roy, "The Preservation of the Peace in Vancouver: The Aftermath of the Anti-Chinese Riot of 1887," *BC Studies*, 31 (1976), 44-59. One history of the NWMP is R. C. MacLeod, *The North-West Mounted Police and Law Enforcement, 1873-1905* (Toronto, 1976). A muckraking account is Lorne and Caroline Brown, *An Unauthorized History of the RCMP* (Toronto, 1973).

Desmond Morton is a member of the Department of History at Erindale College, University of Toronto, and a leading military and labour historian.

Cavalry or Police: Keeping the Peace on Two Adjacent Frontiers, 1870-1900

by Desmond Morton

In an article in the *Pacific Historical Review* for 1955, Professor Paul F. Sharp renewed Frederick Jackson Turner's invitation to test the famous frontier thesis in other settings. Sharp had done so in his own pioneering book on the Canadian-American West, finding the differences more significant than the similarities.[1] In the article, he went on to contrast relations between the Canadian government and the aboriginal people of the Northwest with comparable developments in the United States and Australia: "Against a background of violence and hatred south of the forty-ninth parallel, the Canadian government conceived and executed an orderly, well-planned and honorable policy."[2]

The tribute was overly generous. A century of Indian policy has left the Canadian native people in much the same state of poverty and dependence as their brothers south of the border.[3] Sharp's contrast between Canadian order and American violence may be questioned in detail although north of the forty-ninth parallel it is established as one of those self-congratulatory myths that binds a nation together.[4] While Americans, reputedly, were electing sheriffs, summoning the U.S. Cavalry, and filling the graves on Boot Hill, Canadians were establishing law and order with the aid of a few hundred men of the North West Mounted Police.[5] According to Russell F. Weigley, there were 943 military

From *Journal of Canadian Studies,* X (1977), 27-37; originally presented as a paper at the Seventh Military History Symposium, USAF Academy, Colorado Springs, September 1976.

engagements in the American West between 1866 and 1895; in the Canadian Northwest, there were only six or seven comparable clashes, almost all of them associated with the North-West Campaign of 1885.[6]

Why were the adjacent frontiers apparently so different? Since whites, not Indians, are found at the root of most trouble in the West, Sharp agreed with most American historians that a ten-year lag in settlement had allowed the Canadian tribes and the police to adjust to new patterns of existence.[7] Robert M. Utley, the major historian of the United States Army during the Indian wars, conceded that police methods might sometimes have been more effective than conventional military tactics, but he also concluded that the Canadian approach succeeded only "because the sparsity of settlement prevented serious competition between whites and Indians for the lands and resources of the Northwest Territories."[8]

However, friction between white and native people was not simply a function of numbers but of law, policy, and political philosophy as well.[9] "The fact that the Police arrived before settlement," a young Canadian historian has commented, "is not nearly so significant as what they did when they got there."[10] The predominantly conservative political values of post-Confederation Canada allowed the use of both law and authoritarian structures to protect minority rights. In his recent study of the mounted police, R. C. MacLeod has argued that the force succeeded because, in contrast to British and American practice, it combined judicial and administrative functions in a kind of benevolent despotism moderated, at least until 1905, by the presumption that it would be no more than a temporary expedient.[11]

In the United States, prevailing interpretations of liberty and democracy and a recurrent suspicion of militarism repeatedly undermined the Army's attempts to resume control of Indian policy after 1849.[12] Congress usually preferred the sometimes inept and frequently corrupt agencies of the Department of the Interior. In Canada, one finds only the palest reflection of the ideal of possessive individualism which, in turn, inspired the doctrine of severalty as the ultimate solution of the Indian problem. For good or ill, Canada produced no equivalent to the Dawes Act of 1887.[13] Western Indians on Canadian reserves continued to hold land in common.

Canadian politicians of the Confederation era were preoccupied with avoiding what they considered to be "excesses" in the United States constitution.[14] The concern was bipartisan. "Our chiefest care," insisted Richard Cartwright, a Liberal, "must be to train the majority to respect the rights of the minority, to prevent the claims of the few from being trampled under foot by the caprice or passion of the many."[15] That minority could, of course, be the rich;[16] it could also be the French Canadians, the Catholics, English-speaking Protestants in Quebec – or it could be the Indians.[17] Influential Canadians saw the American West as a manifestation of the dangers of democracy and materialism; they wished no imitation on their side of the border. Visiting Edmonton in 1895, that feminist virago, Lady Aberdeen, noted with satisfaction that most of the newcomers were "heartily glad" to become British subjects but "there is a remnant who would like to introduce American ideas as to what conduct in the West should be. These must be dealt with ruthlessly, & the magistrates & N.W. Mounted Police are determined that this shall be the case if they can manage it."[18]

Canadians may explain the contrast between the frontiers by differing ideologies while Americans point to delayed settlement; both must recognize the role of accident and of defence considerations. Far from learning from American experience and planning a judicious interval between the dispatch of a police force and the advent of white settlers, the Canadian government planned that the costly burden of law enforcement would be assumed only as settlement advanced.[19] Macdonald and his cabinet endured years of well-authenticated reports of murder, violence, and illegal whiskey trading without displaying any of the purported Canadian devotion to law and order. What moved the Prime Minister was a consideration which can hardly have disturbed his Washington counterparts: the threat posed by an expansive and powerful neighbour.

Canadians of Macdonald's generation were obsessed by the American claim of "Manifest Destiny." Sir John both shared the fears and also used them shrewdly for political advantage. A prime goal of British North American confederation in 1867 had been to safeguard the huge, empty territories of the Northwest from American expansion. If Canadians trampled on the feelings of Red River settlers in their haste to possess the Hudson's Bay Company territories in 1869, they remembered how the Company's weakness had cost them the rich Oregon Territory in 1846.[20] After the Civil War, the risk of overt aggression from the

United States faded. The British military withdrawal of 1869-71 and the Treaty of Washington in 1871 served notice that Whitehall would never contemplate a re-match of the War of 1812.[21] The international boundary had been delineated in principle at all but a few points. By 1872, a joint commission was surveying its location on the prairies. An American threat remained only if the young Dominion failed to sustain its own authority. A breakdown in internal order, a movement for secession, a failure to restrain marauding Indian bands might provoke official or unofficial intervention from below the border. Whatever revisionists may believe, most imperial expansion in the nineteenth century owed less to capitalist greed or missionary fervour than to disorder or lawlessness of the frontier. When slave-trading flourished, murder went unpunished and plundering tribesmen found easy sanctuary; the Victorian era found little reprehensible in the forcible extension of government and social order. As the dominant power in the Western Hemisphere, the United States had demonstrated its willingness to enforce its view of international law on Mexico during the nineteenth century. Specifically, Indian wars drew retaliatory U.S. military expeditions deep into Mexican territory in the 1870's.[22]

S. W. Horrall, the official historian of the Royal Canadian Mounted Police, has emphasized Macdonald's view that Canada also could not afford an American-style West: "He feared that a repetition of the American experience would involve the dominion in a series of costly Indian wars, retard development in the Northwest and strain the country's resources."[23] Just as important, Canadian authority had to be firmly imposed so that Americans or their local sympathizers would have no excuse to disrupt the national destiny of a British North America *a mare usque ad marem*. To Edward Watkin, the British railway magnate, Macdonald confessed: "I would be quite willing, personally, to leave that whole country a wilderness for the next half-century, but I fear if Englishmen do not go there, Yankees will. . . ."[24]

How could peace and order be imposed on a huge and potentially turbulent territory at a cost that Canadian taxpayers would suffer? The Americans had solved their problem with a mixture of absent-mindedness and the brilliant inspiration of John C. Calhoun as War Secretary by deploying a tiny regular army on the forward edge of settlement and beyond. The nineteenth century saw a growing distinction between police and military functions in English-speaking countries. To the north, the Hudson's Bay Company had joyfully combined the roles when they occasionally wheedled detachments of British troops from the War Office: "If we succeed in getting a garrison established at Red River," wrote Sir George Simpson in 1845, "we shall be able to put down the illicit trade and keep the settlers in order."[25] However, when Canada acquired the Northwest, it had no standing army apart from the small remaining British garrison, and not the slightest desire to acquire one. To manage its vast new territory, Ottawa proposed to appoint a lieutenant governor and council, backed by a 250-man police force. "It seems to me," Macdonald wrote to the proposed commander, "that the best Force would be *Mounted Riflemen,* trained to act as cavalry, but also instructed in the Rifle exercises. They should also be instructed, as certain of the Line are, in the use of artillery. This body should not be expressly Military but should be styled *Police* and have the military bearing of the Irish Constabulary."[26] An order-in-council allowed fifty men to be recruited in the East (fifteen of them to be French-speaking) and 200 more in the West, where they would reflect the ethnic balance of the population. In short, the prime minister had conceived of a force capable of anything, from firing a cannon to achieving racial harmony, all for a dollar a day and a three-year enlistment.

Macdonald's plan was the genesis for the North West Mounted Police, but the realization was postponed by the first Riel rebellion of 1869-70. To pacify the Metis, Canada was obliged to grant a premature provincial status to Manitoba; for its own peace of mind, it felt compelled to maintain a "provisional" garrison. The few hundred men of the Manitoba Force swallowed the appropriations which the government might otherwise have spent to police the rest of the Northwest. Constitutionally, Manitoba's provincial status prevented Ottawa from creating its proposed "Mounted Police," but Macdonald could retain troops under federal control.[27]

Louis Riel's challenge to Ottawa and his association with W. B. O'Donoghue, Fenian agitator and unofficial U.S. agent, had forcibly reminded Canadians of the vulnerability of their Northwest to the Americans.[28] So had American attempts to prevent Colonel Garnet Wolseley from getting his British-Canadian military expedition through the canals at the Soo.[29] As the winter of 1871 approached, Ottawa again felt compelled to send troops hurrying over the Dawson Trail to meet a reported Fenian threat on the Manitoba border.[30] The militia arrived only to find that the Fenians had been seized at Pembina by a detachment of United States troops. Unfortunately, when Captain Lloyd Wheaton also proclaimed that the little Hudson's Bay post was on American soil, he illustrated the danger of allowing American soldiers to cope with frontier law and order. In due course, the International Boundary Commission restored Pembina to Canada; equally, a Minnesota jury refused to condemn Fenians for looting Canadian property.[31]

The comic-opera Fenian threat proved the loyalty of Manitoba half-breeds to the Canadian regime. However, a militia garrison remained at Winnipeg, largely because winter and the Precambrian shield left Manitoba isolated from the rest of Canada for six months of the year. The American route was hardly trustworthy in a crisis. More immediately, as lieutenant governors soon discovered, negotiation of treaties and land surrenders with Indian bands went more smoothly in the presence of a military escort.[32]

This was no help for the vast regions beyond Manitoba and the Northwest Angle. Far from being threatened by crowds of land-hungry settlers, it was their emptiness that brought trouble. Reports in 1871 by Lieutenant W. F. Butler and in 1873 by the Adjutant-General of the Canadian Militia, Colonel Patrick Robertson Ross, both emphasized the need for policing, preferably by small bodies of mounted troops. Successive governors of Manitoba revived the idea of a mounted police.[33] However, the emptiness of the Great Lone Land, as Butler called it, generated no political pressure. Only the Prime Minister could act and, beset by illness, family problems, and innumerable more immediate political crises, Macdonald was unmoved.[34] Not until the end of March 1873 did he invite Parliament to pass enabling legislation for a mounted police force. "They are to be a purely civil, not a military body," he assured the House of Commons, "with as little gold lace, fuss and fine feathers as possible; not a crack cavalry regiment, but an efficient police force for the rough and ready–particularly ready–enforcement of law and justice."[35] Still they did not exist.

It was Governor Alexander Morris, backed by sensational reports of the massacre of a party of Assiniboines in the Cypress Hills, plus urgings from the American Secretary of State, Hamilton Fish, who finally got Macdonald to move.[36] Although the responsibility for the deaths lay with American and Canadian wolf hunters from Fort Benton, Montana, Ottawa was left with a confused impression that, somehow, American whiskey traders from the notorious Fort Whoop-up were to blame.[37] "It would not be well for us to take the responsibility of slighting Morris' repeated and urgent entreaties," Macdonald advised the Governor General, Lord Dufferin. "If anything went wrong, the blame would lie at our door."[38] On this courageous note, the North West Mounted Police was born. A draft of 150 recruits was assembled and dispatched via the Dawson Trail to Winnipeg. In the spring of 1874, a second contingent travelled by way of Chicago to Fargo, North Dakota, where they donned their scarlet tunics, mounted nervous horses and set off on the first leg of what would be the Mounted Police's epic "March West."[39]

At least two popular myths about the well-known force deserve to be exploded. The first is that the police wore red coats because the Indians had special confidence in the traditional British uniform. The only British redcoats to serve in the West were 300 men of the 6th Foot at Fort Garry from 1846 to 1848. Other British and Canadian troops had worn dark green or more bizarre local costumes. The idea of scarlet tunics came from Governor Morris and, more insistently, from Colonel Robertson Ross, a noted devotee of military finery.[40] Despite the Prime Minister's promise about fuss and feathers, the Mounted Police in full dress soon resembled British dragoon guards. The uniform was elaborate, expensive, and, in the eyes of competent military critics, highly unsuitable.[41] A second myth surrounds the alleged alteration of the title of the force from Mounted Rifles to Mounted Police, presumably to soothe American anxieties about a military expedition along their northern border. The susceptibilities belonged to Sir John A. Macdonald, not the Americans. By 1874, when the NWMP was at last in existence, the Conservative leader was out of office. His successor, Alexander Mackenzie, was a dull, honest man with a major's commission in the militia. Frankly, he would have preferred a military force and a military expedition. Hewitt Bernard, the Deputy Minister of Justice and Macdonald's brother-in-law, had prepared the detailed scheme for the mounted police force and he refused to allow the project to be so cavalierly altered. The new Minister of Justice, A. A. Dorion, wanted the police patronage for his department and, as one of the few experienced members of the new government, he proved a formidable ally. The "mounted police" concept survived.[42]

The new Prime Minister also had to be talked out of an even more dangerous notion. Any major expedition, argued Mackenzie, should be conducted jointly with the Americans. They had the experience and the resources. Problems of law enforcement were their concern, too. A shocked Lord Dufferin headed off any such adventure into internationalism. Not only would Canadian pride be flattered by a national expedition but: "in the next place, we should appear upon the scene, not as the Americans have done, for the purpose of restraining and controlling the Indian tribes, but with a view of avenging injuries inflicted on the red man."[43] The Governor General was right on both counts. Thanks to inexperience and inadequate reconnaissance, the "March West" was a near-disaster but it immediately established the Mounted Police as a Canadian legend. Perhaps more important for its effectiveness in the ensuing ten years, the NWMP proved that it was not simply another regiment of U.S. cavalry. Scarlet jackets may have been inappropriate for hard service on the Prairies but they helped to establish a symbolic distinction between the force and its American counterpart in the eyes of western Canadians, white and Indian alike.

Uniforms and names would not have signified much to the Plains Indians if they had not symbolized more substantive differences in the role and outlook of the Mounted Police and their U.S. counterparts. American cavalrymen and Canadian policemen had much in common. Pay was meagre and often in arrears. Traders at military and police posts were equally rapacious. Barracks were often temporary shacks, ill-constructed, frigid in winter, and sometimes unsanitary. Arms and equipment were sometimes obsolete and often inappropriate for western conditions. Political influence in both countries pervaded every sphere of administration, from forage contracts to promotions. Officers in the NWMP often owed their commissions to party patronage and men in the ranks were by no means always the muscular, adventurous paragons of popular imagery.[44] In 1885, after a few months in the Northwest, General Fred Middleton reported to the Duke of Cambridge: "among them are some of the greatest scamps in the country, broken-down gentlemen who in many cases are called here inebriates, being sent here by their friends because no liquor is admitted in these territories." Since an important duty of the force was prevention of whiskey smuggling, it might be disturbing to learn from Middleton that it had "by no means a good character for sobriety."[45]

There were excellent officers and men in both the American and the Canadian forces in the West. Frontier conditions, hardship, and danger weeded out misfits and chronic failures. Veterans of the Mounted Police played a leading role in many western Canadian communities and their contribution to the economy of the ranching frontier has only begun to be explored.[46] Presumably comparable work is underway for officers and men discharged from the U.S. Army. However, the similarity in the strengths and deficiencies of the two organizations indicates that differences cannot be explained by special qualities in the officers and men nor by exemplary leadership and administration. If the Canadian and the American West developed differently, the sources of divergence must be found in time, law, and society.

By the time the North West Mounted Police took up its station in 1874, the outcome of the Indian struggle was really no longer in question. Bravado or gross miscalculation, as at the Little Big Horn, would be sharply punished. Able leadership and tactical skill would allow Chief Joseph and the Nez Perces to inflict setbacks on American military columns. However, most Canadian Indians, even the warlike Blackfoot Confederacy, could sense their relative safety on the north side of the Medicine Line. The NWMP was not very successful in capturing white exploiters of the Indian–they, too, could find immunity across an international frontier–but at least the force was eager to chase them away. The development of railroads, the concomitant increase in American military effectiveness, and the remorseless annihilation of the buffalo were settling the fate of the native people. By the time the Mounted Police arrived, the Indians of the Great Plains were looking for terms, not triumphs. Sent to administer and to accommodate, the police did not adopt the aggressive mode normal to soldiers nor did minor clashes inevitably produce a warlike response. Proudly military in style, the NWMP was a police force in tactics and attitude.[47]

In contrast to the United States, Canada's political system reinforced the power of the Mounted Police to provide satisfactory terms to the native people. While some American army officers sympathized with the Indians in their plight and sought to offer a paternal protection against white traders, ranchers, and land speculators, they could count on little support in Washington. The anti-militarism of most Americans, both pro-and anti-Indian, almost guaranteed sympathy for any self-professed victim of military tyranny. Far from condemning civilians for the misery inflicted on the Indian, the vocal humanitarians of the "Friends of the Indian" organizations in the East were prone to blame the Army. "The soldiers demoralize the Indian men by whiskey and cards and debauch the women," claimed former Indian agent Alfred B. Meacham in his famous series, "Abolish the Army," "and the officers insult the chiefs by their arrogant assumptions of superior power and authority."[48]

On the relatively rare occasions when Canadian politicians considered Indian affairs in this period, such sentiments might be echoed. George Landerkin, an Ontario Liberal, suggested benignly that the Indians might soon become civilized "if they were not menaced day by day by the force."[49] He was one of a minority of Opposition members who kept insisting that the Mounted Police had been a temporary expedient, to be disbanded when white settlement began in earnest. Significantly, only a few Canadian politicians and journalists, almost all of them in the East, ever condemned the enormous power confided in the NWMP;[50] the usual criticism was the annual cost of the force.

In the United States, eastern humanitarians and western expansionists might at least find common ground in condemning the tyranny or the inefficiency of the Army and its officers. Western interests were vehemently argued in state and territorial assemblies and in Congress. In Canada, the price of a tranquil West was apparently a benevolent police despotism, with the officers of the force sitting in judgement on charges laid by their men against white and Indian alike. Not until 1887 were the first members of an independent judiciary appointed for the Territories. In that year, the territorial council was transformed into an elected assembly; a further ten years would pass before the assembly won the cherished powers of responsible government. Paid and administered from Ottawa, the Mounted Police remained largely immune from local pressures and, as long as Sir John A. Macdonald was alive, it could depend on a powerful guardian against attempts to subvert its authority or discipline for political ends.[51] Settler hostility to the NWMP as a "whiskey police" or, during the 1885 campaign, as "gophers" was at least comparable to American criticism of the Army on the frontier: it did not substantially influence government policy. When Commissioner L. W. Herchmer was under remorseless fire from a swarm of angry western newspapers, an earnest suitor for his position was assured: "Sir John always stands by and defends an 'official' and makes every allowance for pecularities of temper and disposition-and I may say even unpopularity, provided the results of an official's actions are satisfactory."[52] However, even Macdonald's support might not have saved the force from united western anger. Instead, nowhere was it more vehemently defended.

In the decade between its arrival and the grim years before the 1885 outbreak, the NWMP could help the Indians adjust to the constraints of the treaty system with only occasional concern for the impact of white settlement. The early years-when the buffalo were still plentiful, the tribal structure still had resilience, and the police were sufficiently trusted that a couple of constables could make an arrest in the heart of an Indian camp-could not last. While Canadians had been suitably apprehensive about the arrival of Sitting Bull and his band of Sioux in the aftermath of the Little Big Horn, the ensuing relations between the Indians and Superintendent James Walsh rapidly became part of a self-congratulatory mythology for both Canadians and the NWMP.[53]

If Ottawa had shown some inventiveness in creating the NWMP, other features of its western policy bear a dreary resemblance to American practice. Canadian dealings with the Indian, with treaties, land surrenders, annuities, agents, and land reserves, bore a close family resemblance to American methods, if only because both were a heritage of pre-Revolutionary British administration.[54] Like the American Indian administration, the Canadian department was not immune from political patronage, speculation by minor officials, and ill-informed penny-pinching by remote bureaucrats like the notorious Lawrence Vankoughnet, Deputy Superintendent of Indian Affairs.[55] Faced with the enormous and unfamiliar responsibility for feeding the Indians following the failure of the buffalo, Ottawa and most of its agents were unequal to the task. The best of them, Cecil Denny, a former NWMP inspector, resigned in disgust. Pressed to reduce public spending, Ottawa officials found logical economics by reducing rations, substituting bacon for beef on the Blackfoot reserves, and dismissing junior employees.[56]

The era of starvation more than the advent of white settlement cost the NWMP its former standing with the native people. Obliged to defend insensitive and sometimes incompetent officials from the wrath of starving Indians, the force no longer appeared as an even-handed dispenser of justice. The influence of the chiefs, enormously elevated by the police to provide a convenient authority system, plummeted with the waning of the buffalo. By 1883, making an arrest required a small military operation. The arrival of the Canadian Pacific Railway and of speculators in the vast grazing lands suddenly opened by the government only aggravated a problem already created by destitution.[57]

In 1885 came the explosion. Still, the uprising was essentially a Metis rebellion, not an Indian war. Support for Louis Riel was concentrated in half-breed settlements near Prince Albert. Only in the Cree bands of Poundmaker and Big Bear were more than a minority of Indians involved. It was the white settlers, panic-stricken by memories of the Minnesota massacres or the Sioux wars of the 1870's, who fled to the police forts and who spread their terror by telegraph as far as Winnipeg. Only at Frog Lake, where nine whites and half-breeds were murdered, was the terror justified. Few Indians joined Louis Riel at Batoche; most pillaged whatever the settlers had abandoned and then waited nervously for a retribution they knew would follow. Within three months of the outbreak, the campaign was over with the loss of about eighty lives.[58]

For the NWMP, expanded to 500 men on the eve of the outbreak, the 1885 operations brought little glory. Most of the force, hurriedly concentrated in the troubled district, spent the campaign waiting for orders and protecting the white settlement at Prince Albert. At Fort Pitt, a timid Inspector Francis Dickens allowed civilian men, women, and children to surrender to the Indians and then loaded his men on a barge and fled downstream. At Battleford, in a fort jammed with able-bodied men, Inspector W. S. Morris used his telegraph wire to send piteous appeals for help. More redoubtable officers, like Superintendent Herchmer and Inspector Sam Steele, demonstrated unusual fortitude and leadership.[59] However, it is hard to disagree with General Middleton, the British officer responsible for bringing the campaign to an early conclusion, that, when good, well-trained troops were needed, the Mounted Police did not qualify.[60]

Middleton's solution was to transform the force into mounted infantry, clad in workmanlike Khaki and firmly under military discipline. Instead, it was as apparent to Canadians as it was to Americans that the era of Indian wars was over. In Parliament, there was now discernible pressure for the elimination of the Mounted Police, a possibility brought to a head in 1889 when the government proposed long-service pensions for members of the force.[61] At last, with the Indians planted disconsolately on their reserves, the tide of white settlement began to have political consequences for the NWMP. Liquor prohibition became the bitterest issue until licensing triumphed in 1892. "Why any Mounted Police Officer should dictate to any Canadian citizen as to what and when he should drink is more than any fellow can tell," complained the Fort MacLeod *Gazette* in 1887;[62] most westerners would have agreed. A constable, posted in full uniform to watch a notorious Prince Albert saloon, was arrested and fined $25 by a locally appointed magistrate. Another magistrate insisted that he had no proof that liquor was an intoxicant and turned Calgary into a wide-open town.[63] Since the force's own records indicate that some of its own senior officers were notoriously heavy drinkers, the struggle to keep the Canadian West dry was almost hopeless until the triumph of women's suffrage in 1916 brought a new army into the fray.[64]

Although the liquor issue provoked continual conflict within the NWMP and between the force and civilians, the prestige of the Mounted Police grew steadily. Exaggerated accounts of its prowess brought recruits from all corners of the British Empire and it became the beneficiary of the sentimental adulation that marked the late heyday of British imperialism. Commissioner L. W. Herchmer, appointed in 1886, may have been loathed by officers and men but he restored discipline, improved training, equipment, and welfare, and outfought most of his critics.[65] Of these, the most remorseless was Nicholas Flood Davin, poet, editor, and, after 1882, Member of Parliament for Assiniboia West. Davin's grievance began when Herchmer's brother fined him $50 for bringing liquor into the Territories,[66] but it easily encompassed the entire family and reached a climax in a sensational judicial investigation of 137 separate charges against the commissioner. Herchmer emerged with both honour and reputation intact. What is significant about the Davin charges is that the editor-politician felt obliged, for the sake of his political career, to accompany his assault on Herchmer with the most fulsome praise of the NWMP as a whole. Moreover, despite his claim that the commissioner was a tyrant, hated across the West, not a single western member of either party supported Davin.[67] One suspects that Davin would have found more friends if he had sat in the U.S. Congress attacking an army general.

The fundamental critics of the force, R. C. MacLeod has

argued, tended to come from western Ontario and to be heirs of the Clear Grit tradition with its clear links to American democratic ideology. The most articulate of them was David Mills, a former Liberal cabinet minister who had attempted in 1877 to negotiate Sitting Bull's return to the United States. Mills' philosophy was in evidence when he attacked the proposed police pension bill in 1889: "I say that a man who has served fifteen years and, much more, twenty-five years in the force, would be utterly unfit for any other pursuit in life afterwards. The hon. gentleman knows that a man who has served a great many years in the idle life of a soldier or policeman becomes, so far as industrial pursuits are concerned, a poor member of the community."[68] Later, Mills argued that interposing the police between the whites and the Indians and providing for their welfare frustrated the natural law of the survival of the fittest. The Americans, he insisted, had managed their Indians more wisely.[69]

Such a commitment to Social Darwinism, common enough in American debate on Indian policy, was rare in Canada. Indeed, there was relatively little debate in Parliament or elsewhere beyond the time-honoured propositions that economies could be made and that officials would be more prudent and successful if they were only chosen from the party not currently in power. The Indian as an equal citizen was hardly conceived save by idealists or radicals. In 1885, as part of an ingenious extension of the franchise, Macdonald proposed to include all Indians in the electorate. With a rebellion about to begin, the proposal could hardly have come at a less propitious moment and the absurdity of votes for Indians (as well as for certain categories of women) provided the Opposition with ammunition for a largely successful filibuster. However, it was apparent that Macdonald, like his critics, expected the native people to march to the polls not as independent yeomen but under the guidance of dependable Conservative agents and officials.[70]

When the Liberals finally returned to power in 1896, both the reserves policy and the Mounted Police survived the transition. In the aggressive campaign to attract immigrants to the Canadian West from the United States, Britain, and Europe, the presence of the firm, kindly authority of the force became a major selling point. Older settlers were reassured that the Mounted Police would guarantee that newcomers would rapidly appreciate and respect the principles of British justice. Discovery of gold in the Klondike gave the NWMP a new frontier just as the old one was running out. Canadians could soon take appropriate pride in the relative order and respectability of Dawson in the Yukon in contrast to the sordid regime of "Soapy" Smith at Skagway.[71]

Pressed by jeering Tories in 1897 to state whether power had indeed changed his party's attitude to the Mounted Police, the new Liberal Prime Minister rose to the bait. He was, Sir Wilfrid Laurier confessed, "inclined to be rather conservative with regard to this force."[72] So were most Canadians. Perhaps the Mounted Police deserved only incidental credit for avoiding Indian wars in Canada: it was the U.S. Army that demonstrated the invincibility of white weapons. It was easier to mediate the contact of white and Indian when the settlers came in a trickle, not an expected flood. Examined closely, there was little to choose between the blue-clad soldiers below the border and the red-coated Canadian policemen. Both were shabbily treated by government; both could furnish ample evidence of human frailty; both lived at odds with the surrounding communities, white and Indian.

Many nations are in love with their army; fondness for a police force is so rare as almost to be a perversion. For Canadians, the excuse must be that, almost absent-mindedly, they had created a national institution in a country that has very few. By the turn of the century, Canadians took extraordinary pride in offering the world the "last, best West." They could be excused for believing that their Mounted Police had made it so.[73]

NOTES

1. Paul F. Sharp, *Whoop-up Country: The Canadian American West, 1865-1885* (Minneapolis, 1955, 2 vols.).
2. Paul F. Sharp, "Three Frontiers: Some Comparative Studies of Canadian, American and Australian Settlement," *Pacific Historical Review*, XXIV (1955), 373.
3. See Roy W. Meyer, "The Canadian Sioux: Refugees from Minnesota," in Roger L. Nichols and George R. Adams, eds., *The American Indian: Past and Present* (Waltham, Mass., 1971), for a generous account. On Canadian Indians, see G. F. G. Stanley, "The Indian Background of Canadian History," Canadian Historical Association, *Historical Papers*, 1952; Heather Robertson, *Reservations are for Indians* (Toronto, 1970); Harold Cardinal, *The Unjust Society: The Tragedy of Canadian Indians* (Edmonton, 1971).
4. See, for example, the essays in William Kilbourn, ed., *Canada: The Peaceable Kingdom* (Toronto, 1971).

5. See, for example, S. W. Horrall, "Sir John A. Macdonald and the Mounted Police Force for the Northwest Territories," *CHR,* LIII (1972), 179-80. To illustrate, see D. G. Creighton, *Dominion of the North* (Toronto, 1957, rev. ed.), 360; Douglas Hill, *The Opening of the Canadian West* (London, 1967), 133. A perceptive study of one of the most celebrated police-Indian counters, Inspector James Walsh and Sitting Bull, is C. Frank Turner, *Across the Medicine Line* (Toronto, 1973).
6. Russell F. Weigley, *History of the United States Army* (New York, 1967), 267. Canadian engagements would include Duck Lake, Fish Creek, Cut Knife Hill, Batoche, and Frenchman's Butte, all in 1885, with perhaps the battle with Almighty Voice in 1897 as a final conflict.
7. Sharp, "Three Frontiers," 373.
8. Robert M. Utley, *Frontier Regulars: The United States Army and the Indian, 1866-1891* (New York, 1973), 55-6. The sparsity was certainly striking. In 1880, the Dakotas boasted 133,147 people while the 1881 census found only 6,974 whites and Metis in the entire Canadian Northwest. See G. F. G. Stanley, *The Birth of Western Canada: A History of the Riel Rebellions* (Toronto, 1961, rev. ed.), 187. The significance of the Metis as a mediating force in white-Indian relations also appears to have little United States counterpart.
9. See, for example, President Jackson's response to the decision in Worcester v. Georgia, 1832. On American Indian policy, see Francis P. Prucha, *American Indian Policy in the Formative Years* (Cambridge, Mass., 1962); Lorring Benson Priest, *Uncle Sam's Stepchildren* (New Brunswick, N.J., 1942; Lincoln, Neb., 1969).
10. John Jennings, "The Plains Indians and the Law," in Hugh A. Dempsey, ed., *Men in Scarlet* (Calgary [1974]), 50, 54.
11. R. C. MacLeod, *The North-West Mounted Police and Law Enforcement, 1873-1905* (Toronto, 1976), 4-6 and *passim*.
12. On the U.S. Army officers and Indian-white relations, see, for example, Robert G. Athearn, "War Paint against Brass: The Army and the Plains Indians," *Montana: The Magazine of Western History*, VI (1956); Priest, *Uncle Sam's Stepchildren*, ch. II; Robert M. Utley, "The Celebrated Peace Policy of General Grant," *North Dakota History*, XX (July, 1953).
13. On the Dawes Act, see Priest, *Uncle Sam's Stepchildren,* chs. XIII-XIX; William T. Hagan, *American Indians* (Chicago, 1961), 139-48.
14. On Canadian political attitudes, see, for example, Bruce W. Hodgins, "Democracy and the Ontario Fathers of Confederation," in *Profiles of a Province* (Toronto, 1967), 83-91.
15. Cited in R. C. Brown, "Canadian Opinion after Confederation," in S. F. Wise and R. C. Brown, eds., *Canada Views the United States: Nineteenth Century Political Attitudes* (Seattle, 1967), 113.

16. "The rights of the minority must be protected, and the rich are always fewer in number than the poor." (Macdonald's comment on the proposed Canadian Senate, 6 April, 1865, *Confederation Debates.*)
17. Jennings, "Indians and the Law," 51.
18. PAC, Aberdeen Papers, Journal of Lady Aberdeen, 5 August 1895.
19. Horrall, "A Mounted Police Force," 185-8.
20. See, for example, A. C. Gluek, *Minnesota and the Manifest Destiny of the Canadian North West* (Toronto, 1965).
21. On the implications of the British withdrawal, see C. P. Stacey, *Canada and the British Army, 1846-1871* (Toronto, 1963, rev. ed.); and J. M. Hitsman, *Safeguarding Canada, 1763-1871* (Toronto, 1968), ch. X.
22. Utley, *Frontier Regulars*, ch. VIII, esp. 355.
23. Horrall, "A Mounted Police Force," 180-1. The twenty million dollars spent annually on Indian wars by Congress was comparable to Canada's entire federal budget. MacLeod, *Mounted Police*, 3.
24. Cited by P. B. Waite, *The Life and Times of Confederation* (Toronto, 1962), 307. The most thorough treatment of defence considerations in Canada's policy in the Northwest remains C. P. Stacey's "The Military Aspect of Canada's Winning of the West, 1870-1885," *CHR*, XXI (1940), 1-24.
25. E. E. Rich, *Hudson's Bay Company*, vol. III, *1821-1870* (Toronto, 1960), 542. See also A. S. Morton, *A History of the Canadian West to 1870-71* (Toronto, 1973, 2nd ed.), 809; A. C. Gluek, "Imperial Protection for the Trading Interest of the Hudson's Bay Company, 1857-1861," *CHR*, XXXVII (1956), 119-40.
26. Horrall, "Mounted Police Force," 181. See also MacLeod, *Mounted Police*, 8-11.
27. On the Manitoba Force, see Stacey, "Military Aspect," 15-18.
28. Stanley, *Western Canada*, 164-6.
29. *Ibid.*, ch. VI.
30. See C. P. Stacey, "The Second Red River Expedition, 1871," *Canadian Defence Quarterly* (January, 1931), 1ff.
31. See PAC, Macdonald Papers, vol. 329, Return to Parliament, 1884, 148570-2. On the raid, see J. P. Pritchett, "The Origin of the So-called Fenian Raid on Manitoba in 1871," *CHR,* X (1929); Stacey, "Military Aspect," 12-14.
32. J. L. Taylor, "The Development of an Indian Policy for the Canadian North West, 1869-79" (Ph.D. thesis, Queen's University, Kingston, 1976), 56 and *passim*. See Alexander Morris, *The Treaties of Canada with the Indians* (Toronto, 1880), 32 ("Military display has always a great effect on savages, and the presence, even of a few troops, will have a good tendency," in A. G. Archibald's report on Treaty No. 2).
33. See W. F. Butler, *The Great Lone Land* (London, 1872); Edward

McCourt, *Remember Butler: The Story of Sir William Butler* (London, 1967), ch. VI; Colonel Patrick Robertson Ross, "Reconnaissance of the North West Provinces and Indian Territories of the Dominion of Canada . . .," Canada, *Sessional Papers*, 1873, no. 9, cvii-cxxvii.

34. On Macdonald in this period, see D. G. Creighton, *John A. Macdonald: The Old Chieftain* (Toronto, 1955), 111-79. The Prime Minister's best known nickname, "Old Tomorrow," was given by Commissioner A. G. Irvine of the NWMP in 1881.
35. Canada, House of Commons, *Debates* (reported in the Toronto *Globe*), 3 May 1873. See also *ibid.*, 31 March 1873.
36. Horrall, "Mounted Police Force," 192-3.
37. *Ibid.*, 192-4; Taylor, "Indian Policy," 88-114.
38. PAC, Macdonald Papers, vol. 523, Macdonald to Dufferin, 24 September 1873.
39. On the trek, see S. W. Horrall, "The March West," in Dempsey, *Men in Scarlet*, 13-26, reviewing the literature.
40. On Robertson Ross, see D. P. Morton, *Ministers and Generals: Politics and the Canadian Militia, 1868-1904* (Toronto, 1970), 25-6. See also PAC, Macdonald Papers, vol. 252, Morris to Macdonald, 17 January 1873.
41. See Royal Archives, Windsor, Cambridge Papers, Middleton to Duke of Cambridge, 31 July 1885.
42. Horrall, "Mounted Police Force," 198-9.
43. Public Record Office, London, Kimberley Papers, Dufferin to Kimberley, 24 December 1873.
44. Ronald Atkin, *Maintain the Right: The Early History of the North West Mounted Police, 1873-1900* (London, 1973), 124-36, 257-69, giving the best brief review of conditions of service. See also J. P. Turner, *The North West Mounted Police* (Ottawa, 1950, 2 vols.), *passim*, together with many personal memoirs of service in the Force. On patronage and politics, see MacLeod, *Mounted Police*, ch. VII.
45. Cambridge Papers, Middleton to Cambridge, 31 July 1885.
46. D. H. Breen, "The Mounted Police and the Ranching Frontier," in Dempsey, *Men in Scarlet*, 115-37.
47. See MacLeod, *Mounted Police*, ch. VIII.
48. See Arthur A. Ekirch, Jr., *The Civilian and the Military: A History of American Anti-Militarist Tradition* (Colorado Springs, 1972), 115. See also Francis P. Prucha, *Americanizing the American Indian: Writings by the "Friends of the Indian," 1880-1900* (Cambridge, Mass., 1973).
49. Canada, House of Commons, *Debates*, 1 September 1891, 4820.
50. R. C. MacLeod, "The Mounted Police and Politics," in Dempsey, *Men in Scarlet*, 101-5.
51. Jennings, "Indians and the Law," 57-65.

52. Fred White to Colonel W. D. Otter, 18 May 1890, cited in Desmond Morton, *The Canadian General: Sir William Otter* (Toronto, 1974), 139.
53. Turner, *Medicine Line*; "Sitting Bull Tests the Mettle of the Redcoats," in Dempsey, *Men in Scarlet*, 67-76. See also S. W. Horrall, *The Pictorial History of the Royal Canadian Mounted Police* (Toronto, 1973), 70-4; MacLeod, *Mounted Police*, 30-2.
54. Taylor, "Indian Policy," 19-22; Morris, *Treaties*, 9-12, 16.
55. See Stanley, *Western Canada*, ch. XIII; Hugh A. Dempsey, *Crowfoot: Chief of the Blackfeet* (Edmonton, 1972), 108-45.
56. C. E. Denny, *The Law Marches West* (Toronto, 1972, 2nd ed.), 204-5; Dempsey, *Crowfoot*, 161-2.
57. Atkin, *Maintain the Right*, 196-211. See *Settlers and Rebels: Official Reports of the North-West Mounted Police, 1882-1885* (facsimile edition, Toronto, 1973), *passim*.
58. On the campaign, see Stanley, *Western Canada*, 327-80; Desmond Morton, *The Last War Drum: The North West Campaign of 1885* (Toronto, 1972); and, from the viewpoint of a contemporary participant, C. A. Boulton, *Reminiscences of the North-West Rebellions* (Toronto, 1886).
59. See Atkin, *Maintain the Right*, 217-53.
60. On Middleton and the NWMP during the 1885 campaign, see PAC, Caron Papers, vol. 199, Middleton to Caron, 2 May 1885. See also Canada, Department of Militia and Defence, *Report upon the Suppression of the Rebellion in the North-West Territories and Matters in Connection Therewith in 1885* (Canada, Sessional Papers, 1886, no. 6a), 5; Desmond Morton and R. H. Roy, eds., *Telegrams of the North-West Campaign, 1885* (Toronto, 1972), lxxxi, xcii, 230, 357.
61. Canada, House of Commons, *Debates*, 21 March 1889; 15 April 1889. See MacLeod, "Mounted Police and Politics," 103-4.
62. Fort MacLeod *Gazette*, 21 February 1887.
63. Atkin, *Maintain the Right*, 274-7.
64. On the later history of the issue and correction of the notion of a quiet, law-abiding Canadian West, see J. H. Gray, *Booze: The Impact of Whiskey on the Prairie West* (Toronto, 1972); and his *Red Lights on the Prairie* (Toronto, 1971). See MacLeod, *Mounted Police*, ch. X.
65. Atkin, *Maintain the Right*, 257-73; R. B. Deane, *Mounted Police Life in Canada: A Record of Thirty-One Years' Service, 1883-1914* (London, 1916), 30-42.
66. On Davin, see MacLeod, "Mounted Police and Politics," 99-105.
67. The Davin debate may be found in Canada, House of Commons, *Debates*, 31 March 1890, 2674-99.
68. *Ibid.*, 21 March 1889, 770.
69. *Ibid*,, 16 May 1892, 2688.

70. On the Indian franchise, see J. E. Chamberlin, *The Harrowing of Eden: White Attitudes Toward North American Natives* (Toronto, 1975), 200-2 and *passim*; Morris Davis and Joseph Krauter, *The Other Canadians* (Toronto, 1971), 12-14. The Indian franchise was withdrawn by the Liberals in 1898.
71. Atkin, *Maintain the Right*, 298-359. A personal account with appropriate flourishes is S. B. Steele, *Forty Years in Canada: Reminiscences of the Great North-West* (London, 1915), 288-337.
72. Canada, House of Commons, *Debates*, 10 May 1897, 2039.
73. MacLeod, "Mounted Police and Politics," 113.

V
Social Control

In this essay Wendy Mitchinson takes us to the centre of the middle-class women's social reform movement. The Woman's Christian Temperance Union was undoubtedly the most successful of the various women's organizations in late nineteenth-century Canada. Crusading militantly for temperance measures, women found themselves active in political life. As Mitchinson argues, support for suffrage followed naturally. Equally important, however, is the rationale which underlay the WCTU's notions of social reform and subsequently their arguments for the vote. This "maternal feminism," which bestowed upon women a special female responsibility for "cleaning up" society, ironically incorporated much of the sexual stereotyping of the age. In addition, it was often based on questionable socio-biological concepts derived from British social thinker, Herbert Spencer. This tendency would later undercut much of the radicalism implicit in the early women's movement.

There has been a considerable debate in women's history about overall evaluation of conservative elements of the women's movement such as the WCTU. Clearly associated with the middle class, elements of the women's movement paved the way for the social reformism of the Progressive period at the beginning of the twentieth century. The reforms passed then, while ameliorating some of the worst evils of industrial capitalist development, did little to change the underlying causes of those problems. Or so, some historians have argued. Mitchinson here chooses to put a more positive value on the achievements of these women.

FURTHER READING:

Other historians, writing in the American context very recently, have credited feminism as the major source of the Progressive movement itself. See, for example, William Leach, *True Love and Perfect Union: The Feminist Reform of Sex and Society* (New York, 1980). Christopher Lasch has associated middle-class feminism with the rise of the twentieth-century "expert" on the family and other social problems. The later development of what he terms "the therapeutic state" he sees in movements such as the one described here. See Christopher Lasch, *Haven in a Heartless World* (New York, 1977); and Lasch, *The Culture of Narcissism* (New York, 1978). Whether these arguments apply in Canada remains to be seen.

On women and social reform, see Linda Kealey, ed., *A Not Unreasonable Claim* (Toronto, 1979); Veronica Strong-Boag, *Parliament of Women: The National Council of Women of Canada 1893-1929* (Ottawa, 1976); and W. R. Morrison, " 'Their Proper Sphere': Feminism, the Family and Child-centered Social Reform in Ontario 1875-1900," *Ontario History,* 68 (1976), 45-74. The classic work on the Canadian suffrage movement is Catherine Cleverdon, *The Women's Suffrage Movement in Canada* (Toronto, 1950).

Wendy Mitchinson is an historian at the University of Windsor specializing in women's history and, more recently, in medical history.

The WCTU: "For God, Home, and Native Land": A Study of Nineteenth-Century Feminism

by Wendy Mitchinson

The organizational woman is a familiar phenomenon today whether she belongs to a feminist group, a church society, or one of a myriad of other women's organizations. But this was not always the case. In the early part of the nineteenth century women were seldom organized, prevented by distance, poor transportation facilities, and lack of time. Only the more privileged could overcome these obstacles and those who did tended to form local church and benevolent societies. By 1900, however, this situation had altered greatly. Women's organizations had increased in number: many continued the work of the church and benevolent societies that had formed earlier in the century; others formed to provide new expressive outlets for women; still others organized to reform what women saw as problems in society. All represented the ability and desire of many Canadian women to become active outside the domestic sphere.[1]

Several reasons account for this extraordinary expansion of women's activities: transportation had improved, making it easier for groups of women to meet together; towns and cities were growing in size, thus enlarging the membership potential of women's groups; and the increasing affluence of Canadian society meant that more middle-class women had leisure time to devote to women's organizations. In 1871, 81.2 per cent of the

From Linda Kealey, ed., *A Not Unreasonable Claim: Women and Reform in Canada, 1880s-1920s* (Toronto: Women's Press, 1979), 152-67.

Canadian population lived in areas classed as rural. By 1901 this had declined to 62.5 per cent. The greater population density of cities heightened the need for institutional responses on the part of society-orphanages, refuge homes, and hospitals-philanthropic areas in which women had long been involved. Cities also accentuated the problems of poverty, crime, and intemperance. Many Canadian women realized such problems could not be offset through traditional benevolent activities and responded by searching for the causes of these problems. The result was the formation of reform organizations designed to eradicate the source of a specific social ill and not simply to ameliorate its symptoms. The willingness of many women to become so involved reflected an important change that was occurring in their lives.[2]

Throughout the latter half of the nineteenth century, Canada was slowly emerging from a commercial to an industrialized society. At the same time it was becoming more urbanized. As both these processes occurred, the workplace became separated from the home, where women were increasingly isolated. The domestic isolation of women was complemented by what historians have referred to as the "cult of domesticity," the dominating image of which was "woman as mother." Ironically, as woman's prestige in society was being enhanced by her maternal role, the actual fertility of women was declining. In 1871 the registered legitimate fertility rate in Canada was similar to what it had been in the eighteenth century, 378 births per 1,000 women aged 15 to 49 years. By 1891, however, it had declined by 24 per cent to 285 births per 1,000 women aged 15 to 49 years. This decline was especially extreme in urban areas. Although women were having fewer children than had been the case earlier in the century, this did not necessarily lessen women's commitment to the domestic sphere; indeed, through an intensification of the mother-child relationship it may have increased it. Women were becoming, in fact as well as in ideal, the emotional centre of the home and family.[3]

Women may have had influence within the home but the ideal of domesticity certainly limited them outside it. The emergence of women from the domestic sphere through women's organizations was a response to their dissatisfaction with this situation. Many women wanted to preserve their status within and control of the family by becoming active in society. As well, the seeming increase in power and prestige that women had gained through the rise of the domestic ideal led to a desire to publicly assert and extend that power outside the home. The easiest way to accomplish this, given the context of Canadian society at the time, was to rationalize it by an appeal to domesticity.[4]

Women's reform organizations were one way in which Canadian women hoped to protect the family and assert themselves in an acceptable way. Each organization was initially formed to right a specific wrong, but once formed, each tended to involve itself in a number of reform enterprises. The Woman's Christian Temperance Union was such an organization. It provides an example of the emergence of women from the domestic sphere to an active participation in society.

FORMATION AND PLATFORM

The first local WCTU was formed in Ontario in 1874, the first provincial union in 1877 in Ontario, and the Dominion Union in 1883. By 1900, the Woman's Christian Temperance Union had approximately 10,000 members. This made the WCTU one of the largest women's organizations of the time and certainly much larger than any of the suffrage societies. As well, the WCTU was a truly national organization and was located in both small towns and urban centres across Canada, whereas the Dominion Women's Enfranchisement Association, the one national suffrage organization, was essentially based in Toronto.

The Union very early adopted prohibition as its main platform. While most reform organizations in the nineteenth century emphasized the importance of adjusting the individual to the existing norms of society, temperance organizations emphasized the adjustment of society to create an atmosphere of temperance for the individual. By mid-century, temperance advocates had concluded that voluntary appeal did not work. When the state of Maine introduced a compulsory temperance law–that is, prohibition–Canadian temperance advocates quickly followed its lead. Consequently, by the time the WCTU was formed in 1874, prohibition had become *the* weapon against intemperance. But because it depended on government support, its adoption by the WCTU paved the way to an eventual confrontation between the temperance union and the elected representatives of male society, if and when the latter refused to adopt prohibition.[5]

The WCTU had few qualms about supporting prohibition. Its

members believed it to be a radical reform but an essential one. The atrocities of war were negligible beside the atrocities of the liquor trade. As a foe of morality "it turns men into demons, and makes women an easy prey to lust." Because the majority of convicted criminals were known to drink, the WCTU concluded that alcohol caused crime and argued that supporting such a criminal population was uneconomical. Intemperance was ruining the physical health of Canadians as well, one member of the WCTU even linking the spread of cholera with the consumption of alcohol. The statistics of alcohol consumption served only to increase these fears. In 1871 the total alcohol consumption per capita, 15 years of age and older, was 1.19 imperial gallons, rising to 1.29 in 1873 and in 1874, the year in which the WCTU formed, to 1.42. WCTU members were convinced something had to be done to prevent the terrible toll in human suffering that this increase represented to them.[6]

They believed women, as innocent victims of an invasion of alcohol into their homes, suffered most from the liquor trade, and they exploited this appeal to the fullest. "How can Christian women sit still and be quiet while women's cries for help are in their ears?" they asked. Children's cries were also heard. The Children's Aid Society in Vancouver noted in its first annual report that, with one exception, "Every case which has been brought before us had been brought about through drink." Temperance women felt they had a special duty as women to protect these children. Certainly men did not seem willing to do anything about alcohol abuse, perhaps because they were the main consumers of alcohol and profiteers from the liquor trade. The WCTU believed most women did not drink. Where men were seemingly unable to act, then, women could and would. A social ill such as intemperance could not be kept isolated; it reached out and affected temperate and intemperate alike. It had to be stopped.[7]

The WCTU was not particularly concerned about the individual inebriate – the union had neither the resources nor the time to help individuals. They were more concerned with the effects of intemperance on society, the way in which the inebriate hurt innocent people such as his wife and children, and the way in which he undermined the strength of society.

Blaming alcohol for society's ills was a comfortable belief. It did not threaten the economic status of the temperance women or their families because they did not talk about intemperance in personal terms. In fact, their belief in prohibition was a reflection of their class status. Most executive members of the WCTU were married to lawyers, businessmen, doctors, journalists, and clergymen. Considering the connection temperance women made between intemperance, crime, and sexual immorality, it is not surprising that they saw in intemperance a challenge to their middle-class way of life. It was the foreign element in an otherwise ordered society.[8]

THE POLITICIZATION PROCESS

Only the state, through legislation, could ensure a temperate society. To persuade the various levels of government to respond, the WCTU became actively involved in the public sphere. Its members believed they had a responsibility as *women* to protect not only their own but all homes.[9]

One of the WCTU's methods was the use of petitions. They were circulated for signatures, then forwarded to the appropriate level of government in the hope that once officials realized there was a good deal of support for prohibition, they would act. This naive view of the democratic process assumed a common morality for all and, in fact, the existence of an absolute "right" in society, a notion which derived from a fundamentalist interpretation of Christian morality and the members' own political inexperience.[10]

These petitions did have limited success. Through them, governments became aware of the demand for prohibition, and usually responded by granting a plebiscite on the question. The plebiscite was a good tactic, for it allowed Canadians to inform the government of their views on a controversial problem on which the government was hesitant to act. If supported by an overwhelming majority, plebiscites permitted the government to act with few fears of political reprisals. Prohibition was undoubtedly a controversial question. It not only attracted opposition from the liquor interests, but also from those opposed to government intervention in the day-to-day lives of individuals, especially in a practice that was as widespread as drinking was in the nineteenth century.

Petitions and plebiscites were the high points in the preventive public work of the WCTU. They both legitimized temperance work and forced Canadians to consider the question of control.

Generally the WCTU's activity was more mundane. Members painstakingly distributed literature and called on electors to vote for temperance advocates. They appealed to "their fathers, husbands, brothers, sons and friends who possessed the right of suffrage to exercise this right in the interest of temperance and total abstinence." The WCTU approached clergymen, church members, teachers of Sunday schools and public schools, and heads of organizations such as the Knights of Labor, requesting them to use their influence to dissuade people from drinking. It asked doctors to stop prescribing liquor as medicine. Members tried to persuade anyone in a position of prestige to recognize their work, or any part of it, thus using their influence as women in a very traditional way, that is, through moral suasion.[11]

Yet they did not limit themselves to this tactic. The WCTU was so determined to achieve prohibition that it even gave guarded support to a new political party. In March 1888, through the efforts of male temperance organizations, Canada's New Party was formed. Soon afterwards, in the WCTU publication, the *Woman's Journal,* Mrs. Rockwell, a prominent member of the Union, appealed to her readers to use their "influence with husbands, fathers and brothers, for the first and only Political Party committed to the accomplishment of the prohibition of the liquor traffic." The Dominion WCTU resolved to give "individual support to the party which will unequivocally put the plan of Prohibition in its platform." This resolution could only apply to the New Party; however, the party floundered. Old party loyalties remained entrenched and, as the corresponding secretary of the Ontario WCTU reported, "Politics first, politics last, politics everytime, each party afraid of the temperance question."[12]

This was proven again and again. In provincial plebiscites in Manitoba, Prince Edward Island, Ontario, and Nova Scotia, prohibition seemed, to the WCTU, overwhelmingly endorsed; yet the respective governments did nothing. Unfortunately for the temperance women, greater disillusionment lay ahead.

In 1896 the Liberal Party under Wilfrid Laurier promised a national plebiscite on prohibition. Great excitement pervaded the temperance forces. As the president of the Nova Scotia WCTU declared,

> The question of Prohibition is at last a Political issue. Not as a weak, struggling Third Party, but a live question with which both parties feel that they must deal whether they will or

> not. . . . The world is turning to our country today, with great interest for a solution of the Liquor Question. It is nearer a solution with us than anywhere else on earth.[13]

The women naturally felt they should be able to vote in the plebiscite. When this was refused, even the Nova Scotia WCTU, usually more quiescent than others about the enfranchisement of women, showed its exasperation.

> Dear women, are we free and intelligent citizens of a civilized country, or are we the irresponsible nonentities that our government reckons us? If the former in the name of all that is just and right in the name of all that is pure and lovely and of good report; in the name of God and home and humanity, let us rise and claim the citizen's heritage–the right of self-government! If the latter then may we write 'failure,' not only of the cause of prohibition, but of every other righteous reform for the stream never rises above the mothers of men. If they be 'small, slight . . . miserable,' how shall we grow?

Once again the women argued that they should be allowed to enter society in order to protect their homes; moreover, as the domestic force in society they should be encouraged to do so. Many of these women were becoming increasingly frustrated and bitter about being dependent on men to determine the nature of the society in which they lived. They used all the power they had as women to obtain a favourable result, but in the end they could only watch while men voted. The plebiscite took place on September 28, 1898. Every province with the exception of Quebec voted for prohibition, for a net majority of 13,687. The temperance forces felt this was a victory; the government, whose support lay in the province of Quebec, did not.[14]

With this defeat the women of the WCTU lost their faith that governments act in the best interests of the people. In their eyes, prohibition was never a question of individual rights but of moral rights, and it believed no government had the power to make what was morally wrong a legal right. The state was an active agent in society and as such had a responsibility to do "not what shall punish wrong-doing so much as what shall tend to right doing." The Canadian government legalized the liquor trade and, "for a price, for revenue, makes the whole nation, women and all, party to its own degradation." The only solution was for temperance women to have representation at all levels of government.[15]

One reform essential to this process was the enfranchisement of women. Appealing to the good will of men in power had failed. The alternative, then, was for women to represent themselves. By supporting a controversial reform, the WCTU women had confronted their own lack of power as women. With their espousal of suffrage they went on record as supporting two of the most controversial reforms of nineteenth-century Canada. From a desire to protect their homes through the protection of society, these Canadian temperance women had come far. One way in which they met the challenge was to hold fast to the traditional concept of themselves as women, that is, they did not support suffrage as a right owed to them as individuals, but as a useful means by which to meet their feminine responsibility – the care of the family.

THE WCTU, WOMEN'S SUFFRAGE, AND A SENSE OF IDENTITY

The WCTU had not always supported the enfranchisement of women. In the early years of organization Letitia Youmans, WCTU president, deliberately avoided the issue of women's rights and stressed the protection of home and children. In this way she hoped to gain support for the Union.

> So strong was the opposition in Canada to what was commonly termed 'women's rights,' that I had good reason to believe that should I advocate the ballot for women in connection with my temperance work, it would most effectively block the way, and it was already uphill work for a woman to appear on a public platform.[16]

In the 1870's the suffrage question had been a divisive issue. By the 1890's, after the WCTU had come face to face with government intransigence, it was acknowledged as *the* weapon against the liquor interests.

The WCTU stressed the good that would result if women were given the vote. Mrs. Jacob Spence, first superintendent of the Ontario WCTU's Franchise Department and mother of Canadian temperance leader F. S. Spence, explained the reasons best:

> It is not the clamor of ambition, ignorance or frivolity trying to gain position. It is the prayer of earnest, thoughtful, Christian women in behalf of their children and their children's children. It is in the interest of our homes, our divinely-appointed place, to protect the home against the licensed evil which is the enemy of the home, and also to aid in our efforts to advance God's kingdom beyond the bounds of our homes.
>
> It is only by legislation that the roots of great evils can be touched, and for want of the ballot we stand powerless in face of our most terrible foe, the legalized liquor traffic. The liquor sellers are not afraid of our conventions, but they are afraid of our ballots.

The appeal to woman's maternal role attracted many women who might otherwise have rejected such a reform. Home and family were the cornerstones of society; an attack on one was an attack on the other.[17]

The connection between prohibition and votes for women was made clear. Where it was not, support for the franchise was weakened. In the Maritimes, for example, there seemed to be little concern over the ballot except among the WCTU, and even this was negligible when compared to other provincial unions. One reason was that the Maritimes, more than the other provinces, took advantage of the Scott Act, the local option law, with the result that they had the lowest per capita alcohol consumption in Canada. Because of this virtual prohibition in the Maritimes, the connection between temperance and the enfranchisement of women could not be easily made. There, only the justice argument for suffrage remained. It was a political appeal, one that suggested a challenge to the established order that would force women out from behind their concerns of home and family into the world. Few women in the nineteenth century identified with this concept, for it negated the altruism which was seen as the source of their influence in Canadian society.

The struggle for the franchise was the epitome of the temperance women's confidence in themselves, a confidence which had emerged only slowly. In the early years they were very hesitant, even to the point of discussing whether a woman should lead a public prayer unless careful scrutiny of the audience revealed the absence of men. Such timidity was understandable. The WCTU had formed at a time when women were not used to speaking in public, and although this timidity lessened as the women learned to run meetings and publicly express themselves, it never disappeared. Certainly their attitude toward working with men remained ambivalent. On the one hand, they encouraged men's support through honorary memberships and the occasional men's auxiliaries. On the other hand, men were not allowed to vote in their meetings. There were other men's-only and mixed temperance organizations, but there was only one *Woman's* Christian Temperance Union. Its members formed a wholly female society in which they were comfortable and in which their individual efforts were recognized.[18]

The campaign for prohibition was a significant one for the temperance women. The liquor interests represented "the heaviest monied monopoly on the continent. It has an outpost in every town. It cows legislation. Its grip is upon the throttle valve of all political enginery." To counter such evil, the women of the WCTU had to be strong. Their special mission allowed no compromise, even to attract new members.

> I have heard it hinted by some, by both within and without our fold, that our burning need was an influx of the upper tendom, 'to give tone to the movement,' to popularize it. If the money and influence secured in this way were not counter-balanced by some shrinkage of our principles, to accommodate the less rigid notions of those educated to a polite tolerance of wrong, we would doubtless be the gainers. Yet, the 'if' is a large and serious one. It is to be feared that the Dons would have more to get than to give. The common people have ever been the bond and sinew of successful revolution, whether in morals or estates.[19]

The revolution they wanted was one of morals and attitudes. It was a world where their position as leaders would be recognized and where they would receive the accolades which normally went to "society" women. As one member explained, "While we believe there are many good women leading a social life, yet we believe no true woman whose spiritual sensibilities have not been benumbed by habit and custom, finds in this a satisfying portion." A woman was to be admired for what she did herself and not for her husband or family connections. This belief provided these organizational women with a feeling of unity and devotion to one another and to their leaders.[20]

This feeling of solidarity is evident in the following description of Frances Willard, president of the American and World WCTU. One member of the Canadian WCTU recalled with quiet reverence her first contact with Miss Willard:

> At the first appearance of her calm sweet face, I was enraptured and before she had closed, her thrilling words and the spirit within her had so filled my heart that I too would have been more than willing to have left all and followed her. . . . As I look back through the vista of years to this first knowledge of Miss Willard, I think I have a dim realization of the feelings of the disciples when our Master and Saviour stood revealed to them in all purity and truth of His manhood and called to them 'come and follow me.'

Feminine friendships were particularly strong in the nineteenth century because women were expected to remain within their own, separate sphere. In the rarefied atmosphere of women's organizations, women could find congenial company and develop friendships which, as revealed by the love shown to Frances Willard, were very deep. Such devotion and trust in one another and their leaders was also necessary. WCTU members faced great opposition to their advocacy of prohibition and suffrage and they undoubtedly found needed support in these friendships.[21]

THE STRUGGLE FOR A MORAL SOCIETY

Support for women's suffrage did not negate the belief in separate spheres for men and women. Temperance women made it clear that their espousal of suffrage did not make them "new" women. "A man is to a woman and a woman is to a man, a stronghold; a completeness such as no two women or two men ever can be to one another," they declared. Mothers were urged to train their daughters in the duties of housekeeping. The Union stressed the adoption of manual training in schools to ensure that children received the practical skills requisite for their future careers; in the case of girls this meant domestic science. Better fulfilment of the domestic role even justified support for higher education. The WCTU also advocated the appointment of female school trustees, factory inspectors, physicians at girls' reformatories, matrons, bailiffs, and police matrons. The limited acceptance of these demands resulted in the creation of new work roles that extended women's participation and involvement in society and did so on a premise which most could accept, that is, the domestic ideal of woman.[22]

The women of the WCTU also wanted to protect children. The British Columbia WCTU endeavoured to secure a Children's Protection Act similar to the one in Ontario; the Dominion WCTU supported the establishment of cottage homes as reformatories for boys and girls so that juvenile offenders could be reformed in a home atmosphere; and several provincial WCTU's tried to institute curfew bells which would ring at a certain hour, usually nine o'clock, after which time no child was to be on the street unless accompanied by parent or guardian. The WCTU hoped a curfew would prevent late hours, "that most subtle of stimulants," and thus lessen the number of children who would be tempted to drink. It began to realize, however, that curfew bells only controlled the actions of children to a limited extent, whereas education encouraged them to voluntarily restrain their actions, and in 1896 the women of the New Brunswick WCTU supported compulsory education for this reason. Education for its own sake was not their goal, but it could offset a bad home influence and teach children to be well-behaved.[23]

The WCTU was equally concerned about young girls and women. Its members felt that all girls did not have the advantages of a decent home life and a loving and protecting mother, and as mothers themselves they wanted to help them. They believed that young girls kept ignorant about the beginnings of life were especially vulnerable and urged that mothers and educators be honest about sex, arguing that ignorance was not a protector of purity but a weapon against it. Society was seen by them as dangerous to women; man was the seducer, woman his victim, and unfortunately, the law favoured the former. The WCTU of British Columbia pointed out that the law did not appear concerned with the protection of girls since it allowed them to give sexual consent at the age of sixteen, yet did not prosecute the seducer until the age of twenty-one. The WCTU protested that when police raided houses of ill fame only the names of the prostitutes were published. It demanded that the names of the men be published as well, so that respectable women would know which men to shun.[24]

In many areas the WCTU was over-zealous, its members responding in a drastic way to what appeared harmless to most Canadians at the time. Concern for the moral health of society led them to condemn certain styles of evening dress, round dances, nude art, gambling, theatre, prize fights, and the use of women as bar maids. For members of the WCTU these were serious problems which had dire consequences.

> What had produced the almost numberless bands of young thieves, murderers, and train-wreckers, of whom we read in every day's paper? Dime novels, indiscriminately sold. . . .
>
> Why are there so many divorces among young married people, now-a-days, where they have not the Bible ground of excuse to plead. Distorted views of life gathered from the trashy novel, where the heroes are all strong, tender and wealthy, and the heroines are beautiful, pure, and loving. Real life proves a different thing, and there is not strength of character to meet and bear the common discipline of plain human nature.

The WCTU invited confrontation in its advocacy of prohibition and suffrage. Because of the continued rejection by the majority of Canadians of their two central reforms, WCTU members developed a siege mentality. They saw the foundations of their world – that is, the sanctity of the home – attacked on all sides. As a result, they became more entrenched in their own principles.[25]

Any compromise in the struggle for a moral society was unthinkable. The WCTU protested vehemently when the British government reintroduced the Contagious Diseases Act, whereby brothels were legally licensed. When Isabella Somerset, vice-president of the World WCTU, apparently approved of the Act, she was criticized severely. At the quarterly meeting on February 4, 1898, the Stanstead County WCTU resolved, "That we have no sympathy with the propositions of Lady Henry Somerset in relation to the C.D. Act and we reaffirm that the first plank in our platform is no compromise with sin." Dr. Amelia Yeomans, a vice-president of the Dominion WCTU, condemned the re-election of Somerset by the World WCTU and urged the Canadian Union to resign from the international body. By this time, however, Somerset had recanted and the Dominion executive, with the exception of Dr. Yeomans, voted full confidence in her.[26]

The WCTU accepted the view that woman was and should be the moral guardian of society and so took a particular interest in the campaign for purity. Its campaign emphasized a single standard of sexual morality for both men and women, the standard being that dictated to women–control. This standard would not only help individuals, but would safeguard the future of the race. "Impure living," whether represented in sexual promiscuity, reading licentious novels (any novels), or the "secret vice" (masturbation) had, the WCTU believed, horrendous results on subsequent generations. The WCTU held that a mother's thoughts could influence her child before birth, warning that "sensuality may be transmitted to the yet unborn child by . . . want of care in this respect." The new science of eugenics confirmed it. Heredity was important physically and morally and therefore men and women had a responsibility to choose their spouses wisely. Intemperance itself was hereditary, they thought, and its consequences reached out to maim the innocent, as the 1892 Report of the Department of Heredity and Hygiene was meant to illustrate:

> Recently a friend of mine was urging a little boy two years of age to join the Band of Hope, when he startled her by saying, 'You don't know what you are asking of me. *Never drink any more liquor?* I love it better than my life, I could not live without it.' Think you that was an acquired taste with that child? No, no; his parents are responsible for it. 'A corrupt tree cannot bring forth good fruit.'

The purpose of this obviously fantastic story is clear.[27]

The belief in heredity created a problem. If intemperance was inherited, the WCTU could to little to prevent it, and this would mean defeat, a negation of its entire educational and preventive program. Fortunately, the members of the WCTU had a strong belief in the spiritual power of man. As upholders of morality they were upholders of the Christian faith. The two were inseparable in their eyes and so to fully understand their determination it is important to understand the source of it.

THE WCTU AND THE CHURCH

The WCTU wanted a Protestant Christian society. For most of its members, faith and temperance went hand in hand. The fight for prohibition was part of a religious battle, and one which women were determined to win. In the early years of its existence this religious strain probably did much to attract the initial WCTU membership and make it a respectable organization. Certainly the WCTU was closely aligned with those churches which endorsed prohibition, as revealed by the religious affiliation of its executive. Forty-three per cent of its executive were Methodist, 18 per cent were Presbyterians, and only 10 per cent were adherents to the Church of England. Methodists had long disapproved of the consumption of alcohol and had been active in condemning it, although Presbyterians had not. Except for the more evangelical among them, Church of England supporters were uncomfortable in an organization which disapproved strongly of their church's use of wine as part of its religious service. The WCTU, then, was aligned to the church most active in its social involvement and strongest in its encouragement to women to become involved, to accept personal responsibility and to follow Christ's teachings.[28]

The Union patterned itself after the church. Its meetings opened with a prayer and a hymn and ended with a benediction. During the meeting there was more hymn singing, a collection, and often an address by a minister. The WCTU believed that religious faith was the cornerstone of a temperate society and supported anything which strengthened the church. It firmly endorsed the movement to maintain Sabbath Observance and devoted a department to this end. Sunday laws allowed families to be united by granting workers one day of rest, but Sunday laws also made it difficult for the working man and his family to have outings together. In the same way that curfew bells limited the freedom of children, Sunday laws limited the freedom of working men on the one day they had to call their own.[29]

The WCTU's religious faith was strong. Uppermost in its members' minds was the spiritual welfare of the people they were trying to help, for although they rejected the denominational exclusiveness of missionary societies, they still retained the "spirit of Faith and Prayer" which characterized them. They believed that they could help men stop drinking if they could only bring them back to the Christian faith. They did not advocate temperance as simply a rational economic philosophy, but as a moral ethical one which was necessary if man was to live through Christ. Because reform of men's temporal state came only through Christ, the WCTU wanted "to carry the Gospel cure to the drinking classes." Its only approach to the individual inebriate, then, came through an evangelical commitment.[30]

Many work departments reflected this evangelical tendency: Flower Mission, Work Among Sailors (Immigrants, Lumbermen, Railwaymen), Sabbath Observance and Sabbath Schools, and Work in Jails. The women attempted to comfort those in need with the solace of religion. They often visited the inmates of prisons, hoping to win these men and women away from their former intemperate habits by bringing them the word of God. Yet when faced with prison conditions, they were led to demand prison reform. They became the advocates of prisoner classification, work for the incarcerated, the indeterminate sentence (an open-ended sentence which would terminate only when the individual had reformed), the parole system, and schoolrooms within the jail. However, the women of the WCTU were worried that prison reform might take the spotlight away from their evangelical work and so continually stressed the need to remember the power of prayer and maintained a vigilance over their own spiritual well-being.

The church was the one institution in which women had been permitted and encouraged to work, even if only in a subordinate role. More importantly, the women of the WCTU believed a common Christianity bound them together as women, allowing them the freedom to think and act. They were convinced that Christianity and its handmaiden, the Protestant church, recognized women as being equal to men. Believing this, their involvement in public agitation to support prohibition and suffrage was not a denial of their proper sphere but a fulfilment of it. Their activism was justified by faith.

WCTU members were part of a movement to rectify wrong. As individuals they counted for little; as part of a great crusade they believed they became worthy of Christ.

> The Woman's Christian Temperance Union is no accident, but one of God's special creations. Throughout the ages since the fall of man Divine Love has been raising up instrumentalities for the restoration of our race to its original standard of moral rectitude.[31]

CONCLUSION

The Woman's Christian Temperance Union played a significant role in the lives of many Canadian women in the nineteenth century. Its advocacy of prohibition necessitated state intervention, which meant the WCTU was forced to appeal to the public in order to persuade the government to implement such a controversial policy. This made the Union much more visible than most other women's organizations and hastened the time when its members would be faced with their own powerlessness as women. Through this politicization process the members of the WCTU confronted the reality of their lives in nineteenth-century Canada – they had little concrete power. As a solution they advocated women's suffrage, not so they could represent themselves as individuals, but so they could extend their domestic power as women in their effort to protect their homes by protecting society from the problems within it that could undermine both. They did not reject society's view of women, but argued that what made them different from men and what made them the centre of domestic life necessitated their involvement in temporal society. Their belief in an active Christianity supported them in this endeavour. That their actions and beliefs might appear contradictory did not concern them. They were practical women; they did what they felt had to be done and rationalized it by any means possible.

The rationales they used were the domestic ideal of woman and Christian duty. These were successful because the members really believed in them and these were also two supports which could not be attacked by those disapproving of women's activism. There were limits to what women could do using the ideal of domesticity to justify their actions. It meant an acknowledgement that woman's role was to care for the home. However, few Canadian women in the nineteenth century perceived this as a limitation. For them there was no contradiction between their actions and belief. Their interpretation of the domestic ideal of womanhood was a dynamic one, one that could and did encompass the women's rights movement. They were social feminists, not feminists.

As a precursor for the experience of other women's groups the WCTU's significance is great. It exposed the importance of the domestic ideal and Christian duty for women in the nineteenth century and demonstrated how Canadian women were able to use what some historians have seen as restrictive concepts to extend and exert their power in society.[32]

NOTES

1. The following is only a partial list of the women's clubs which were formed in the latter part of the last century: the Woman's Auxiliary

to the Board of the Domestic and Foreign Missionary Society of the Church of England in Canada (1885); The Women's Baptist Missionary Union of the Maritime Provinces (1885); The Woman's Foreign Missionary Society of the Presbyterian Church in Canada, Eastern and Western Division (1876); the Woman's Missionary Society of the Methodist Church (1881); The Woman's Art Association of Canada (1890); the National Council of Women (1893); the Woman's Christian Temperance Union of Canada (1885); the Young Women's Christian Association (1893); the Dominion Order of the King's Daughters (1891); the Victorian Order of Nurses (1898); the National Home Reading Union (1895); the Aberdeen Association (1897); the Girls' Friendly Society of Canada (1882); the Imperial Order of the Daughters of the Empire (1900); the Dominion Women's Enfranchisement Association (1889); plus numerous local musical clubs, historical societies, literary societies, dramatic, athletic, and charitable associations.

2. In Ontario and Quebec, the most populated provinces, 22.8 per cent of the population lived in centres classed as urban in 1881. By 1891 this had increased to 33.2 per cent and 29.2 per cent respectively. No province, however, matched British Columbia, whose urban population increased by 30.6 per cent between 1881 and 1891. *Census of Canada 1890-1891*, vol. 4, 401; *Sixth Census of Canada*, 1921, vol.1, 346.
3. Barbara Welter, "The Cult of True Womanhood 1820-1860," *American Quarterly*, 18 (1966), 258-71; Jacques Henripin, *Trends and Factors of Fertility in Canada* (Ottawa, 1972), 39, 36. See Ann D. Gordon and Mari Jo Buhle, "Sex and Class in Colonial and Nineteenth-Century America," in Bernice Carroll, ed., *Liberating Women's History* (Chicago, 1976), 286, for a discussion of the intensification of the mother-child relationship in the American context.
4. The second hypothesis has been suggested by Daniel Scott Smith's concept of domestic feminism. See Daniel Scott Smith, "Family Limitation, Sexual Control, and Domestic Feminism in Victorian America," in Mary Hartman and Lois W. Banner, eds., *Clio's Consciousness Raised* (New York, 1974), 119-37.
5. For a discussion of the early temperance movement in Canada and the way in which it was influenced by the American, see J. K. Chapman, "The Mid-19th Century Temperance Movements in New Brunswick and Maine," *CHR*, xxxv (1954), 43-60. The confrontation with government was experienced by other women's organizations much later since few advocated such controversial reforms. Eventually, however, most women's groups were faced with government reluctance to implement their reforms.
6. Annual Report, Woman's Christian Temperance Union of Ontario, 1898, 96; *ibid.*, 1899, 50-1; Robert Popham and Wolfgang

Schmidt, *Statistics of Alcohol Use and Alcoholism in Canada 1871-1956* (Toronto, 1958), 15-25.

7. Annual Report, WCTU, Ontario, 1882, 5-6; Anne Angus, *Children's Aid Society of Vancouver 1901-1951* (Vancouver, 1951), 5.
8. The percentage of the WCTU executive who were traceable was small, only 38 per cent.

WCTU Executive 1890-1901; Occupation of Husband

	Traceable	%
Business	8	19
Law	6	14
Ministry	9	21
Medicine	4	9.5
Journalism	5	12

(These figures represent only the professions with the largest representations.)

9. State intervention was gradually adopted by most women's reform organizations. It was the method by which they could cope with an increasingly complex society.
10. The importance of religious faith for the WCTU will be examined later.
11. Annual Report, WCTU, Ontario, October 24, 1878, Resolutions; Annual Report, Woman's Christian Temperance Union of British Columbia, 1889, 18.
12. Ruth Spence, *Prohibition in Canada* (Toronto, 1919), 144; Annual Report, WCTU of the Dominion of Canada, 1889, 3; *ibid.*, 18; *ibid.*, 1891, 43.
13. Annual Report, WCTU, Nova Scotia, 1896, 27.
14. *Ibid.*, 1897, 3; Rev. W. Peck, *A Short History of the Liquor Traffic* (n.p., 1929), 14.
15. Annual Report, WCTU, Nova Scotia, 1897, 24; Annual Report, WCTU Canada, 1892, 53.
16. Letitia Youmans, *Campaign Echoes* (Toronto, 1893), 206-7.
17. Annual Report, WCTU Ontario, 1880, 10. For further information on the suffrage movement in Canada and the role the WCTU played, see Catherine Cleverdon, *The Woman Suffrage Movement in Canada*, 2nd ed. (Toronto, 1974).
18. *The Templar Quarterly* (August, 1897), 28.
19. Annual Report, WCTU New Brunswick, 1899, 26; Annual Report, WCTU Ontario, 1898, 66.
20. Annual Report, WCTU Manitoba, 1890-91, 43-4; Smith, "Family Limitation," 125. There is a suggestion in Alison Prentice, "Educa-

tion and the Metaphor of the Family: the Upper Canadian Example," *History of Education Quarterly*, XII, 3 (1972), 286, that the family as a source of identification in mid-nineteenth-century Canadian society was declining, due to the discredit brought upon the concept by the Family Compact.

21. Scrapbook, WCTU, 1898, lent to the author by Mrs. Harris Magog, Quebec. For information on feminine friendships in the United States, see Carroll Smith-Rosenberg, "The Female World of Love and Ritual: Relations Between Women in Nineteenth-Century America," *Signs*, 1 (Autumn, 1975), 1-31.
22. Annual Report, WCTU of the Maritime Provinces, 1890, 43.
23. Annual Report, WCTU Ontario, 1893, 117; Annual Report, WCTU B.C., 1899, 58.
24. Annual Report, WCTU B.C., 1897, 32; Annual Report, WCTU Ontario, 1894, 140.
25. Annual Report, WCTU Maritimes, 1890, 49.
26. Scrapbook, Stanstead County WCTU, 1898.
27. Annual Report, WCTU B.C., 1899, 60; Annual Report, WCTU Canada, 1892, 76. This emphasis on heredity was common in the latter nineteenth century. See Michael Bliss, "Pure Books on Avoided Subjects," Canadian Historical Association, *Historical Papers*, 1970, 89-108.
28. **WCTU Executive:**

	Number	%
Presbyterian	7	18
Church of England	4	10
Catholic	—	—
Methodist	17	44
Baptist	6	15
Congregational	5	13

29. Annual Report, WCTU Canada, 1891, 93.
30. Annual Report, WCTU Ontario, October 23, 1878, Resolutions; Annual Report, WCTU Quebec, 1884-85, 70.
31. Annual Report, WCTU B.C., 1893, 23.
32. See Jill Conway, "Women Reformers and American Culture," *Journal of Social History*, 5 (Winter, 1971-72), 164-77, for an expression of this phenomenon in the American context.

VI
Women

Analysing the testimony of women workers before the 1886-89 Royal Commission on the Relations of Labour and Capital, Susan Trofimenkoff concludes that even their "muffled" voices tell us much about late nineteenth-century social attitudes toward working women. A relatively new field of historical inquiry, women's history is now beginning to try to recreate the lives of women who did not make a major impression on the historical record. The methodological problems in this attempt, discussed briefly here, are great, but a start is being made.

Most women working in late nineteenth-century industry were young and single. Labouring usually only until marriage, their youth and short work lives made them highly exploitable. Although their meagre earnings were often all that separated their families from dire want, the notion that they were earning additional income for a family provided employers with a heartless rationale for abysmally low wages. Regarded ambiguously by their male comrades, only with the coming of the Knights of Labor in the 1880's were women organized into the labour movement. Skilled unionists in their jealous and desperate attempts to retain control of their crafts sometimes excluded women. This process became especially severe in the early twentieth century.

FURTHER READING:

On women workers, see Janice Acton *et al.*, eds., *Women at*

Work: Ontario 1850-1930 (Toronto, 1974); and Wayne Roberts, *Honest Womanhood: Feminism, Femininity and Class Consciousness Among Toronto Working Women 1893-1914* (Toronto, 1976). On the Royal Commission, see Greg Kealey, ed., *Canada Investigates Industrialism* (Toronto, 1973); and Fernand Harvey, *Révolution industrielle et travailleurs* (Montreal, 1978). On women in the Knights of Labor, see Gregory S. Kealey and Bryan Palmer, *"Dreaming of What Might Be": The Knights of Labor in Ontario* (New York, 1982). For a description of the life cycle of women workers, see Michael Katz, *The People of Hamilton, Canada West: Family and Class in a Mid-Nineteenth-Century City* (Cambridge, Mass., 1975).

Susan Trofimenkoff teaches history at the University of Ottawa and is the author of studies on French-Canadian nationalism in the twentieth century.

One Hundred and Two Muffled Voices: Canada's Industrial Women in the 1880's

by Susan Trofimenkoff

The Royal Commissioners studying the relations between capital and labour searched diligently but in the end they could only find Georgina Loiselle. Since the Commissioners were well aware of inquiries similar to their own in the United States and in Great Britain, they fully expected to find many cases like Georgina's.[1] But after months of roving Canada's four eastern provinces, persistently questioning workingmen and their employers, they found only the one. And even that one had occurred some five years before, in the early 1880's, when "modern" factories were just beginning in Canada and when one might expect the accompanying tensions to burst into flagrant abuse. Still, it was too bad that only the one case could be found. The Commissioners, all of whom were political appointments[2] and most of whom shared solidly middle-class values, somehow expected the lower orders to misbehave, particularly when those lower orders were sexually mixed in the new factories. But there was only Georgina.

Mademoiselle Georgina Loiselle was an apprentice in Fortier's cigar factory in Montreal. She was one of a number of children supporting a widowed mother. But sometimes she was cheeky, speaking back and refusing to do extra work demanded by M. Fortier. Fortier was determined to give her a lesson; when she refused to make 100 more cigars, Fortier seized her, intending to put her over his knee and spank her. But Georgina fell to the factory floor; Fortier pinned her there and beat her with a cigar

From *Atlantis*, 3 (1978), 66-82.

mould. When reporting the incident to the Royal Commission on Labour and Capital in 1888, neither Georgina nor Fortier seemed particularly perturbed. Georgina had left Fortier's at the end of her apprenticeship but had returned some time later and appeared quite docile; Fortier had not had to touch her again. Fortier, in fact, considered it his duty to correct the young people entrusted to his "care" by their parents.[3] And others shared his sense of duty: the Recorder of Montreal believed young factory workers probably received the same treatment at home; moreover, it was certainly better to have young people safely in factories, no matter what the treatment, than to see them running the streets. The Commissioners may well have agreed, for their concern with Georgina was less the physical abuse of the young woman than the moral decency of "a man placing a girl of eighteen in that position."[4] In their investigations, the Commissioners would find other evidence to shake their sense of moral propriety but this was the only case of physical abuse to be found among the one hundred and two female witnesses before the Royal Commission on Labour and Capital.

There is, however, other information that can be discovered about women workers in the 1880's from that Royal Commission. One can, for example, hear the voices of some of Canada's industrial women recounting the kind of work they did, describing their working and living conditions and voicing their complaints. One can also glean the views of male workers and male employers on the question of female labour. And finally one can decipher, by the very questions asked, the attitudes of the male commissioners towards Canada's industrial women. In the pages that follow these three areas will be explored.

Needless to say, the Royal Commission on Labour and Capital was not an enquiry into the nature of female labour in the 1880's. Female labour was only one of a multitude of subjects that the Commissioners were to investigate. Indeed, aside from the 102 women witnesses before the Commission, only another 218 spokesmen offered any information or opinions on the subject of female labour. The remaining witnesses (close to 1,800 people testified during the year and a half of hearings in cities and towns in Ontario, Quebec, New Brunswick, and Nova Scotia) spoke of everything from factory laws to wages, from apprenticeships to rents, from arbitration to immigration, and from convict labour to strikes.[5] The inquiry, in short, was an investigation of all aspects of that great nineteenth-century worry: labour and its relation to capital. Women were only a small part of such an inquiry.

The inquiry itself was also politically inspired, and, in spite of early efforts to obtain female suffrage and even some early successes in terms of the municipal franchise, women really had very little to do with politics in the 1800's[6] and even less so, it would seem, with labour politics.[7] But because of some labour agitation in the 1880's–including radical papers, political candidates, and attempts to create national trade union centrals–the aging Prime Minister, John A. Macdonald, decided to establish the inquiry. Macdonald was also feeling pressure from the two central provinces. Both Ontario and Quebec, in the mid-1880's, passed factory legislation regulating hours and ages for working people. The Prime Minister had never shown the same keen interest in factory legislation; he was still counting on his political reputation as a friend of labour established back in 1872 when he accorded trade unions in Canada some legal status. However, he was not anxious to have the provinces establish an undisputed claim for sovereign jurisdiction in the area. In many ways, therefore, the Commission was as much a political manoeuvre as a labour inquiry. And, of course, women's place in that kind of activity was virtually non-existent. As an added incentive for the establishment of the Royal Commission, Macdonald had the unsettled economic conditions of the mid-1880's. The Prime Minister was anxious to show that his National Policy of 1879 had been and could continue to be beneficial to the Canadian economy and to the Canadian working class. The Commissioners in fact took this part of their undertaking very seriously; their reports credited the industrialization of the country to the National Policy.

But again, none of that had much to do with women. Hence the muffled quality of their voices: no one really wanted to hear from them. As witnesses before the Commission they constituted only one-fortieth of the Ontario witnesses, one-tenth of the Quebec witnesses, one-twentieth of the New Brunswick witnesses, and one-thirtieth of the Nova Scotia witnesses. To understand the muffling that those figures reveal, one need only contrast them with the census figures for 1891. In the category "manufactures and mechanical industries," working women made up almost one-fifth of the labour force in Ontario, Quebec, and New Brunswick and slightly more than one-fifth in Nova Scotia.[8] Another illustration of this muted quality is the anonymity of so many of the women witnesses. Forty-three of the 102 voices had no name at all. And the women were decidedly more reticent than their male counterparts: in all, seventy-three people chose to testify anonymously; only thirty of the close to 1,700 male witnesses wished to hide their names.

Given the purpose of the Commission and the muffling of the women witnesses, it is surprising that much at all can be gleaned about Canada's industrial women. But historians of women are becoming used to squeezing every drop of information from every kind of source, and this particular source can be subjected to the same treatment. The women themselves give description; the men, attitudes.

From the 102 voices there emerges clearly the type of work these women undertook. Textile workers in cotton mills constituted the largest group overall and for each of the four provinces except Ontario. Other kinds of textile workers made up the next largest group: women in woollen and knitting factories. Then there were women in shoemaking factories, in match factories, in tobacco industries, and in printing offices, where the women did the folding and stitching, not the typesetting. And finally there was an odd assortment of milliners, dressmakers, ropemakers, and paper bag makers. One portent of the future appeared before the Commission – a telephone operator; and one caricature-before-her-time appeared in the form of a WCTU executive member who had no answers at all for the Commissioners' probing questions.

Behind the 102 lurked even more women workers. When male employers commented upon female labour they often told the Commissioners how many "hands" they employed. In this way they revealed another, much larger group of women – some 5,000 – not merely muffled but entirely voiceless and shadowy as well. Still their occupations are clear. In descending numerical order they were tobacco workers, cotton mill operatives, shoemakers, clothing makers, matchmakers, and woollen mill workers. The occupations are similar to those of the 102; only the order is somewhat different. But how representative were these one hundred and two voices or these 5,000 shadowy "hands"? Compared once again with the "manufactures and mechanical industries" category of the census of 1891 (where the majority of women in the labour force did not in fact appear; that majority was rather in the service and professional categories as servants and teachers), the occupational structure of the women is quite different. From the census, the occupations, in descending numerical order, were dressmakers, seamstresses, tailoresses, milliners, cotton mill operatives, mill workers, boot and shoe workers, and woollen mill operatives.[9] Even adding all the mill workers together would only move them to third place in the list of industrial occupations. But such a ranking might, however, put them in first place in terms of factory workers, since many dressmakers and seamstresses would work in their own homes, in private homes, in very small establishments, or as "outside workers" for retail clothing shops. And it was, after all, the factory workers who most interested the Royal Commissioners. By that very fact, factory workers would be more likely to hear of the existence of the Commission; hence they turned up in relatively larger numbers than their sisters in other occupations.

Nonetheless, 102 voices remain a very small sample of the 57,283 women who worked in manufactures and mechanical industries in 1891.[10] And as the list of occupations given above indicates, their work was almost as limited as their numbers. But still some generalizations can be made, both about women workers and about Canada's nascent factory system. All those textile workers merely represented a transfer from home to factory of the traditional female skills and tasks. For the women, the role would be familiar; only the surroundings and perhaps the pace would differ. But the shoe workers tell us something else. They were a direct result of the factory system with its logic of breaking down attained skills into simple, repetitive, and mechanical tasks. Where once the shoe trade required long apprenticeships and highly skilled men, now the factory-made shoes simply required highly attentive women to watch the machines. Women were, of course, cheaper. And finally, the matchmakers and the printing employees represented the flourishing of light industry in certain parts of Canada. Light industries required vast numbers of unskilled and therefore cheap labour. All of the industries were, in fact, welcomed by the women involved; in a society where domestic service and school teaching were the only independent economic paths women could take, the factory system opened new areas of paid employment.

The 102 voices also provide a glimpse of the working conditions of Canada's industrial women. The hours of work appeared to vary from west to east, with the women witnesses from Ontario working a nine-hour day, those in Quebec a ten-hour day, and those in the Maritimes an eleven-hour day. Such a variation would obviously produce the Commissioners' findings of an average ten-hour day in the factories of eastern Canada,[11] but it does not reveal much more. More can be gleaned from the women's remarks about their wages. As perhaps might be expected, the wages varied with the age of the woman and her skill. For example, a fourteen-year-old folding in a printing plant earned $2 per week; a twenty-year-old in a cotton factory earned $4 per week; a middle-aged expert dressmaker earned $7 per week, and a middle-aged forewoman in a tannery earned $10 per week.[12] But there were catches in those salaries. The women (as did most factory men at the time) earned their wages by piece-work; they were paid by the number of items they produced, not by the day or by the week. But in order to make the items and in order to make enough of them to earn a "living wage,"[13] the workers had to be provided with the material for their work. If there was no material provided, they might hang around the factory all day waiting for non-existent work. The result would be a slimmer pay packet at the end of the week. Nor could the women count on those wages for the entire year. At a time of over-production, a factory simply stopped its machines, closed its doors, and turned its workers out. Then, too, many occupations were of a seasonal nature: printing, dressmaking, and millinery followed demand and fashion, which determined thereby that women would not have year-round work. And women's wages were consistently lower than those paid to male workers. A final catch in the wage rates of women (and of men, too) was the number of fines exacted for defective work or unseemly behaviour. A snag in a piece of cloth, a defective shoe sole, a late arrival, a chat, a giggle, a pincurl fabricated with paper from the factory "closet" would bring the foreman's ire and financial exaction.[14] For the most part women appear to have accepted without complaint this "muffling" of their behaviour.

Perhaps the women were used to similar curtailments of their activities at home. Although very few of the 102 talk at all about their living conditions, those who do admit that they could not afford to board out. The $2 per week demanded by private homemakers or a higher amount demanded by boarding houses or institutions[15] would put independent living beyond the reach of all but the most skilled of women workers. They lived at home, dependent upon their families to house and feed them, just as the families were dependent on the income that the young women could bring home. Where ages were mentioned at all, the women appeared to be between sixteen and twenty-four and many of them had been working since they were twelve or fourteen. It would seem then that a working-class family required the wages of its youngsters and that, from about the age of twelve, a girl would be expected to contribute to the family income. Employers could count on this kind of interdependency; they were assured of a constant supply of willing workers and, because of those workers' living arrangements, they could also pay them low wages.[16]

Although the 102 women were relatively open and forthright when describing their work and their working and living conditions, when the time came to voice complaints, their voices fell silent. The women were very reticent, even with the sympathetic probing of some of the Commissioners. Only when women gave their testimony anonymously would they dare to utter a word of complaint. In effect, only when they muffled their own voices would they speak out. And they spoke of badly ventilated workrooms: they were either too hot, or too cold, or too dusty: "We have all got frightful colds; it is not good for the health, I assure you." They complained of extra time added to the work day without financial compensation. They argued that they did not receive enough pay for the work they did. One woman even carried a personal feud into the hearing of the Commissioners: she claimed she worked much harder than the previous witness but she received the same pay. Other women complained that, on leaving a job, they did not receive the pay owing to them. Still others had to have the tiniest of complaints put into their mouths by the Commissioners:

Q. Wouldn't a half-day holiday on Saturday be a boon?
A. Yes.
Q. Do you think that you would not wish for anything more?
A. I think we would wish for a great many more things that we do not get.[17]

Where the women were willing to identify themselves, either their remarks were of a different nature or they themselves were different. For example, two factory workers in Ontario freely gave their names, but when the time came to voice complaints they stated that everything was fine in their factory. Another young factory worker and her mother gladly furnished their names, but the younger woman, it turned out, had been dismissed from her job: indeed the two complained that the daughter had lost her job because of testimony she had given at a court investigation of a workman's injuries. She had refused to be silenced but she had paid for that refusal. And finally there were the skilled dressmaker and milliner, employers of other women. They, too, were quite willing to give their names and to use the occasion to voice their complaints about the shoddy workers they were obliged to hire. The school system, they contended, simply had not prepared young girls for needlework jobs. Moreover, the girls were more interested in getting married than in being trained for a steady job.[18] Thus complaints from women workers only reached the ears of the Commissioners in indirect ways. Only those women who were removed from the immediate work at hand, by anonymity, by dismissal, or by status would dare say anything critical. Even Georgina Loiselle did not complain about the treatment she had received at the hands of cigar manufacturer Fortier. But then Fortier was present during her testimony. It can only be concluded that the women were afraid and so muffled their own voices.

From the 102 themselves, there is little more to be heard. Fortunately, the Commissioners pursued the question of female labour with both male workers and male employers. Again one must remember that the inquiry was not primarily about female labour; indeed, the question was by no means a major concern of either the Commissioners or the male witnesses.

Only 218 other witnesses out of the 1,800 spoke of female labour at all. Often there was a one-word or at most a one-sentence reply to a question about female labour and a quick passing on to a totally different subject. For example, one male witness all in one breath agreed that women teachers should receive the same salary for the same work as men teachers and then launched into a lengthy discussion of the drainage and sewers in London, Ontario.[19] In spite of these handicaps to a clear picture of industrial women in the 1880's, there are a number of things that can be wrenched from the comments, first of the male workers, and then of the male employers.

Men factory workers were decidedly ambiguous about the question of female labour. They had, it would seem, not yet come to terms with it. Where, for example, one cigar worker readily admitted that women could do the same work as well as men and that, therefore, they should receive the same wages, others, in printing, tailoring, and cigarmaking, would justify the lower salaries paid to women by the contention that the women did an inferior job. Still other men, working in dry goods shops or tailoring establishments, recognized that the lower salaries paid to women encouraged employers to hire them rather than men; these men were fully aware that the wage difference was a means both of cutting into job opportunities for men and of depressing their wage rates. But the men had no ready solution to the vexing problem; they voiced only their personal concern. Other workers pointed out that there was a sexual division of labour in many factories: men and women worked at different tasks. There could be, therefore, neither comparison nor competition between the two and the women were paid less.[20] In short, the factory system itself was another highly effective means of muting the voices of such women.

Some of the male workers were more direct. They believed, for example, that young girls should not be working in the large mills because there they would hear "immoral words" and thus become immoral. And they suggested that women, if they were working in factories, should leave their workplace at a different time from the men. In that way they would not hear the "bad words" uttered as the hands left the factories.[21] In both these cases the male workers voiced an opinion that was much more pronounced among the Commissioners: morally corruptible women had to be protected from the ill effect of words. Perhaps this moral concern on the part of the male workers was one way of covering their bewilderment at the economic competition they were suddenly facing from women factory workers. Certainly it suggested an effective way of controlling the women. But other male workers were even more blunt: one simply need not listen to the women. There was no need, remarked one man, to pay any attention to women factory workers complaining about dust in the workroom because they were always "grumbling about something or other all the time."[22] The men warned the Commissioners thereby that they should not take the few complaints they heard from women workers too seriously. Women were always complaining. Short of muffling them directly by removing them from the factories, the men should do so indirectly, simply by not listening.

In fact, there were almost as many opinions about female labour as there were workingmen witnesses. This very diversity of opinion suggests that the male factory workers were unsure of just what female labour meant to them. As household heads they knew perfectly well that the wife's or daughter's wages were necessary to the family's survival. As union men they also recognized the necessity of equal pay for equal work.[23] As members of the working class they had always known that women worked. And yet, whether their backgrounds were rural or urban, these men also knew that women's work was different from theirs. Now the existence of factories implied – although did not always ensure – that women's work could be the same as men's, might even be better, and usually was cheaper. Female labour did not augur well for men. Their uneasiness about it rings through their testimony.

Male employers, however, were quite direct and forthright. None of the worries of the male workers appeared. The employers liked female labour because it was "more profitable to us or we would not employ them."[24] Yet, that very profitability was based on certain expectations about the nature of women workers. The employers expected the women to be docile, clean, quick, cheap, and sober.[25] As long as women maintained those characteristics, traits which rendered them superior to male employees, they would be sure of jobs. The employers had very effective means of ensuring that women workers did maintain those qualities. Should the women protest any of their working conditions, should they, in effect, cease to be docile, clean, quick, cheap, or sober, they could be "muffled" very easily. There was always another group of women with the appropriate behaviour ready to replace the protesters. This tactic worked well in the Stormont Cotton Mills in Cornwall when striking women, protesting the foreman's demand that they be quiet and orderly during the dinner hour, returned docilely to work under threat of being replaced.[26] And, as happened in another case, the employer simply moved his factory away from the offending women.[27] Muffling could take many forms, all equally effective.

Employers expressed still other expectations of women workers. They fully expected their female employees to be temporary workers;[28] the women would work a few years before marriage and then would vanish, to be replaced by another group of young women. This continual turnover not only enabled the employers to keep the wages of women low but also permitted them to dub the women unreliable, uninterested in learning a trade or in applying themselves seriously to it. That characterization, while perhaps applicable to the women, effectively concealed the fact that the women's *positions* were steady, unchanging, and profitable. The employers reaped the benefits but justified them by muffling the women in terms of male expectations. Sometimes, too, the employers justified those benefits by claiming a paternal interest in their women workers. Fortier believed he was replacing Georgina Loiselle's dead father when he admonished her physically for disobedience.[29] And a master baker believed that the women working in his new, modern bakery would be better wives and mothers for their experience.[30] Women workers were so beneficial to male employers that the employers had to believe that they, too, were of benefit to the workers.

Finally, the employers counted on the women being less skilled than men. Such an expectation enabled the employers to justify the lower wages they paid their female hands. Some employers even enforced this particular characteristic of their women employees. Certain factories maintained a strict sexual division of labour, with the women assigned to the least skilled tasks. Other workshops maintained a sexual division of wages by which, for example, a male tailor would be paid by the week and a woman tailor by the piece.[31] The piecework rate ensured that the woman would work constantly and quickly, in order to produce enough garments to fill a pay packet. She may have succeeded in that task but the comment from the employer was that the man's work was finer. She could not win; nor was she intended to.

Male employers were quite clear in expressing, and often in enforcing, their economic interest in a certain type of female labour. Noticeably absent from their calculations was the moral interest which some working men had shown. Where that moral interest found full expression was in the Commissioners themselves. Just what that moral concern meant is, however, another matter. The workers' interest in protecting the morality of their female co-workers probably reflected their uneasiness at the prospect of economic competition from women. But obviously the middle-class Commissioners had no such worries. Were they vaguely aware that the factory system was undermining their sense of family and of propriety? Were they afraid? Was something "catching" going on in the factories?[32] Or were the Commissioners simply revealing their middle-class notions of the time: that women were both the guardians of morality and the most easily corruptible, and that the poor were poor because of some flaw, usually a moral one, in their character? What then of poor working women? They truly were a scandal.

Certainly the Commissioners were not interested in the women as workers. Even when women constituted the majority in a given factory, the Commissioners' questions concerned the male employees.[33] And when the women witnesses were factory hands, their voices were effectively muffled by perfunctory questioning. The Commissioners asked about hours of work, about wages, about language, and about closets. And that was all. But if the women witnesses happened to be employers of women, they had free rein to express their opinions on a wide variety of subjects, notably one dear perhaps to the hearts of the wives of the Commissioners: why young girls were unwilling to go into domestic service.[34] Women as workers were not the primary concern of the Commissioners.

Instead they searched diligently for what they most expected from working-class women–scandal. Assuming that immoral behaviour was a necessary consequence of the mingling of the sexes in the factories, the Commissioners painstakingly hunted down every instance of immorality. They found it, they thought, in the language women heard. Immorality, it seems, was some kind of disease spread through language and particularly catching for women. Women should not therefore hear, much less use, violent language. But the working women obviously had a different set of values. While one Commissioner fretted over the kind of language a certain woman might hear in a factory, the witness in question took it all very casually. She must have shrugged as she replied offhandedly that the language was not violent–"just cursing; that is all."[35]

Undeterred, the Commissioners continued to track down instances of, or occasions for, immorality. They found them, they thought, in the "conveniences" that the working people had to use. Hence their recurring question: were there separate "closets" for the male and female workers? Here, immorality, at least in the minds of the Commissioners, seems to have something to do with toilets. The state of factory toilets amounted to a virtual obsession. "Did you ever see the men try to get into the females' closets when the females were in there?" "What is the height of the water closets separating the men from the women?"[36] Etc. etc. The concern probably reveals more about the strange inner workings of middle-class Victorian minds than it does about the state of working conditions in Canadian factories, but any investigation of that will have to await the flowering of psycho-history in this country. Certainly the Commissioners did find a sufficient number of "combined conveniences" to cluck about. But what the connection was with the morality of women workers remains unexplained.

Still they pressed on. How, they wanted to know, did the foremen and the factory owners behave toward the female employees? Was their behaviour "gentlemanly"?[37] The lower orders, it seems were expected to misbehave, and the men in particular were expected to take advantage of women in subordinate economic positions. The Commissioners' self-appointed role of moral watchdog for the factory women may have been truly a part of their own gentlemanly protective impulse or it may have been an unwitting revelation of middle-class behaviour. In the Canada of the 1880's there were far more women working as domestic servants than as factory workers and the domestics were far more susceptible to male (and middle-class) aggressions. Indeed, studies of the period indicate that most prostitutes began their careers as servants.[38] The Commissioners may thus have revealed more of their own class attitudes to women than of the class reality of factory women. In any case, just as for their other questions, they were never able to find sufficient evidence to support their worries. There was only M. Fortier smacking Georgina while she lay on the factory floor.

And yet the Commissioners would not give up. They persisted in inquiring about the presence of "persons not married, in such a condition as they ought not to have been in" – a roundabout Victorian way of looking for unwed mothers. And when they finally did discover a few such women, they referred to them as "the guilty party."[39] Only one of the Commissioners indicated any economic awareness of the problem when he asked whether a witness believed that low wages drove women into prostitution. But even that searching question was to be deflected, this time by the solidly middle-class witness. Mayor Howland of Toronto restored the questioning to its proper level by remarking icily: "A good woman will die first."[40]

Finally the Commissioners were able to find one factory in Montreal that did confirm many of their preconceptions. At the St. Anne's Cotton Factory they discovered men and women throwing water at each other over the partition in the closets, "pretty free" conduct on the part of men and women workers, "tough acts" by the manager and superintendent, and "young unmarried persons . . . in such a state that it was not fitting they should associate with others."[41] But even in this case, the workers were not willing to have the Commissioners confirm their preconceived notions. One of the women witnesses complained to the Commission that the local press had exaggerated the "goings-on" at the mill.[42]

Perhaps the Commissioners took the complaint to heart. Or perhaps they convinced themselves by their own scrupulous investigation. Certainly they left no stone unturned in their quest for misbehaviour. But in the end, when they made their reports, they had to conclude–albeit somewhat reluctantly, one suspects–that there were no signs of "serious immorality" in Canadian factories. Indeed, in a grand gesture, they even conceded that the moral character of Canadian working women was "as high as that of other classes."[43] No one had asked them to inquire into the moral state of Canadian women but they had done so anyway and in the process had managed to muffle not only the women themselves but also the crucial economic and social questions raised by the factory system and by women's place in it. Given their moral concern they could not help reiterating the notion that women constituted a helpless class, that they needed both moral and physical protection from the dangers of the work world. In that, of course, the Commissioners were no different from their contemporaries who were passing factory legislation and demanding female factory inspectors. Protecting women from the world was a common concern in the 1880's.

The four groups of people discussed above seem to have been living in four different worlds. Working women, working men, male employers, and male Commissioners constituted so many voices speaking in the dark. The women tried to speak of the reality of their working days but they did so in muffled tones. The working men hid their confusion about female labour in a flurry of contradictory opinions. The male employers spoke clearly: women were an economic asset in a factory as long as they fulfilled certain requirements. And the male Commissioners deliberately confused the entire question of female labour by treating it as synonymous with morality. The only characteristic that the four groups had in common was the muffling itself. And that muffling was omnipresent in the women's anonymity, in the male workers' ambiguity, in the employers' economic interest, and in the Commissioners' moral interest. Perhaps one has here an aspect of "female culture,"[44] the silence that is both imposed upon and accepted by women. That silence may be both cause and consequence of the economic dependency of women in the family and in the factory. Certainly the injunction to be silent accompanied young women as they eagerly sought the variety of jobs the factory system offered. The trick for the historian remains, however: how to crack that silence.

NOTES

1. The Canadian Royal Commission on the Relations of Labour and Capital, named in December 1886, had been drawn up by Justice Minister J. S. Thompson. To do so he studied similar inquiries in Pennsylvania, Connecticut, New Jersey, and Kansas. PAC, Macdonald Papers, Thompson to Macdonald, 2 September 1886. The Commission reported in 1889 with a single volume containing a majority and a minority report and five volumes of testimony.
2. See, for example, PAC, Macdonald Papers, T. Stewart to Macdonald, 21 September 1887; A. T. Freed to Macdonald, 22 September 1886; A. H. Blackeby to Macdonald, 26 January 1887. Blackeby, the secretary of the Commission, wanted to receive a salary before the Commission had begun its work, not for himself but to assist the local Conservative candidate, Cowan, in his campaign!
3. *Report of the Royal Commission on the Relations of Labour and Capital* (hereafter cited as RCLC), Quebec Evidence, 91-2, 125-6.
4. *Ibid.*, 126.
5. For a complete list of the subjects of interest to the Commission, most of which were also of interest to the trade union movement at the time, see RCLC, *Report*, 5-6.
6. See Catherine Cleverdon, *The Woman Suffrage Movement in Canada* (Toronto, 1974), 19-26, 105-11; Carol Bacchi, "Liberation Deferred: the Ideas of the English Canadian Suffragists, 1877-1918" (Ph.D. thesis, McGill University, 1976), ch. 2.
7. One of the many aims of the Knights of Labor was equal pay for equal work, but not many women have shown up in Knights of Labor Assemblies. The radical *Palladium of Labor*, 7 December 1886, insisted on female suffrage as part of its Labour Reform platform for the Ontario election of 1886 and it had the occasional article from a working woman, but the *Palladium* was far from being a mass paper. The Trades and Labour Congress also endorsed the suffrage at its convention in 1886 but the trade unions, based as they were on skilled trades, also had few women members. See Jean Scott, *Conditions of Female Labour* (Toronto, 1892), 27.
8. Calculated from Canada, *Census* (1891), vol. II, 152-5, 158-60, 164-7, 175-9.

	Women	*Men*	*Total*	*% women*
Ontario	30,757	128,074	158,831	19.4
Quebec	17,792	75,414	93,206	19.1
New Brunswick	3,648	15,059	18,707	19.5
Nova Scotia	5,086	17,425	22,511	22.6
Total	**57,283**	**235,972**	**293,255**	**19.5**

For some reason the Quebec women witnesses seem to have been less easily muffled than their sisters in the other provinces!

9. *Ibid.*, dressmakers: 22,054; seamstresses: 10,083; tailoresses: 7,731; milliners: 3,141; cotton mill operatives: 2,954; mill operatives: 11,811; boot and shoe workers: 1,720; woollen mill operatives: 1,671. For purposes of comparison, there were 73,652 domestic servants and 14,787 teachers recorded in the same census.
10. As in note 8 above. The total is only for the four provinces visited by the Royal Commission.
11. RCLC, *Report*, 37, 99, 135-95.
12. RCLC, Ontario Evidence, 1163; Quebec Evidence, 484; Ontario Evidence, 347; Quebec Evidence, 1311.
13. Somehow more significant than the "Living Profit" that businessmen in the same period have tried to make us believe was their just dessert. M. Bliss, *A Living Profit* (Toronto, 1974). As Terry Copp makes clear in his *Anatomy of Poverty* (Toronto, 1974), no one, except the poor themselves, worried too much about their inability to earn a living wage.
14. RCLC, Quebec Evidence, 482, 987, 1146, 1147, 273.
15. *Ibid.*, Ontario Evidence, 358; Quebec Evidence, 989, 1147, 1284, 818-19, 1350-1; New Brunswick Evidence, 192, 196, 146; Nova Scotia Evidence, 201, 203.
16. One workman, a weaver in charge of a woollen factory in Sherbrooke, believed, however, that those who boarded worked harder, since they had to earn more in order to pay their keep. *Ibid.*, Quebec Evidence, 1192. The piece-rate would then be an incentive.
17. *Ibid.*, Quebec Evidence, 984, 988, 1145, 1148, 1120, 1296-7, 1294, 1282-3, 1284-5; Ontario Evidence, 1173.
18. *Ibid.*, Ontario Evidence, 1086, 1087; Quebec Evidence, 639-40, 641; Ontario Evidence, 358, 347, 348.
19. *Ibid.*, Ontario Evidence, 662.
20. *Ibid.*, 919; Quebec Evidence, 356; Ontario Evidence, 810, 41, 48, 627; New Brunswick Evidence, 73, 74, 211; Quebec Evidence, 1072; Ontario Evidence, 150; Nova Scotia Evidence, 71.
21. *Ibid.*, Ontario Evidence, 665; Quebec Evidence, 320.
22. *Ibid.*, Nova Scotia Evidence, 210.

23. Printers' unions insisted on equal pay; however, they had few female members. *Ibid.*, Ontario Evidence, 44, 48, 108, 596.
24. *Ibid.*, 617.
25. *Ibid.*, 621.
26. *Ibid.*, 1074-5.
27. *Ibid.*, 288.
28. *Ibid.*, 289; New Brunswick Evidence, 4.
29. *Ibid.*, Quebec Evidence, 126.
30. *Ibid.*, 598.
31. *Ibid.*, Ontario Evidence, 691, 628, 1164; Quebec Evidence, 854; New Brunswick Evidence, 117, 339.
32. This sense of something dubious spreading from the lower orders to infect those above is something that Shorter has turned on its head to posit a revolution in romance and sentiment spreading with industrialization from the working class to the middle class. Edward Shorter, *The Making of the Modern Family* (New York, 1976). The book has been subject to severe, and convincing, criticism in part on the grounds that the author has used middle-class evidence to reveal peasant and working-class reality. See, for example, Joan Scott's review in *Signs*, 2 (Spring, 1977), 692-6. I hope I have avoided that particular trap in this discussion. There certainly is no denying the uneasiness the middle-class Commissioners felt in the face of female labour, but whether that uneasiness was based on any working-class female reality is quite another question.
33. For example, RCLC, Quebec Evidence, 1157.
34. *Ibid.*, Ontario Evidence, 358-9, 1009. The question of the declining number of domestic servants bothered all middle-class reformers throughout the last third of the nineteenth century and first quarter of the twentieth century. See National Council of Women, *Yearbooks*; G. Leslie, "Domestic Service in Canada 1880-1920," in J. Acton *et al.*, eds., *Women at Work: Ontario, 1850-1930* (Toronto, 1974), 71-117.
35. RCLC, Ontario Evidence, 1162.
36. *Ibid.*, Ontario Evidence, 1079; Quebec Evidence, 476.
37. *Ibid.*, New Brunswick Evidence, 193.
38. L. Rotenberg, "The Wayward Worker: Toronto's Prostitute at the Turn of the Century," in Acton *et al.*, eds., *Women at Work*, 33-63.
39. RCLC, Quebec Evidence, 476, 483.
40. *Ibid.*, Ontario Evidence, 168. A. T. Freed was the curious Commissioner.
41. *Ibid.*, Quebec Evidence, 481.
42. *Ibid.*, 485.
43. *Ibid.*, *Report* I, 9; *Report* II, 79. Historians have begun to spill a lot of ink over the fact that the Commissioners divided among themselves and produced two reports. See B. Ostry, "Conser-

vatives, Liberals and Labour in the 1880's," *Canadian Journal of Economics and Political Science*, 27 (1961), 150-3; G. Kealey, introduction to his one-volume edited version of the Royal Commission, *Canada Investigates Industrialism* (Toronto, 1973); F. Harvey, "Une enquéte ouvrière au XIXe siècle: la Commission du travail, 1886-1889," *Revue d'histoire de l'Amérique française,* 30 (juin 1976), 35-53; and G. Vallières, "La Commission royale sur les relations du travail avec le capital au Canada 1886-89" (M.A. thesis, University of Ottawa, 1973). The two reports are in fact quite similar, although there does seem to be slightly more sympathy for the workers displayed in the second report, which was written by those more closely connected with workers' associations. But on the question of female labour, the two reports differ only in wording.

44. Berit Äs, "On Female Culture," *Acta Sociologica*, 18, 2-3 (1975), 142-61.

Readings in Canadian Social History

Volume 1 Economy and Society During the French Regime, to 1759
Volume 2 Pre-Industrial Canada, 1760-1849
Volume 3 Canada's Age of Industry, 1849-1896
Volume 4 The Consolidation of Capitalism, 1896-1929
Volume 5 Modern Canada, 1930-1980's